Panning for Pleasure

• AN ALASKA COOKBOOK •

Introduced by Ed Rombauer

Especially for Shirley & Geraldo
Loretta's best cooking couple

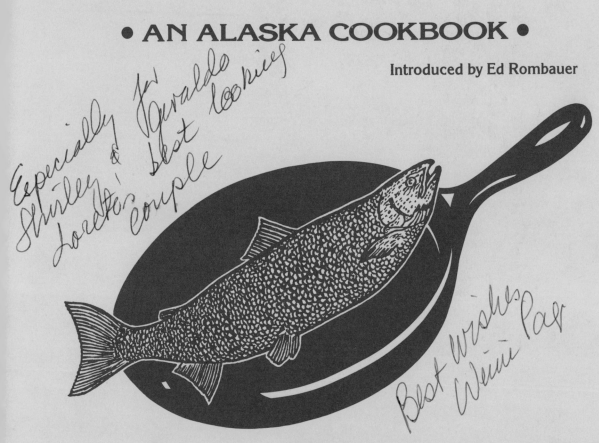

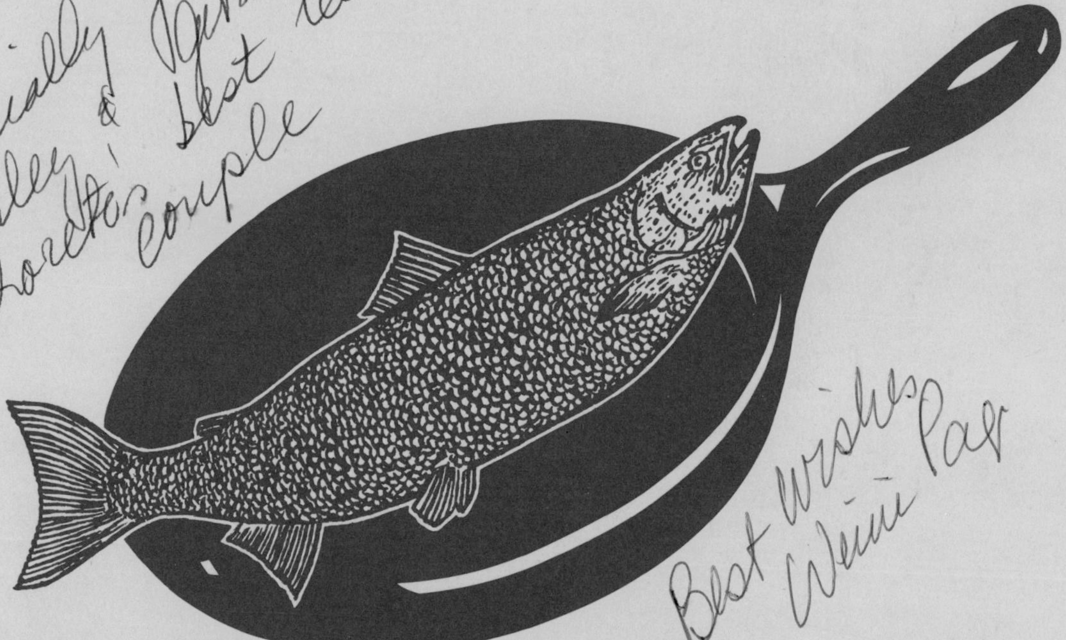

Best wishes
Winni Page

by
Winni Page

PANNING FOR PLEASURE
by WINNI PAGE

For additional copies, please use order form in back of book or write:

Winni Page
Panning for Pleasure
18065 Trails End Drive
Juneau, Alaska 99801

Cover design by: Kathy Brann & Steve Williams
Illustrations by: Betsy Andrews
Title contributed by: Rosewell Page III

Edited by:
Betsy Andrews
Donna Page
Pia Davis

1st Printing December, 1988
2nd Printing June, 1989

Library of Congress Catalog Card Number: 88-092470

International Standard Book Number: 9-9621777-0-9

Printed by

WIMMER BROTHERS

Memphis Dallas

FOREWORD

I was raised in the kitchen of a fair to middling cook, who to get me out from under foot at age five (circa 1912) plunked me on a stool broadside a chopping board heaped high with steaming spinach, armed me with a cleaver and had me chop it finer than a modern blender for the making of creamed spinach, a staple in our house in my youth. With this start I early on developed an avid interest in the culinary arts.

Neither friend nor family then would dream that in 1932 Mother would privately publish a work smaller than yours, but like it containing tried and true recipes from diversified cuisines, called the JOY OF COOKING, the tremendous success of which gave birth to a publishing gold rush.

Having inherited some one hundred of her favorite cookbooks which I added to some fifty of my own, I was delighted to receive a copy of your first edition of PANNING FOR PLEASURE. The clarity of recipe presentation and variety of dishes has put it on my kitchen workshelf.

Best wishes for your second edition.

Sincerely,

Edgar R. Rombauer

Edgar R. Rombauer

THANKS. . .

To my husband, Bob, for making this book a dream come true, and for his constant love and support.

A special thanks to my wonderful family and friends, who sat through many tasting and testing sessions, and after that, still urged me to write this book. This has truly been a "family affair."

TABLE OF CONTENTS

For Openers

FOR OPENERS

CHEESE AND OLIVE BALLS

Makes 40 cheese balls

Something about warmed olives that makes me think of sunshine and Mexico.

1/4 cup butter, softened
1/4 pound cheddar cheese, grated
3/4 cup flour
1/2 teaspoon paprika
40 small stuffed green olives

- Combine butter and grated cheese. Blend well. Add the flour and paprika. Stir until mixture has the texture of pie dough. Set aside and chill for 20 minutes. Drain olives. Take pinches of dough and seal olives completely inside. Place on ungreased cookie sheet. Set aside to chill for 10 minutes. Meanwhile, preheat oven to 275 degrees. Bake olives for 20 minutes.
- These freeze well, and do not need to thaw before baking; just increase baking time to 30 minutes.

SAVORY SHRIMP BITES

Makes 40 appetizers

Quick appetizers

2 cups large cooked shrimp, cleaned
1 clove garlic, minced
1 cup chili sauce
20 slices bacon

- Mix shrimp and garlic, pour chili sauce over. Cover and let flavors blend for a few hours. Cut bacon slices in half and cook until limp, not crisp.
- Remove shrimp and wrap a piece of bacon around each, securing with a wooden pick.
- Set oven to broil. Place shrimp in oven 3 inches from heat source and cook until bacon is crisp, turning once.

PECAN STUFFED MUSHROOMS

Makes 1 dozen appetizers

My friend Violet Davis was willing to share this outstanding stuffed mushroom recipe with us all.

1	**pound mushrooms, large**	**1/2**	**teaspoon salt**
1	**cup pecans, finely chopped**	**1/4**	**teaspoon thyme**
3	**tablespoons parsley, chopped**		**Pepper to taste**
1/4	**cup margarine, softened**		**Cream for basting**
1	**clove garlic, minced**		

- Wipe mushrooms clean. Remove stems, chop and reserve. Mix all ingredients except cream, with chopped stems. Pack this filling into mushroom caps, and place on greased cookie sheet. Bake at 350 degrees for about 20 minutes. Baste often with cream.

PICNIC PORK PÂTÉ

Serves 10 to 12

Bring along some pumpernickel bread, a cluster of green grapes and some good mustard for this picnic dish.

2	**pounds bulk pork sausage**	**1/2**	**teaspoon cinnamon**
2	**pounds fresh spinach, chopped**	**1/2**	**teaspoon thyme**
2	**teaspoons salt**	**1 1/2**	**teaspoons basil**
1/2	**teaspoon mace**		

- Mix all the ingredients in food processor or blender.
- Fold into a 9-inch loaf pan, making sure it is well-packed and is hiding no air pockets.
- Bake in preheated oven at 350 degrees for 45 minutes. Remove from oven. Immediately compress pâté by placing a brick wrapped in foil or a couple of heavy cans on top. Cool and wrap well. Refrigerate for at least 2 hours. Unmold and remove any fat. Slice and serve.

EMERGENCY PÂTÉ

Makes 1 1/2 cups

This is terrific for a quick appetizer.

- **1/2 pound braunschwiger or liverwurst roll**
- **3 green onions, chopped**
- **1/4 cup black olives, chopped**
- **3 tablespoons sour cream**
- **3 tablespoons cream cheese, room temperature**
- **2 tablespoons brandy**

- Blend all the ingredients and spoon into crock. Chill several hours to let flavors mingle.

BRIE PÂTÉ

Makes 2 1/2 cups

- **1 8-ounce package Brie, rind discarded**
- **1 1/2 sticks butter, softened**
- **1/2 cup almond slivers, toasted**
- **2 tablespoons dry sherry**
- **1/4 teaspoon dried thyme**

- Whip all the ingredients together. Spoon into crock; cover and let stand at room temperature for 2 hours.
- Serve on crackers.

BAKED BRIE

Serves 4

One of my favorites. It's a snap to make.

1 8-ounce wheel Brie
1/4 stick butter, room temperature
1/4 cup almonds, sliced

- Preheat oven to 350 degrees. Place Brie in oven proof dish. Spread butter on cheese. Arrange almonds on top. Bake for 12 minutes or until heated through.
- Serve warm with Flute bread and some pear or apple slices.

PEANUT BUTTER ON THE RITZ

I suppose it would be nice to apologize for adding this kind of recipe. All I ask you is, try it. Guaranteed to surprise you.

Ritz crackers
peanut butter
small onions, sliced

- That's it; spread peanut butter on cracker and top with a slice of onion.
- Do not make these too far in advance, as the crackers do tend to get soft.

GRAVLAX

There are so many ways to prepare Gravlax; this recipe came from Denmark, and it is terrific. We serve it on toasted French bread topped with a little scrambled egg and chives for brunch.

2 2-pound fillets red king salmon
1 1/4 cups salad oil
2 tablespoons sugar
1 teaspoon salt
1 teaspoon white pepper
4-5 tablespoons fresh dill, chopped

- Wipe salmon with a damp dish towel. Dip salmon in oil and pour the remaining oil over fillets before adding spices.
- Combine sugar, salt and pepper, set aside.
- Place some fresh dill in bottom of a pan as close in size as possible to the fish you use.
- Place one fillet skin-side up. Place the other fillet on top, skin to skin, then top with more dill and spices. Cover with plastic wrap and place a heavy object on top, a couple of heavy cans will do.
- Refrigerate for 24 hours, turning several times.
- Slice into thin slices very sharp knife.
- Very tasty served on pumpernickel bread, spread with cream cheese.

FIESTA FONDUE

Serve with corn chips

This is a wonderful Mexican dip we often enjoyed at the home of Jeannie Sturrock.

3 cups sharp Cheddar cheese, grated
1 teaspoon salt
1 teaspoon garlic, minced
1/4 cup green onions, chopped
1 4 1/2-ounce can refried beans
1 tablespoon horseradish sauce
1/2 cup green chilies, chopped
1/2 teaspoon Tabasco sauce

- Heat above and mix thoroughly.
- Top with the following:

1 cup Swiss cheese, grated
1 cup sharp Cheddar cheese, grated
1/2 cup black olives, chopped
1/2 cup green chilies, chopped
1/2 cup green onions, chopped
1/2 cup green olives, chopped

- Place in ovenproof dish and heat until all the cheese has melted. About 15 minutes.

SWEDISH MEATBALLS

Makes about 40 appetizers

Always one of the favorite things on the buffet table, and the first to need refilling.

1/2 pound veal, ground
1/2 pound moose or beef, ground
1/4 cup pine nuts
1 clove garlic, minced
1 small onion, grated
2 eggs, slightly beaten
1/2 cup soft bread crumbs
1 teaspoon salt
1 teaspoon basil
Bacon grease and butter for frying

- Mix all ingredients in mixer. Form into small meatballs and fry in half bacon grease and half butter. Or, deep fat fry.

SWEET-AND-SOUR SAUCE:

1 cup chicken broth
1/2 cup sugar
1/2 cup pineapple juice
1/2 cup vinegar
2 tablespoons cornstarch
3 tablespoons soy sauce
1/2 green bell pepper, chopped
1/2 red bell pepper, chopped
1 8-ounce can pineapple chunks

- Combine broth, sugar, juice and vinegar. Dissolve cornstarch in soy sauce. Add to broth mixture and cook until thickened.
- Add bell peppers, meatballs and pineapple and let simmer for 20 minutes. Serve in chafing dish at low heat.

COUNTRY PÂTÉ

Serves 12 to 16

A wonderful combination of many flavors and not hard to do with the help of a food processor or a willing husband to chop for you. When sliced, this pâté has a marbled appearance. This looks nice served with fresh grapes and toasted triangles of pumpernickel bread.

1/2 pound ground pork
1/2 pound pork fat
1/2 pound chicken breast
1/2 pound chicken livers, or calf liver
1 onion, chopped
1 garlic, minced
1/3 cup parsley, chopped
1 piece ham, fully cooked,
1/4 cup mushrooms, chopped
1/4 cup pistachio nuts, shelled
2 tablespoons pimento, chopped
1 tablespoon butter
1/2 teaspoon thyme
1/2 teaspoon oregano
1/2 teaspoon chervil
1/2 teaspoon pepper
1/4 teaspoon ground clove
2 tablespoons flour
1 egg
4 tablespoons brandy
12 slices bacon
Parsley or lettuce

- Chop pork, pork fat, chicken in food processor, using the on/off method, or use meat grinder. Set aside.
- Sauté garlic, onion, parsley and liver for 5 minutes. Remove and chop liver coarsely.
- Chop the ham into small cubes. Combine all three meat combinations in a large bowl with mushrooms and pistachio nuts. Stir well and add all ingredients except egg, brandy and bacon. Finally add egg and brandy: mix thoroughly.
- Place the bacon slices in loaf pan and pour mixture in. Overlapping bacon on top. Place loaf pan inside larger pan holding water to measure 3/4 up sides of loaf pan.
- Bake at 350 for 1 1/4 hours.
- Remove bacon slices and discard.
- Arrange on top of a bed of parsley or lettuce.

PARMESAN CHICKEN BITES

Makes about 50 pieces

Tasty little morsels. Very easy to serve at an informal cocktail party.

- **2 pounds chicken breasts**
- **1/2 cup plain bread crumbs**
- **1/4 cup Parmesan cheese, grated**
- **2 teaspoons basil**
- **1 teaspoon thyme**
- **1/2 teaspoon marjoram**
- **1/2 teaspoon paprika**
- **1/2 cup butter, melted**

- Cut chicken into bite size pieces. In a medium size bowl, combine bread crumbs with cheese and basil, thyme, marjoram and paprika. Mix well. Dip the cubed chicken into butter and roll it in the seasoned bread crumbs. Place on cookie sheet. Bake in oven at 350 degrees for about 10 minutes or until lightly browned.

HOT SAUCE FOR DIPPING:

- **1/2 cup apricot preserves**
- **2 tablespoons catsup**
- **2 teaspoon prepared hot Chinese mustard**

- Mix well. Serve with chicken bites. This sauce is also very good served with egg rolls.

CHICKEN LIVER PÂTÉ

Serves 12 to 16

We rarely have a gathering without this easy pâté on the table.

- **1 quart water**
- **2 teaspoons whole peppercorns**
- **1 teaspoon whole cloves**
- **1 bay leaf**
- **2 sprigs parsley**
- **1 1/4 pounds chicken livers**

- Combine and simmer the above gently for 10 minutes.
- Remove the chicken livers after they have cooked, discard the spices and liquid. Place chicken livers in blender or food processor with the following ingredients except brandy:

- **2 sticks butter, softened**
- **1 small onion, grated**
- **1 clove garlic, minced**
- **1/2 teaspoon salt**
- **1 teaspoon dry mustard**
- **1/4 teaspoon nutmeg**
- **Dash of Tabasco sauce**
- **1/4 cup brandy**

- Chop, or process using the on/off method until you have a smooth pâté. Add brandy and stir gently. Place in refrigerator until serving time. If you find the pâté a little dry, add a couple of tablespoons of mayonnaise.
- I usually serve this with pumpernickel bread.

PLUMP MUSHROOMS

Serves 6 to 8

One of the "you can't eat just one" appetizers.

- **1 teaspoon paprika**
- **1/2 teaspoon salt**
- **1/4 teaspoon pepper**
- **1 1/4 cups flour**
- **6 ounces beer**
- **Oil for deep frying**
- **24 uniformly sized mushrooms**

• Wash mushrooms well and remove stems. Combine the seasonings with flour and whisk in beer until smooth.

• Heat oil. Add the mushrooms to batter and dip them into oil, about five at a time. Turn them a couple of times, until they are golden brown. Remove and place on paper towel to absorb grease.

• Continue with the remaining mushrooms. Serve with Horseradish Sauce. This batter will last up to 1 week in the refrigerator.

HORSERADISH SAUCE:

- **1 cup mayonnaise**
- **3-4 tablespoons prepared horseradish**
- **2 tablespoons sour cream**
- **2 tablespoons cream, Half-and-Half**
- **Dash of Worcestershire sauce**

• Blend well and keep cool until serving time.

WIN'S CHUTNEY CHEESE BALL

Serves 8

Keep on hand for unexpected company. This freezes well.

- **1/4 pound Gorgonzola cheese, or Blue cheese**
- **1/2 pound cream cheese**
- **1/4 cup chutney, like Peter Page's Chutney, chopped**
- **1/2 cup toasted almonds, chopped**

• Mix Gorgonzola cheese, cream cheese and chutney; form into ball. Roll cheese ball in toasted almonds. Chill. Serve on toasted pumpernickel triangles.

HOMEMADE LOX

My husband, Bob, was not sure he could part with this secret and very easy way to have delicious lox all year round. I think this was because it is so simple and he has had nothing but praise for his culinary talent. Now you'll all know the tremendous work involved.

- Start by catching a King salmon, preferably 40 pounds or larger. A red one is nice, only because it looks prettier. The whites are just as tasty though; perhaps even better.
- Fillet the salmon, removing the ribs from both fillets. Cut fillets into equal thirds, or pieces that will fit flat into a crock or other non-metallic container that you will not need very soon.
- Wash and wipe salmon clean. Cover bottom of crock with a thick layer of Morton's Salt and Sugar Cure. Layer salmon fillets flesh to flesh, beginning with skin side down. Cover each piece with a liberal amount of sugar and salt cure, making sure the top layer is well covered with the brining mixture. The salmon will make it's own brine, do not add any liquids. Place in a cool place for 3 months. This will remain good for up to 1 year.
- When serving, rinse all the cure off and soak salmon in cold water, changing water several times. Soak overnight or longer, depending on your taste.
- Wipe clean and place skin side down. With a very sharp, thin-bladed knife, cut paper-thin slices on a slight diagonal, slicing to the skin.
- Serve on cream cheese covered bagels with a thin ring of red onion and a touch of capers.

The following recipes give you some idea's of how to enjoy Lox.

LOX WITH CANTALOUPE:
Simply wrap a thin slice of lox around a piece of cantaloupe.

LOX ON PUMPERNICKEL BREAD:
Cut bread into attractive triangles. Spread with cream cheese. Top with lox, garnish with fresh chives. Do not substitute with green onions.

LOX WITH PISTACHIOS:
Mix cream cheese with nuts and a little curry powder. Spread on crackers, top with lox.

LOX WITH ASPARAGUS:
Wrap thin slices of lox around crispy cooked, cooled asparagus.

LOX AND CREAM CHEESE:
Cut logs of cream cheese, wrap lox around cheese. Place a touch of parsley on each end of logs.

LOX WITH MUSTARD SAUCE

- 2 tablespoons Dijon mustard
- 1 tablespoon sugar
- 1 1/2 tablespoons wine vinegar
- 1 teaspoon dill, chopped
- 1/2 teaspoon salt
- 1/3 cup vegetable oil
- French bread

- Mix all the ingredients except oil, blending until sugar crunch is gone. Add oil a little at a time, stirring constantly. Toast a thick piece of French bread. Spread with Mustard Sauce, top with lox and fresh chives or dill.

LOX WITH HEART OF PALM

- 1 cup oil
- 1/2 cup white wine vinegar
- 1/4 fresh cup lemon juice
- 1/4 cup capers, rinsed, dried
- 1/2 tablespoon sugar
- 1/2 teaspoon salt
- 1/4 teaspoon pepper

- Combine all the ingredients in mixing bowl and blend well. Cover and refrigerate until serving time. To serve, wrap a piece of lox around a heart of palm; pour dressing over. This can be made up to 3 days before and kept cold.

HERB CREAM CHEESE

Makes 1 1/2 cups

Making them yourself is so much less costly than buying cheese spreads in the supermarket. Use fresh spices if possible.

12 ounces cream cheese, softened
1/2 cup butter, softened
3 cloves garlic, minced
2 tablespoons chive
1 1/2 teaspoons chervil
1 1/2 teaspoons tarragon
1 teaspoon parsley, chopped
1 1/2 teaspoons thyme
1/2 teaspoon white pepper
Couple of shakes of Tabasco sauce

- Cream cheese and butter and add remaining ingredients. Let rest in refrigerator overnight or longer to blend flavors.
- Pretty served inside a red bell pepper.

HUNGARIAN COCKTAIL STICKS

Makes 4 dozen appetizers

There is a surprise in the middle. This comes from one of the cooking classes I attended.

1 cup mashed potatoes
1/2 cup butter
1/2 teaspoon salt
1 cup flour
1 egg yolk, beaten
1 tablespoon cream
4 tablespoons sesame seeds
2 teaspoons caraway seeds
4 tablespoons Parmesan cheese
1/4 teaspoon paprika

- Preheat oven to 375 degrees.
- In a bowl, mix the potatoes, flour, butter and salt to form a smooth dough. Shape into a ball; roll out making a flat sheet, 1/4-inch thick. Brush the beaten egg thinned with cream. Cut dough into quarters; sprinkle two sections with sesame seeds and two with caraway seeds. Sprinkle Parmesan cheese and paprika on two sections, one of each with a different seed topping. Cut into 1/2-inch wide and 3 inches long strips. Bake at 375 degrees for 12 minutes or until light brown.

MUSHROOM/VEAL TERRINE

Serves 8

A simple, delicious preparation for an elegant terrine.

1/2 pound ground veal
1 cup fresh bread crumbs
5 shallots, chopped
1/4 pound butter
1/2 cup heavy cream
1 egg white
1/4 teaspoon salt
1/4 teaspoon pepper
Pinch of ground ginger and allspice
2 pounds mushrooms, diced
1/4 cup oil
1 clove garlic, minced
1 cup chicken broth
1/2 teaspoon each dried sage, basil, and thyme

- In medium bowl, combine veal and bread crumbs. Sauté half the shallots in 2 tablespoons of butter until limp. Add to bowl with veal. Beat egg white and half of cream until thick with salt, pepper, ginger and allspice. Add to veal mixture. Set aside in a cool place for 1 hour.
- Sauté mushrooms in oil for a couple of minutes. Reserve liquid. Set aside.
- Melt the remaining butter, add to it garlic, remaining shallots, mushroom juice, broth, sage, basil and thyme. Bring this to a boil and let simmer until reduced to half. Strain and pour over the cooked mushrooms.
- Add remaining cream, meat mixture and mushrooms with the liquid, blend well.
- Heat oven to 350 degrees.
- Fold ingredients into greased terrine. Cover with foil and cook in water bath by placing terrine inside roasting pan filled with hot water. Make sure water reaches 1/2 way up the sides.
- Bake for 1 1/4 hours.
- This is a delightful first course.

GUACAMOLE DIP

Serves 6

4	**small Italian tomatoes**	2	**tablespoons fresh lemon juice**
2	**ripe avocados**	2	**cloves garlic, minced**
4	**green onions, finely chopped**	1	**tablespoon cilantro, minced, optional**
1/2	**teaspoon Jalopeño pepper, minced**		**Salt and pepper to taste**

- Finely dice tomatoes. Peel avocados and sprinkle with lemon juice, this prevents them from turning dark. Mash avocados with a fork, and fold in the chopped tomatoes. Add onions, pepper, garlic, lemon juice and spices. Line bowl with lettuce leaves, spoon in the guacamole and serve with taco chips.

BREN'S LORETO GUACAMOLE

Serves 4

One very used recipe when we are in Loreto, but always a good one anywhere.

2	**ripe avocados**	1/2	**cup chilies, minced**
1/2	**cup onion, finely chopped**	1	**lemon, juice of**
1/2	**cup tomatoes, finely chopped**		**Salt and pepper to taste**

- Combine all the ingredients in a blender and blend to your liking. We like it smooth but for a few avocado chunks.

CURRY SAUCE FOR PICKLED HERRING

Sauce for 4 jars of herring

Follow the recipe for Thompson's Pickled Herring, or the commercial kind from Vita is a nice substitute. Drain herring and discard onions first. Serve with a glass of ice-cold Akvavit.

MIX THE FOLLOWING:

2 tablespoons sugar
2 tablespoons hot water
1/2 cup cider vinegar
2 teaspoons curry powder
1 cup mayonnaise
1 medium red onion, sliced

- Pour sugar into hot water and stir until dissolved. Add vinegar and curry powder, making sure to blend really well; set aside to cool.
- Stir the mixture into mayonnaise a little at a time, blend thoroughly.
- Add the sliced red onion and allow flavors to mingle, by storing covered in refrigerator. This will last several weeks.
- Serve on crackers or on triangles of pumpernickel bread.

FETA STUFFED MUSHROOMS

Makes 24 appetizers

Good for dieters.

1 pound fresh spinach
1/2 cup grated Parmesan cheese
4 ounces feta cheese, crumbled
1/2 cup green onions, finely chopped
1/2 cup parsley, finely chopped
24 medium-sized mushrooms

- Cook spinach; squeeze all liquid from greens and combine with all ingredients except mushrooms. Clean mushrooms and stuff with feta mixture. Sprinkle each with a little extra Parmesan cheese. Bake at 400 degrees for 15 minutes.

DUNGENESS CRAB DIP

Serves 8

Zippy and tasty.

1/2 pound crab meat
1/2 cup sour cream
1/4 cup mayonnaise
1 teaspoon lemon juice
1/2 teaspoon Tabasco sauce
1/2 teaspoon horseradish
1/2 teaspoon salt
2 tablespoons parsley, finely chopped
Dash paprika

- Combine all the ingredients, carefully folding in the crab. Serve on crackers. Garnish with small sprigs of parsley.

DIJON SHRIMP RAMEKIN

Serves 4

Easy first course, or for a light luncheon.

1 cup celery, finely chopped
1/4 cup mayonnaise
2 tablespoons Dijon mustard
2 tablespoons onion, minced
20 large shrimp, cooked
1/2 cup croutons

- Combine mustard, mayonnaise, onion and celery. Scoop sauce into 4 ramekins, reserving a little for top. Place 5 shrimp in each ramekin. Pour remaining sauce over.
- Top with croutons and bake for 8 minutes at 350 degrees.

DANISH SILDESALAT

Serves 6

Herring Salad is the translation. Best served on small triangles of pumpernickel bread.

1 1-pound jar herring in wine sauce, drained
1 cup cucumber pickles, diced
1 cup tart apples, peeled, diced
1 cup canned, pickled beets, diced
1/4 stick butter
1 1/2 tablespoons flour
1/4 cup chicken broth
1/2 teaspoon Dijon mustard
1/2 cup liquid from pickled beets
1/2 teaspoon salt
1/4 teaspoon pepper
2 hard-boiled eggs for garnish
Watercress for garnish

- Cut drained herring into small squares. Combine with pickles, apples and beets, mix gently. Melt butter in small sauce pan. Add flour and let bubble for 2 minutes, stirring constantly. Thin with broth and liquid from beets, until a smooth sauce is obtained. Blend in the mustard, salt and pepper and stir infrequently until cool. Combine with herring mixture. Chop or slice eggs and garnish salad with both eggs and watercress, or I sometimes use alfalfa sprouts.

HOLIDAY CHEESE BALL

Makes 2 1/2 cups

2 8-ounce packages cream cheese
1 6-ounce wedge Bleu cheese, room temperature
1 tablespoon garlic salt
1 teaspoon Worchestershire sauce
2 tablespoons parsley, chopped
1 teaspoon paprika
1/4 cup walnuts, chopped

- Combine cheeses with garlic salt and Worchestershire sauce. Form into ball. Roll first in parsley, then in paprika and then finally in walnuts. This is best served at room temperature.

MURDER COVE SMOKED SALMON SPREAD

Makes 1 1/2 cups

1/2 pound smoked salmon, or 1 7-ounce can
1 3-ounce package cream cheese
3 tablespoons mayonnaise
1/2 cup celery, diced
1/2 teaspoon Dijon mustard
1/4 teaspoon salt
Dash of Tabasco sauce

- Drain salmon, if using canned. Finely chop. Cream together cheese and mayonnaise. Add salmon, celery and seasonings.
- Serve on crackers or pilot bread.

DIABLO EGGS

Makes 8 appetizers

4 eggs, hard-boiled
1 1/2 tablespoons mayonnaise
2 tablespoons chutney
1/2 teaspoon curry powder

- Remove yolks from eggs and blend with mayonnaise and chutney. Season with curry powder. Stuff egg whites with mixture.
- Arrange on lettuce leaves.

Brunch Favorites

BRUNCH FAVORITES

DANISH PANCAKE BALLS (Aebleskiver)

Makes 2 dozen

For these you will need a special Danish pan called an aebleskive pan. They can be found in any large kitchen shop and are well worth the purchase.

8 eggs, separated
1 tablespoon sugar
2 cups flour
1/2 cup butter, melted
1 1/2 cups cream
1 teaspoon cardamom
Jam
Powdered sugar

- Separate eggs. Beat egg yolks and sugar together well.
- Sift flour into yolk mixture and blend thoroughly. Add the melted butter and cream. Whip egg whites and fold into the mixture. Add the cardamom.
- Heat the pan over medium heat, melt a dot of margarine or butter in each hole. Fill the holes 3/4 full, let cook for 3 minutes. Turn over and cook other side. Fry until golden brown. Sprinkle with powdered sugar and keep warm until all the dough has been used up.
- Serve hot with jam and powdered sugar.

AEBLESKIVER WITH YEAST (Apple Pancake Balls)

Makes 1 dozen

1 teaspoon sugar
1/2 teaspoon salt
2 cups flour
1/2 teaspoon cardamom
1 package dry yeast
1/4 cup warm milk
2 cups milk
3 eggs
Apple sauce
Powdered sugar

- Sift the first four dry ingredients into a large bowl; mix well.
- Dissolve the yeast in warm milk. Add milk, eggs and the yeast mixture to flour mixture and blend thoroughly. Set aside and let rise for 2 hours. Bake in the Danish aebleskive pan until golden brown.
- Serve with apple sauce and powder sugar.

MONTPELIER BREAKFAST DISH

Serves 8

This is such an easy dish to make. This was given to me at the Legion Hall in Montpelier, Virginia. "They" were there for a chitlin breakfast. This was my first and may I add, my last chitlin feast, but this dish was great, and most of the things can be found in the refrigerator and whipped up in no time.

2 pounds hot Jimmy Dean Sausage
10 eggs
1 1/2 cups milk
1/2 teaspoon salt
1/2 teaspoon pepper
1/2 teaspoon paprika
6 slices white bread
1 1/2 cups sharp Cheddar cheese

- Heat oven to 350 degrees. Grease a lasagne pan well.
- Whip eggs with milk, salt, pepper and paprika. Remove crust from bread slices. Place bread in pan. Crumble and fry sausage until done.
- Mix egg mixture with cooked sausage and pour over bread. Top with shredded cheese and bake at 350 degrees for 25 minutes.

ARTICHOKE/EGG DISH

Serves 4

My sister-in-law, Melinda, served this unusual combination at a brunch last time we visited New York City. We loved it and have served it many times. I like to French scramble the eggs by cooking them over a double boiler.

1 can artichoke hearts, in water
8 eggs
Dash of salt
Dash of white pepper
2 tablespoons butter

- In an ovenproof dish warm the artichoke hearts in oven until ready to use, at about 300 degrees for 15 minutes. Scramble the eggs with salt and pepper in butter. Remove artichoke hearts from oven and drain. To serve, place hearts in a circle with scrambled eggs in the middle.

SOUTHERN FRIED APPLES

Serves 8

Perfect when served with sliced Virginia ham and Potato Pancakes.

8 Granny Smith apples, unpeeled
2 tablespoons bacon drippings
2 tablespoons butter
1/2 cup Maple syrup
3/4 cup brown sugar
1 teaspoon cinnamon

- Core apples and slice. Melt bacon grease and butter in skillet. Add apples, syrup and brown sugar. Bring it to a boil, stir gently for 30 seconds, lower heat and let simmer until apples are soft, but not mushy, or about 45 minutes. Just before serving, sprinkle apples with cinnamon.

POACHED EASTER NESTS

Serves 4

This looks very attractive, a perfect Easter Brunch dish.

8 eggs, separated
4 tablespoons tarragon vinegar
Water for poaching eggs
Pinch of paprika

- Separate yolks from whites and whip whites until stiff.
- In a large skillet, heat water and vinegar and bring to a boil. Lower heat, let simmer while preparing eggs.
- Place 8 separate ''nests'' of whipped egg whites in water, now place 1 egg yolk on top of each nest. Cover with lid and let simmer for 4 minutes, or until whites are set and yolk still soft.
- Sprinkle with paprika.
- Serve on top of grilled muffins.

VIKING SPECIAL

Serves 6

All can be prepared ahead, kept cold and baked just before serving the crowd. Our stand by on the Damn Yankee.

1/2 pound Cheddar cheese, sliced
1/2 pound Cheddar cheese, shredded
1 cup sour cream
1/2 teaspoon dry mustard
1/2 teaspoon paprika
1 teaspoon salt
1 pound hot Jimmy Dean Sausage
10 large eggs
2 shakes of Tabasco sauce

- Grease casserole dish; place sliced cheese in bottom. Mix sour cream with mustard, paprika, salt and Tabasco sauce; spread half of mixture on top of cheese.
- Cook sausage; drain on paper towel. Layer crumbled sausage over sour cream mixture. Break eggs on top of sausage trying to keep yolk from breaking. Pour the remaining sour cream mixture on top of eggs.
- Top with shredded cheese and bake at 325 degrees for 25 minutes.

PEYTON'S GERMAN PANCAKE

Serves 4

While we were fishing in Pybus bay one morning our niece grew tired of waiting for someone to break away and think "breakfast" and not "fishing". I suggested she do something about it. This is what she served. Fantastic!

6 eggs
1/4 teaspoon salt
1 teaspoon sugar
1 cup flour
1 1/2 cups milk
1 stick butter, melted
Powdered sugar for topping
Fresh lemon juice for topping

- Preheat oven to 400 degrees. Beat eggs with salt and sugar. Blend flour and milk until smooth. Combine the two mixtures. Melt butter. Pour butter into round pan or two 8-inch square baking pans. Add batter, bake for 15 minutes or until golden brown and set. Keep an eye on it, cover if it gets too brown. It will be puffy and light.
- Top with powdered sugar and freshly squeezed lemon juice.

GARDEN QUICHE

Serves 6

Use any combination of fresh vegetables you might have on hand. Great luncheon dish. Even men like it.

CRUST:

1 1/2	**cups flour**
1/4	**teaspoon salt**
1/3	**cup butter**
1	**egg**

FILLING:

1/2	**cup Romano cheese**
1/4	**cup flour**
2	**medium tomatoes, peeled**
1/2	**cup green onions, sliced**

FILLING (continued):

8	**mushrooms, sliced**
1/2	**cup zucchini, in chunks**
4	**eggs**
1/2	**cup milk**
1/2	**teaspoon mustard, dry**
1/4	**teaspoon salt**
1/2	**teaspoon fresh basil, or 1/4 teaspoon dried**
1/4	**teaspoon white pepper**

- Preheat oven to 375 degrees.
- For crust, combine flour, salt and butter in medium bowl. Add egg; stir well. Shape into ball and press into bottom of a quiche pan, or any 9 inch, deep dish pan. Sprinkle with 2 tablespoons of Romano cheese. For filling, place flour in a bowl; dip tomatoes, onions, mushrooms and zucchini into flour. Layer over crust. Sprinkle with the remaining cheese.
- Mix eggs, milk and seasonings in bowl, beat well. Pour mixture over vegetables.
- Bake at 375 degrees for 40 minutes or until set.
- Cool 5 minutes before serving. Slice like a pie.

BRUNCH CHAMPAGNE

Serves 6

2	**cups fresh orange juice**
2	**cups champagne**
1/2	**cup orange-flavored liqueur**
	Strawberries

- Mix all the ingredients in a blender. Serve in tall champagne glasses with a strawberry set afloat on each.

CHEESY ONION AND EGG GRATIN

Serves 8

This can be made ahead, popped in the oven and on the table in 12 minutes.

8	**eggs, hard-boiled**	**1**	**cup milk**
1	**cup mushrooms, sliced**		**Salt and pepper to taste**
1/2	**tablespoon butter**	**1/4**	**teaspoon paprika**
1	**cup green onions, chopped**	**2**	**tablespoons coarse grain mustard**
2	**tablespoons flour**	**3**	**shakes Tabasco sauce**
1/2	**cup Half-and-Half**	**3/4**	**cup Swiss cheese, shredded**

- The perfect hard-boiled egg ?
- Place eggs in cold water; bring to a boil. Upon boiling, remove from heat and set aside in water exactly 10 minutes. Remove and run under cold water. Perfect!
- Slice eggs in half lengthwise and place in ovenproof pan. I usually cut a tiny part off round edge so the eggs rests firmly in pan. Cover with mushrooms.
- Melt butter in sauce pan, sauté green onions until limp; add flour and stir for 2 minutes. Slowly add Half-and-Half and milk, stirring constantly. Sprinkle with salt, pepper and paprika. Stir in mustard and keep stirring until thick, then add Tabasco sauce.
- Pour over eggs and mushrooms. Cover top with shredded cheese and bake for 12 minutes at 400 degrees.
- Serve on buttered muffins.

OUR TAILGATE BRUNCH

Many of the North Americans living either full time or part of the year in Loreto, Mexico, have their Loreto Breakfast Club meetings on selected Sundays, outside of town on some scenic beach. As we drove we passed Brahma bulls, donkey's, road runners, rabbits and a few stray burrows. Beautiful cactus trees grow everywhere; some small, some tall, but all completely unhuggable. Here is a sample of some good things cooked over the open fire.

- Sandy: She prepared duck gizzards in a heavy cast iron skillet. She sautéed the gizzards in butter. Once in awhile tipping a bottle of cream sherry over the pan, and continuing to cook them, sometimes with a lid, sometimes not. They were out of this world.

- Anne: Anne willingly shared with us a most treasured buck-wheat pancake mix she had obtained on a recent trip to Virginia. I happen to know this was her last package. We poured some wonderful, ''the real thing'', maple syrup over the cakes.

- Joanne: Came loaded with thick slabs of honey cured bacon they had carted down in their motor home from Long Beach. After the bacon was done, she fried some potatoes in the same pan, blending them with a mess of crisp onions. Scrumptious.

- Cathy: Fluffed up some serious scrambled eggs, light as air. We donated some slices of Virginia ham and some homemade jam, nothing compared with all the other delicacies. It was all appreciated.

- The men folks: They mostly fished, made some of Fred's cool Bloody Merry drinks, and fished some more. Took some walks, and made the dogs retrieve sticks. In a few words, they had a great time too.

EGGS FLORENTINE

Serves 6

- 6 eggs
- 2 tablespoons tarragon vinegar
- 6 baked patty shells, like Pillsbury Farms
- 1 cup spinach
- 1 tablespoon butter
- 2 teaspoons lemon juice
- 1/4 teaspoon salt
- 1/8 teaspoon pepper
- 2 tablespoons Parmesan cheese
- Mornay sauce, see below

- Poach eggs gently in tarragon vinegar and water. Set aside.
- Chop spinach and cook until done. Drain well.
- Heat cooked spinach in butter and stir in lemon juice, salt and pepper. Make a layer of spinach in bottom of each shell. Spoon 1 tablespoon of Mornay Sauce over spinach and place poached egg on top. Fill the shells with remaining sauce and sprinkle with cheese. Bake in a 350 degree oven for 15 minutes.

MORNAY SAUCE:

- 3 tablespoons butter
- 3 tablespoons flour
- 1/2 teaspoon salt
- 1/8 teaspoon pepper
- 1 cup hot milk
- 2 tablespoons Swiss cheese, grated
- 2 tablespoons Parmesan cheese

- Melt butter over low heat, add flour and seasonings. Stir in the hot milk, a little at a time, until thick and smooth. Simmer for about 10 minutes under lid, stir frequently. Blend in the cheeses.

SPINACH FLORENTINE

- Follow recipe for Eggs Florentine, but replace shells with artichoke bottoms.

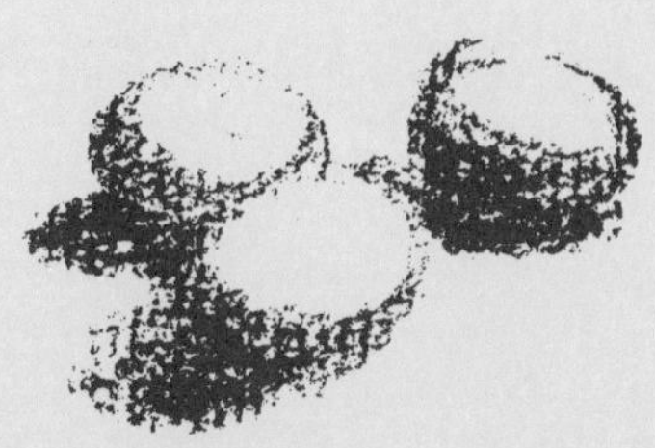

From the Bread Basket

FROM THE BREAD BASKET

BRAIDED EGG BREAD

Makes 2 loaves

2	**packages dry yeast**	1	**tablespoon salt**
2	**cups water**	9	**cups flour**
6	**tablespoons honey**	1	**egg yolk**
4	**eggs**	1	**tablespoon water**
1/3	**cup vegetable oil**	1 1/2	**teaspoons poppy seeds**

- Dissolve yeast in warm water for 5 minutes. Add honey.
- Mix eggs, oil and salt with 2 cups flour. Beat well. Place in mixer with dough hook on, add yeast mixture and another 4 cups of flour. Keep kneading, adding flour as you go, until all used.
- Place in greased bowl and let rise until double in bulk, about 2 hours. Punch down and divide into 2 equal parts.
- Divide each of these into thirds and braid.
- Place both loaves on cookie sheet. Brush with egg yolk mixed with 1 tablespoon water. Sprinkle with 1 1/2 teaspoons poppy seeds.
- Bake at 325 degrees for 25 to 30 minutes. Cool on racks.

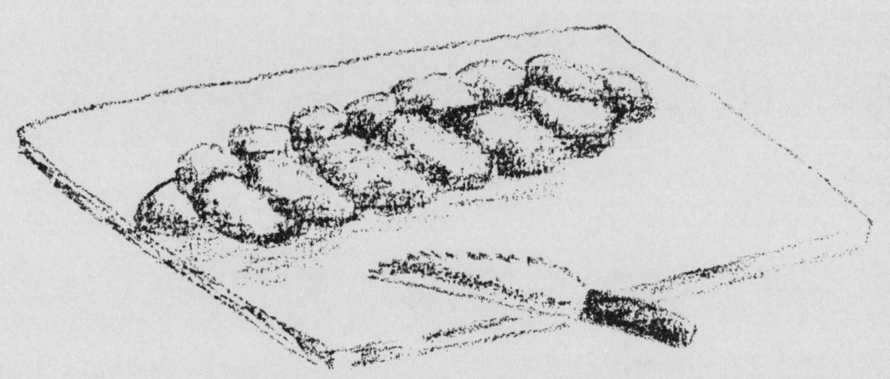

COTTAGE CHEESE BREAD

Makes 2 loaves

Nice and moist. Plan to use within a day or two, it doesn't keep very well.

1 package yeast
1/2 cup warm water
2 cups creamed cottage cheese
2 tablespoons butter
2 eggs, beaten
2 teaspoons salt
1/4 cup sugar
1 tablespoon caraway seeds
1/4 teaspoon baking soda
5 cups flour, unbleached

- Combine yeast and water; let sit for 5 minutes.
- Warm cottage cheese and butter. Add to them eggs, salt, sugar, caraways seeds and baking soda and beat until blended. Combine egg mixture and yeast and blend well. Add as much flour as necessary for a smooth dough. In mixer with dough hook or on a floured board, knead until smooth. I usually use up all the flour.
- Place in greased bowl; cover and let rise until double in bulk, about 2 hours. Punch down. Shape into two loaves and place in greased loaf pans. Cover and let rise another hour or until dough swells above pan edge.
- Bake in preheated 375 degree oven for 35 to 40 minutes.
- Cool on racks.

YANKEE BEER BREAD

Bakes 2 loaves

We spend the summers cruising Southeast Alaska and often find the smaller villages short of baking supplies. Beer Bread is known to all Alaskans, and is handy because it has so few ingredients. This is our version of it.

5 cups self rising flour
2 cans beer, flat
6 tablespoons sugar
1 teaspoon salt

- Simply mix together all the ingredients. Place in two greased loaf pans and bake at 350 degrees for 1 hour.

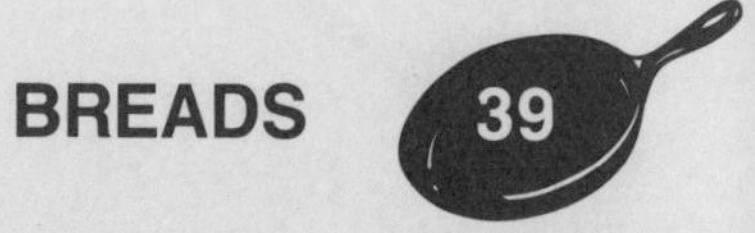

SHIRLEY'S CHEESE BREAD

Serves 6

This crunchy bread is a snap to make and is a perfect companion to any picnic or outdoor barbecue.

1 loaf sourdough bread
1 cup mayonnaise
2 cups sharp Cheddar cheese, shredded
1 bunch green onions with part of stems, chopped
2 tablespoons Romano cheese
1 teaspoon oregano

- Cut bread in half lengthwise. Combine onions, cheese and mayonnaise. Spread on bread. Sprinkle with Romano cheese and oregano.
- Bake in a preheated oven at 350 degrees for 20 minutes.

GRAHAM BREAD

Makes 2 round loaves

This is a nice crunchy bread, somewhat sweet. It makes nice sandwiches.

5	**cups flour**	**1/4**	**cup honey**
2	**packages yeast, Quick rise only**	**2**	**tablespoons oil**
1	**tablespoon salt**	**1 1/2**	**cups graham cracker crumbs**
2	**cups water**		

- Combine 2 cups flour, yeast and salt; mix well.
- Heat water, honey and oil until warm, about 125 degrees.
- Add to flour mixture. Blend on a low speed until moistened. Add the remaining 3 cups of flour and graham cracker crumbs. Knead for 5 minutes, using a mixer or by hand. Place in a greased bowl. Cover and let rise in a warm place for 15 minutes.
- Punch down dough. Divide in half and form into round loaves. Place on greased cookie sheets and let rise for about 30 minutes — it won't rise much. Bake at 375 degrees for 40 minutes.

DANISH PUMPERNICKEL BREAD

Makes 2 loaves

Get a good quality Brie cheese, some green grapes and a bottle of good red wine, mix all the ingredients with some good friends. Enjoy!

3	**packages yeast**	**2**	**tablespoons oil**
1 1/2	**cups water, warmed to 105 degrees**	**4**	**cups rye flour**
1/2	**cup dark molasses**	**2 1/2**	**cups white flour**
1	**tablespoon salt**		

- Dissolve yeast in water in a large bowl. Add molasses, salt and oil, then flours alternately. Knead bread for 10 minutes. Place in greased bowl and let rise until double in bulk.
- Divide dough in half, let rest for 10 minutes. Grease a baking sheet. Form round loaves and let rise again, until double in size.
- Bake at 375 degrees for 55 minutes.

WHOLE-WHEAT BEER BREAD

Makes 2 loaves

The aroma of this bread baking turns anyone into my personal slave for the day, or at least until the bread is gone.

1	**can dark beer, Heinikan**
1/2	**cup water**
1/4	**cup bacon drippings**
2	**packages yeast**
1/3	**cup sugar**
2	**cups whole-wheat flour**
2	**teaspoons salt**
3 1/2	**cups flour**
2	**eggs**
1 1/2	**cups rolled oats**
1	**cup Parmesan cheese, grated**
1	**tablespoon caraway seeds**

- Combine beer, water, and bacon drippings. Heat to 120 degrees. This is easily done in the micro oven, using the temperature probe. Add yeast, sugar, whole-wheat flour and salt to beer mixture; beat for a few minutes. Blend in 2 cups of the flour and eggs. Beat on high speed for a few minutes. Stir in oats and Parmesan cheese and mix well. At this point, the batter will be soft. Keep adding flour until you have the correct ''feel'' of the dough, smooth but firm. Place in greased bowl and let rise until double in bulk, about 1 hour. Punch down, divide into two and press gently into loaf pans. Let rise again in a warm place for about 1 hour, or until double in size.
- Bake at 375 degrees for 20 to 25 minutes.
- Cool on wire racks.

SOURDOUGH STARTER

The best way to have a good starter is to obtain a cup from someone proud of owning a starter with some history. Some sourdough starters date back a 100 years, and are often passed on from friend to friend all over Alaska. The older the starter, the more tangy the flavor.
Never use anything but glass, plastic, wood, or the traditional crocks with sourdough. Metal must never be used, it reacts adversely with the acid in sourdough starter. To start your own, follow this recipe.

2 cups flour
3 tablespoons sugar
1 package dry yeast
2 cups warm water, 105 degrees

- Combine all ingredients in a large, plastic bowl, as this mixture will more than double in volume during fermentation.
- Beat with a plastic or wooden spoon. Cover with plastic wrap punctured in several places to let yeast breathe. We use a light weight shower cap with elastic band and it works well.
- Set in a warm place for 4 to 6 days. Stir the mixture — remember, don't use a metal spoon — several times a day during the fermenting period. Once this starter has been born, do not ever add anything to it other than warm water and flour in equal amounts. If once in awhile you need to boost it up, sprinkle a little dry yeast in and mix it well — nothing else.
- Keep in a container in refrigerator with loosely fitting lid. This is important; the gases formed might explode a sealed jar or crock.
- Starters can be frozen for up to 3 months. If you do freeze it, let it come back to life for 24 hours in refrigerator before using. To use starter, remove from refrigerator the night before and add 1 cup flour and 1 cup warm water. Upon removing the amount needed at cooking time, replace with equal amounts of water and flour, return to refrigerator.

SOURDOUGH RAISIN MUFFINS

Makes 12 muffins

These are somewhat sweet, and full of plump raisins.

1/2 cup whole-wheat flour
1 1/2 cups flour
1/2 cup brown sugar
1 teaspoon salt
3/4 cup sourdough starter
1 teaspoon baking soda
1 egg
1/2 cup vegetable oil
1/2 cup buttermilk
1 cup raisins

- Grease 12 muffin cups; set aside.
- Mix all dry ingredients thoroughly. In medium-sized bowl blend eggs, oil, starter and buttermilk. Combine the two mixtures, stir only to blend. Fold in the raisins.
- Fill muffin cups 3/4 full. Bake at 425 degrees for 20 minutes or until golden brown.

SOURDOUGH ENGLISH MUFFINS

Makes 10

When on the DamnYankee for the summer, and not always near the Le Petit Paris Bakery, I make these. I can't tell you if they keep well, we never have any left over.

1 1/2 cups Sourdough Starter
1 teaspoon salt
1 tablespoon sugar
1/2 teaspoon baking soda
1 1/2 cups flour, sifted
Cornmeal

- In a large warm bowl, place 1 1/2 cups starter, salt, sugar and baking soda, mix well. Sift flour and add a little at a time, reserving 1/4 cup. Knead a few minutes on a floured board using the remaining flour. Roll to a thickness of 1/2 inch. Use an empty tuna can, cut out 10 muffins. Place on cookie sheet, sprinkle with cornmeal and let rise for 1 hour. The muffins will only rise a little, but they puff up when frying.
- Heat a small amount of oil in large frying pan over medium heat or an electric griddle set at 325 degrees and fry muffins 10 minutes on each side.

BOB'S SOURDOUGH BISCUITS

Makes 18-24 biscuits

We have a lot of traffic in the galley, and many offers of help right around the time these biscuits are to come from the oven. You'll know why, just try these light biscuits. Remember to replace the starter you remove.

1 package dry yeast
1/2 cup warm water, 105 degrees
1 1/2 cups sour dough starter
1/2 cup milk
2 1/2 to 3 cups flour
3/4 teaspoon salt
1 tablespoon sugar
1/4 teaspoon baking soda
1 teaspoon melted butter

- Mix yeast and water, let rest 5 minutes.
- Combine milk, starter, yeast mixture, and 1 cup flour. Mix salt, sugar and baking soda, add to batter. Gently knead in the remaining flour. Roll out or pat down dough to 1/2 inch thickness. Cut with biscuit cutter. Place on lightly greased cookie sheet, letting edges touch. Let rest for 1 hour, they will rise a little.
- Dip finger in butter and pat top of each biscuit.
- Bake at 375 degrees for 25 to 30 minutes.

OAKLAND SOURDOUGH ROLLS

Makes 16 rolls

This is a take-off on the original Oakland Roll recipe the Page family has enjoyed for years. I am told that when my husband was a boy, the dinner table always held Oakland Rolls. I added the sour dough starter.

1 package yeast
1/2 cup lukewarm water
2 teaspoons sugar
1 cup sourdough starter
1 egg
1 teaspoon salt
4 cups, more or less, sifted flour

- Dissolve yeast in water with half of sugar. Place starter in a large bowl with egg, salt and remaining sugar. Add flour until a smooth but firm dough is obtained.
- Set aside in warm place, covered with dish towel, and let rise until double in size, about an hour. Punch down and form into dinner rolls. Place on baking sheet so that their sides touch. Let rolls rise again until double in size, about another hour.
- Bake in a preheated oven at 375 degrees for 15 to 20 minutes.

BASIC FRENCH BREAD

Makes 2 loaves

When baking these loaves, I use metal flute pans.

2 packages dry yeast
1/2 teaspoon sugar
1 cup lukewarm water
3 1/2 to 4 cups flour
1 teaspoon salt
2 tablespoons vegetable oil

- Preheat oven to 400 degrees.
- Combine yeast, sugar and water. Have water at 105 degrees.
- Let stand 5 minutes. Mix 2 cups of flour and salt in food processor or mixer with a dough hook attachment. Add the oil and the yeast mixture. With the processor running, add another cup of flour. Keep kneading until smooth and satiny. Turn dough out onto a floured board with the remaining flour and knead until elastic.
- Cover, set aside and let rise until double in bulk, about 2 hours.
- Punch down and divide dough into two parts. Form long flute loaves to fit the pans or use regular bread pans. Let rise for another hour. Make several diagonal slashes in each bread with a sharp knife. Brush bread with water and place in oven.
- Place a pan of hot water in oven.
- Bake bread for 25 minutes if using flute pans or 35 minutes for loaf pans.

RUSSIAN BLACK BREAD

Makes 2 loaves

Very hearty and moist. Is outstanding served with a main meal soup, some good sausage and mild grainy wine mustard.

2 packages dry yeast
2 1/2 cups warm water, about 105 degrees
1 tablespoon sugar
1/4 cup butter
1/4 cup dark molasses
1/4 cup vinegar
2 cups bran flakes
2 teaspoons salt
1 ounce unsweetened chocolate, melted
2 tablespoons caraway seeds, crushed
2 teaspoons strong coffee
2 teaspoons onion flakes, dried
1/2 teaspoon fennel seeds, crushed
4 cups rye flour
3 cups white flour
1 teaspoon cornstarch mixed with 1/4 cup water, for topping

- In a large bowl, blend water with yeast and sugar, set aside for 5 minutes. Add the next 10 ingredients and beat well. (I use a mixer with a dough hook.) Knead in flour a little at a time, and keep kneading for 8 minutes.
- Place dough in a greased bowl, cover and set to rise for about 1 1/2 hours. Punch down on floured board; divide dough in half and shape each loaf into a ball. Place on cookie sheet, cover and let rise for another 1 1/2 hours or until double.
- Heat oven to 350 degrees. Bake loaves for 45 minutes.
- Mix cornstarch and water in a small pan; cook over medium heat for 30 seconds. Brush bread with cornstarch mixture, return bread to oven for another 3 minutes to form glaze.
- Cool on wire racks.

PYBUS BAY FRENCH BREAD

Makes 4 loaves

One of our favorite places to hide out for some good fishing. Remember to replace the starter you remove.

2 packages dry yeast
2 cups warm water
3 cups starter
4 teaspoons salt
8 cups flour
1/2 teaspoon sugar

- Mix yeast and warm water, set aside for 5 minutes.
- In a medium sized bowl, combine starter, salt and 2 cups flour. Mix thoroughly, add sugar and the yeast mixture with another 2 cups of flour. Stir in the remaining flour, knead well. Dust board with flour and knead until all flour is used and dough is smooth and elastic.
- Set aside, cover and let rise until double, about 2 hours.
- Punch down, knead 30 seconds. Form into 4 loaves and place on greased cookie sheet. Make deep slashes on top with sharp knife. Let rise until double in size, about 1 hour.
- Place a loaf pan with hot water in oven, on rack below bread.
- Bake at 400 degrees for 35 to 40 minutes. Brush with water right after removing bread from oven; this gives bread a nice shine.

ITALIAN BREAD STICKS

Makes 1 dozen

Perfect with any main meal soup, or served with a fresh salad.

2/3 cup warm water
1 package yeast
1/2 teaspoon sugar
2 cups flour
1 tablespoon salt
1/4 cup oil
1/4 teaspoon garlic salt
1 egg
1 teaspoon water
Sesame seeds, optional

- Dissolve yeast in warm water with sugar added. Combine flour, salt, oil and garlic salt. Stir into yeast mixture. Knead in your mixer, or by hand for 2 minutes. Set aside in warm place and rise for 1 hour. Punch down, shape into finger-size sticks. Place on greased cookie sheet. Combine egg and, brush on sticks. Sprinkle with toasted sesame seeds.
- Bake at 400 degrees for 20 to 25 minutes.

MONTPELIER ROLLS

Makes 24 rolls

This wonderful recipe comes from Mrs. Brown in Virginia. As explained to me on a recent visit.

2 packages dry yeast
3 cups warm water
1/2 cup sugar
4 tablespoons margarine or shortening
1 egg, well beaten
2 tablespoons salt
4-5 cups white flour

- Grease a cookie sheet lightly.
- Mix the yeast with warm water and 1 tablespoon of the sugar.
- Set aside. In large bowl combine margarine, the remaining sugar, egg and salt, mix well. Add the yeast mixture and 2 cups of the flour, beating well. Keep adding the flour as needed to make a moderately stiff dough. Cover and set aside in warm place until double in bulk, about 45 minutes or longer. Punch down and let it rise a second time, about 45 minutes. When double in size, punch down and form dough into rolls. Place on greased cookie sheet. Then double in size again. Bake at 350 degrees for 15 to 20 minutes.

NEVER-FAIL POPOVERS

Serves 6

Light and fluffy. A must to serve with standing rib roast.

1 1/4 cups flour
1 1/4 cups milk
1/2 teaspoon salt
3 large eggs, room temperature

- Combine salt, flour and milk. Add one egg at a time using a wire whisk. Do not over beat.
- Grease popover pan or use individual cups. Fill cups 3/4 full.
- Bake in a preheated 425 degree oven for 20 minutes. Lower oven temperature to 325 degrees and continue baking for another 15 minutes, or until light brown.

TAKU HARBOR CORN BREAD

Serves 8

Made with sourdough. The millet gives this bread a nice crunch. Remember to replace the starter you use.

- **2** **eggs**
- **1** **cup starter**
- **1** **cup evaporated milk**
- **1/4** **cup vegetable oil**
- **3/4** **cup cornmeal**
- **3/4** **cup flour**
- **3** **tablespoons millet**
- **2** **tablespoons sugar**
- **3/4** **teaspoon baking soda**
- **1** **teaspoon salt**

- Preheat oven to 450 degrees. Grease an 7 1/2 x 11-inch pan.
- Beat eggs. Add all liquid ingredients to eggs. Combine and mix all dry ingredients. Mix the two, and stir just to blend, do not over beat. Pour into prepared pan. Bake for 20 minutes, or until toothpick comes out clean.

JALAPEÑO CORN BREAD

Serves 6

- **1** **cup cornmeal**
- **2** **tablespoons flour**
- **1** **teaspoon salt**
- **1/2** **teaspoon baking soda**
- **1** **cup buttermilk**
- **2** **eggs**
- **1** **cup creamed corn**
- **1** **onion, chopped**
- **3** **Jalapeño peppers, chopped**
- **1/2** **pound sharp Cheddar cheese, shredded**
- **1/3** **cup oil**

- Combine the dry ingredients. Thoroughly blend buttermilk, eggs and corn and add to the dry mixture. Add onion and peppers and fold in the Cheddar cheese.
- Grease a cast-iron skillet with oil, pour in mixture and bake at 400 degrees for 35 minutes.

RUNG'S CORN BREAD

Serves 8

Our friend, one of the moose hunters, Darrell Rung managed to surprise me with a recipe. It is outstanding, and now a favorite in this house.

1 1/2	**cups self-rising cornmeal**
1/2	**cup self rising-flour**
1/3	**cup sugar**
1 1/2	**cups buttermilk**
2	**tablespoons mayonnaise**
2	**eggs**
1/3	**cup Crisco, or other shortening**

- Mix the dry ingredients together. In a separate bowl, mix all the wet ingredients. Combine the two and blend well. Place half of the Crisco in a cast-iron skillet and set an oven preheated to 400 degrees. Add remaining Crisco to batter, stir and pour into pan. Bake for 20 minutes or until light brown, and toothpick comes out clean.
- Cut like a pie.

TENAKEE CORN STICKS

Makes 12 sticks

3/4	**cup yellow cornmeal**
1	**cup flour**
1	**teaspoon baking powder**
2	**tablespoons sugar**
1/4	**teaspoon baking soda**
1/2	**teaspoon salt**
3/4	**cup sour milk**
2	**tablespoons oil**
1	**egg, beaten**
6	**slices bacon, cooked until crisp**

- Combine first six ingredients.
- Add sour milk and oil, blend well. Add the beaten eggs and bacon bits.
- Grease corn stick pans. Preheat pans in a 350 degree oven then pour in the batter. Bake for 30 minutes or until golden brown.

OVERNIGHT PETERSBURG BRAN MUFFINS

Makes 3 1/2 dozen or 3 dozen

Thanks to Mrs. Strand from Petersburg, Alaska. She gave me this recipe many years ago. Make batter up before heading out on your boat, as suggested by my friend Linda, and you have breakfast in no time.

Keeps in refrigerator for about 1 month.

2 cups boiling water
2 cups All-Bran cereal
4 eggs, beaten
1 cup butter, melted
3 cups sugar
1 quart milk
1 tablespoon lemon juice
5 cups flour
4 cups Raisin Bran cereal
5 teaspoons baking soda
1 teaspoon salt
2 cups dates, chopped

- Pour boiling water over All-Bran and set aside. Beat eggs, butter and sugar, and continue to beat. Stir in milk and lemon juice. Add All-Bran, mix well. In a separate bowl, combine flour, Raisin Bran, baking soda, salt and dates. Stir into wet mixture. Place in refrigerator overnight.
- Bake in greased muffin tins at 400 degrees for 25 minutes.

BLUEBERRY MUFFINS

Makes 1 1/2 dozen

1/2 cup melted butter
1 1/4 cups sugar
2 cups flour
2 teaspoons baking powder
1/2 teaspoon salt
2 eggs
1/2 cup milk
1/2 cup walnuts, chopped
2 1/2 cups blueberries = Thawed

- Cream butter and sugar with an electric beater until light and fluffy. Add all the ingredients except nuts and berries; fold these in last. Grease muffin tins, fill them 3/4 full of batter. Bake at 350 degrees for 15 to 20 minutes. Before removing them from oven, check to see if toothpick comes out clean.

BANANA-CRANBERRY BREAD

Makes 1 loaf

Delicious bread for Chistmas presents.

- **3/4 cup butter**
- **1 1/2 cup sugar**
- **3 medium bananas, mashed**
- **2 eggs, well beaten**
- **1 teaspoon vanilla**
- **2 cups flour, sifted**
- **1 teaspoon baking soda**
- **3/4 teaspoon salt**
- **1/2 cup buttermilk**
- **3/4 cups walnuts, chopped**
- **1/2 cup cranberries, fresh**

- Cream butter and sugar. Blend in bananas, eggs and vanilla. Sift dry ingredients. Add the dry ingredients a little at a time, alternating with buttermilk. Fold in nuts and cranberries.
- Pour into large greased loaf pan. Bake at 350 degrees for 1 hour and 15 minutes.

MRS. D'S ZUCCHINI-NUT MUFFINS

Makes 48 muffins

Feel free to cut recipe in half.

- **2 teaspoons baking soda**
- **2 teaspoons baking powder**
- **2 teaspoons cinnamon**
- **6 cups flour**
- **2 teaspoons salt**
- **8 eggs**
- **4 cups sugar**
- **2 cups salad oil, (soybean is best)**
- **1 teaspoon vanilla**
- **4 cups zucchini, raw, washed, grated**
- **1 cup yellow raisins**
- **2 cups walnuts, chopped**

- Mix together soda, baking powder and cinnamon, and salt, set aside.
- In a mixer, beat eggs and sugar until creamy. Slowly add oil. Add vanilla and zucchini, and blend well. Next, add raisins and nuts. Fold in the dry ingredients.
- Mix in flour, don't over beat.
- Grease muffin pans well with solid shortening. Fill each muffin cup 2/3 full. Place in preheated oven at 350 degrees for 15 minutes. Do not peek while cooking, or they will fall.

ZUCCHINI MUFFINS

Makes 12 muffins

This batter keeps well. If stored in refrigerator, stir it well before piling batter into greased muffin pan.

1 1/2 cups flour
3/4 cup sugar
1 teaspoon soda
1/2 teaspoon salt
1 teaspoon cinnamon
1/2 cup oil
1/4 cup milk
1 teaspoon vanilla
1 egg
1 cup zucchini, shredded
1/4 cup currants
1/4 cup pecans, chopped

- Heat oven to 350 degrees. Grease 12 muffin cups. In a large bowl stir together flour, sugar, soda, salt and cinnamon. Add oil, milk, vanilla and egg, blend thoroughly. Fold in the shredded zucchini, currants and pecans. Spoon into cups, filling each about 2/3 full. Bake for 25 to 30 minutes, or until toothpick comes out clean.

OREGON ZUCCHINI-NUT BREAD

Makes 3 loaves

Another delicious recipe from the McGowan farm. This freezes well; good toasted.

3 eggs
2 cups sugar
1 cup oil
2 cups zucchini, peeled and shredded
1 teaspoon vanilla
3 cups flour
1 teaspoon salt
1 teaspoon baking soda
1/2 teaspoon baking powder
3 teaspoons cinnamon
1/2 cup walnuts, chopped
1/2 cup dates, chopped

- Beat eggs and sugar until light and fluffy. Add all other ingredients and stir to blend well.
- Lightly grease 3 medium loaf pans. Pour in batter. Bake at 325 degrees for 1 hour.

In the Salad Bowl

IN THE SALAD BOWL

SALAD DRESSINGS

SPINACH SALAD WITH SWEET AND SOUR DRESSING

Serves 4

When the garden or markets are bursting with fresh spinach, it's time to try out another tasty salads.

6 slices bacon
2 bunches spinach, washed and torn
4 green onions, chopped
2 oranges, in wedges

- Cook bacon until crisp; reserve grease. Combine spinach, onions and orange wedges with crumbled bacon; set aside.

SWEET AND SOUR DRESSING:

4 tablespoons oil
2 tablespoons bacon drippings
3 tablespoons sweet and hot mustard
2 tablespoons honey
1 clove garlic, minced
Freshly ground pepper

- Blend all the ingredients and pour over spinach salad.

Serves 4.

EAST INDIAN SALAD WITH SPUNKY DRESSING

Serves 4

2 cups cooked chicken breast, diced
1 cup celery, chopped
2 mandarin oranges, peeled and sliced
1 Japanese pear, chopped
1 large banana, sliced
1/2 cup cashews, chopped
4 green onions, chopped
Spunky Dressing

- Toss all the ingredients and refrigerate. Arrange on Bibb lettuce leaves and spoon Spunky Dressing over.

SPUNKY DRESSING:

1/2 cup sour cream
5 tablespoons of Peter Page's Chutney
1 teaspoon orange rind, grated
1 teaspoon lemon juice
1/2 teaspoon curry powder
Salt and freshly ground pepper to taste

- Combine all the ingredients and blend well. Double recipe and keep extra in refrigerator - it lasts for weeks.

HARLEQUIN SLAW

Serves 8

Delightful arrangement of many colors. A must with any outdoor cooking party.

6 cups cabbage, finely shredded
1 cup carrots, grated
1 2-ounce jar pimentoes, drained
1 small red onion, chopped
1/2 cup cucumber, diced
2 1/2 ounces black olives, sliced
1 cup mayonnaise
1/2 cup sour cream
2 tablespoons red wine vinegar
2 tablespoons Dijon mustard
1/2 teaspoon caraway seeds
Salt and pepper to taste
1/2 cup parsley, chopped

- Combine all the vegetables in a large bowl. Blend mayonnaise, sour cream and vinegar in a separate bowl, then add mustard and caraway seeds. Season with salt and pepper. Combine dressing with slaw mixture and let flavors blend. Before serving, sprinkle with parsley.

EMERALD GREEN SALAD WITH CHÈVRE

1 serving

Take a combination of fresh lettuce, spinach or any of your favorite greens and arrange on individual salad plates, then add the following ingredients:

5 shrimp
4 Greek olives, pitted
3 slices Mozzarella cheese
2 fresh basil leaves
1 Italian tomato, cut into quarters
1 tablespoon chèvre (goat cheese)

DRESSING: (For 10 servings)

1 1/2 cups good quality olive oil
1/3 cup Balsamic vinegar
1 lemon, juice of
1 cup fresh basil leaves, chopped
1 cup parsley, chopped
1/2 cup Romano cheese
Salt and pepper to taste

- In blender or food processor, blend the above ingredients.

BROCCOLI SALAD

Serves 4

Terrific warm day salad. We find it plenty filling for a luncheon dish. From the files of Mrs. Newton in Pennsylvania.

- **1 stalk broccoli, broken into bite-sized pieces**
- **1 onion, finely chopped**
- **1/2 pound lean bacon. crisp, crumbled**
- **1 cup sharp Cracker Barrel cheese, shredded**
- **1/4 cup or less sugar**
- **1 tablespoon vinegar**
- **1 cup mayonnaise**

- Combine the broccoli, onion, bacon and cheese in a large bowl. Dissolve sugar in vinegar; add to mayonnaise. Fold into the broccoli mixture. Serve cold.

ROMAINE AND SPINACH SALAD

Makes 1 cup dressing

A snap to make and very tasty.

- **4 tablespoons sesame seeds, toasted**
- **1/4 cup sesame oil**
- **1/4 cup honey**
- **1/2 cup red wine vinegar**
- **Dash of garlic juice**
- **Dash of Maggi liquid**
- **Romaine lettuce or spinach leaves**

- Combine everything except lettuce, then store in refrigerator until ready to use.
- Break up Romaine or spinach leaves. Pour dressing over and serve immediately.

CRUNCHY CUCUMBER SALAD

Serves 4

Best made a day ahead of serving.

1 English cucumber, or 3 regular
1 tablespoon salt
3/4 cup vinegar
3 tablespoons sugar
1 tablespoon water
1 tablespoon parsley, chopped
1/2 teaspoon black pepper, freshly ground

- Slice cucumber paper thin, with peel on. Sprinkle salt over and mix well. Set aside for 1/2 hour. Remove and squeeze all the bitter juices from cucumber. Discard juices.
- Combine vinegar, sugar and water. Mix to dissolve sugar.
- Add cucumbers, parsley and pepper. Refrigerate until serving time.

PEA SALAD

Serves 6

I first had this salad served to me in a restaurant in Wrangell. There is nothing to it, but it is one of my favorites to mix in a hurry.

1 bag frozen early peas
6 slices bacon, crisp, crumbled
1/2 cup chopped water chestnuts
1/2 cup sliced green onions
1 cup mayonnaise
Pepper to taste.

- Simply thaw peas. Do not cook.
- Add water chestnuts, onions, peas and bacon to mayonnaise. Sprinkle with pepper and stir well. Keep cool until serving time.

TOP RAMEN SALAD

Serves 6

This is a great crunchy salad that was given to me by Donna Harvey in Wrangell. I make it often and like it especially with seafood.

- **2 ounces almonds**
- **2 tablespoons sesame seeds**
- **1 tablespoon butter**
- **1/2 head cabbage, shredded**
- **4 green onions, chopped**
- **1 package Ramen noodles, chicken flavored, uncooked**

DRESSING:

- **1/2 cup salad oil**
- **1/2 teaspoon sesame oil**
- **3 1/2 tablespoons vinegar**
- **2 tablespoons sugar**
- **1/2 package seasoning from noodles**

- Sauté almonds and sesame seeds in butter until light brown.
- Finely shred the cabbage. In a large bowl add onions to cabbage, stir in the nut mixture. Set aside.
- Mix oil with vinegar, sugar and seasoning. Stir well to dissolve sugar. Using a shaker bottle makes this easy.
- When ready to serve, pour dressing over cabbage and crumble up the Ramen noodles.
- If you make this ahead, the noodles will get soft; you don't want that.

GRAPEFRUIT AND AVOCADO SALAD

Makes 2 cups dressing

Ever since Brenda McGowan served this outstanding salad to us, it has been a favorite.

- **1/4 cup cider vinegar**
- **1/4 to 1/2 cup powder sugar**
- **1 teaspoon salt**
- **1 teaspoon celery seeds**
- **2 teaspoons Dijon or French's mustard**
- **1 teaspoon paprika**
- **1 cup salad oil**
- **Avocado**
- **Grapefruit**

- Mix the first 6 ingredients well. Slowly add oil and whip while pouring. Chill until serving time.
- Serve over sliced avocado and grapefruit wedges.

Also use this Celery dressing over wedges of orange, slices of red onion and avocadoes. Wonderful!

CRAB AND CELERY SALAD IN TARRAGON MAYONNAISE

Serves 4

- 6 tablespoons tarragon wine vinegar
- 6 tablespoons olive oil
- 1/2 teaspoon salt
- 1/4 teaspoon cayenne pepper
- 2 cups cooked crab meat, in chunks
- 4 cups Boston or Bibb lettuce, shredded
- 1 cup celery, finely chopped
- 1 cup mayonnaise
- 1 tablespoon fresh tarragon
- 2 hard-boiled eggs, chilled and sliced
- 2 tablespoons capers, rinsed

- In a small bowl, mix together vinegar, oil, salt and cayenne pepper. Add the crab meat. Stir gently to evenly coat. Set aside to marinate for 1 hour in refrigerator.
- When ready to serve, line a large bowl with lettuce. Drain crab of marinade. Combine crab, celery and 1/2 cup of mayonnaise. Spoon mixture over lettuce leaves. Crumble tarragon into the remaining 1/2 cup mayonnaise. Spread over salad and garnish with sliced eggs, overlapping them around the edge of the bowl. Scatter capers in center.
- Serve at once on chilled plates.

GREEK CRAB SALAD

Serves 4

A light luncheon salad.

- 1/4 cup onion, chopped
- 2 tablespoons parsley, chopped
- 1 tablespoon pimento, chopped
- 1 pound crab meat
- 1/4 cup fresh lemon juice
- 1/2 cup olive oil
- Salt and pepper to taste
- 1/2 teaspoon oregano
- Lettuce
- Green stuffed olives, for garnish
- Black olives, for garnish
- Radishes, for garnish
- Lemon wedges, for garnish

- Add onion, parsley and pimento to crab. Set aside.
- Make dressing by combining lemon juice, olive oil, salt, pepper and oregano; blend well with wire whisk. Pour over crab mixture and toss gently. Refrigerate for several hours.
- Place salad on lettuce-lined platter and top with the garnishings.

CHICKEN AND FRUIT SALAD

Serves 4

A summer salad filled with fresh fruit, served with a refreshing chutney dressing.

1/4 cup almond slivers
2 whole chicken breasts, cooked, cubed
1/2 cup green grapes
1/2 cup sweet cherries, pitted and halved
4 apricots, pitted and cut into bite-sized slivers
1/4 cup green onions, including tops, chopped
Chutney Dressing
Salt, optional
4 cups Bibb lettuce
1 large avocado, sliced
1 orange, cut into wedges

- Toast almonds in oven for about 5 minutes at 350 degrees.
- In a large bowl, combine chicken, grapes, cherries, apricots, green onions and Chutney Dressing. Season with salt, if desired.
- Arrange lettuce on plates with avocado slices. Place chicken salad in middle and sprinkle with toasted almonds. Garnish with orange wedges.

CHUTNEY DRESSING

1/3 cup mayonnaise
1/3 cup sour cream
2 tablespoons chutney, finely chopped
1 teaspoon orange peel, grated
1 tablespoon lemon juice
Dash of nutmeg

- Mix all the ingredients and pour over salad.

APPLE AND SPINACH SALAD

Serves 6

A Page family favorite.

2	red apples with peel, cored and sliced
1/2	head butter lettuce, leaves left whole
1	bunch fresh spinach leaves, torn into bite-sized pieces
3/4	cup pecans, broken into pieces
3/4	cup red onion, sliced
6	slices bacon, crisp, crumbled
1	piece Brie, chilled, cut into small chunks

DRESSING:

1 1/2	teaspoons brown sugar, packed
1/4	cup red wine vinegar
1/4	teaspoon salt
	Pepper to taste

- Combine apples with lettuce and spinach. Dissolve sugar in vinegar, add salt and pepper. Pour dressing over greens and apples. Add nuts, onion, bacon and cheese.
- Toss and serve at once.

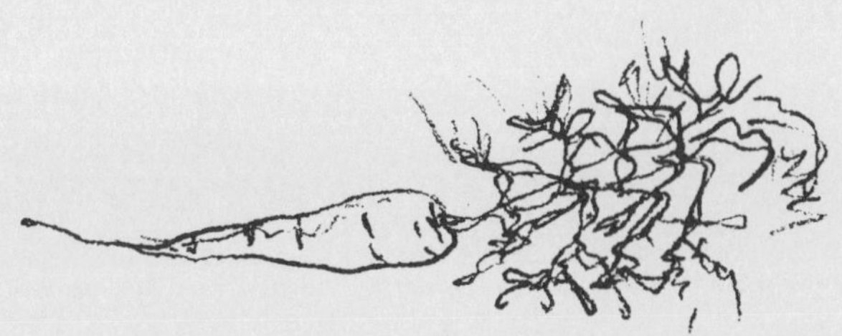

CARROT AND FRUIT SALAD

Serves 6

Both a tasty and colorful salad to serve with almost any meal. And it's good for you, too.

4	cups carrots, shredded
2	medium apples, sliced
1	cup pineapple chunks, drained
1/2	cup yoghurt
2	tablespoons mayonnaise
2	tablespoons wine vinegar
1	teaspoon sugar
1	teaspoon celery seeds

- Combine shredded carrots with apples and pineapple chunks. Blend together yoghurt, mayonnaise and vinegar. Stir in sugar and celery seeds. Add dressing to fruit and stir to coat.

FRESH RASPBERRY FRUIT SALAD

Makes 1/2 cup dressing

When the berries bend the bushes to the ground, take time out for a delicious treat.

2 bunches Bibb lettuce, broken up
2 cups fresh raspberries
1/4 cup almond slivers

DRESSING:
1 clove garlic
1/2 teaspoon salt
1/2 teaspoon freshly ground pepper
2 tablespoons raspberry vinegar
7 tablespoons good-quality olive oil

- Toss together lettuce, raspberries and almonds. Mash garlic with salt and pepper until paste is formed. Add vinegar and blend well. Slowly add olive oil and whisk continuously until nice and thick.
- Pour over salad.

ITALIAN GRAPEFRUIT SALAD

Serves 2

1 large grapefruit, peeled
3 tablespoons olive oil
1 tablespoon parsley, minced
1 teaspoon fresh lemon juice
Salt and pepper to taste
3 cups romaine leaves, torn into pieces
1/2 green pepper, cut into strips
1/2 red pepper, cut into strips
3 tablespoons pine nuts, toasted

- Divide grapefruit into wedges, try catching the juice. Set aside. Mix grapefruit juice with oil, parsley, lemon juice, salt and pepper to taste. Combine the romaine, peppers and grapefruit wedges.
- Pour dressing over and sprinkle with toasted pine nuts.

SUMMER SLAW

Makes 1 gallon

This refreshing slaw comes from North Carolina. The Brann family's favorite aunt ran a barbecue and catering service, and used this recipe for 40 years. I hope it will soon be a favorite of yours. I sometimes use fresh tomatoes in this, and it is wonderful.

- **2 cups sugar**
- **2 cups vinegar**
- **6 pounds cabbage, chopped or shredded**
- **1 small jar pimento, chopped**
- **1 quart canned tomatoes, drained and chopped**
- **1 green pepper, chopped**
- **1 1/2 tablespoons black pepper**
- **1 1/2 tablespoons salt, or to taste**

- Combine sugar and vinegar; heat until dissolved.
- Pour over vegetables. Season with salt and pepper.
- This keeps well in refrigerator for up to a month.

CURRIED COLESLAW

Serves 6

Another refreshing salad from Donna Harvey. She is one of Wrangell's better cooks.

- **6 slices bacon**
- **1/2 cup mayonnaise**
- **1 teaspoon sugar**
- **1/4 teaspoon salt**
- **2 tablespoons vinegar**
- **1/2 teaspoon curry powder**
- **6 cups cabbage, shredded**

- Fry bacon until crisp; set aside. Combine mayonnaise, sugar, salt and vinegar with curry.
- Add dressing to cabbage. Mix well. Add crisp bacon to salad, toss and serve.

SESAME PASTA WITH CHICKEN

Serves 4

Spicy and full of amber-colored good flavors. Serve with chop sticks for a fun take-your-time luncheon.

2	**whole chicken breasts, cooked**	1/4	**cup soy sauce**
1	**package Chinese noodles, cooked**	6	**tablespoons chili oil**
1/4	**cup sesame oil**	7	**tablespoons brown sugar**
1/2	**cup Tahini, sesame paste**	3	**bunches green onion, sliced**
1/4	**cup rice vinegar**		**Lettuce**

- Cut cooked, cooled chicken into bite-sized pieces.
- Cook noodles, drain when done, and immediately place under cold running water. Set aside.
- Mix sesame oil, Tahini, rice vinegar, soy sauce and chili oil with brown sugar and stir until sugar is dissolved. Add green onion, chicken and noodles. Toss and serve in lettuce-lined bowl.

ROTINI IN CURRY MAYONNAISE

Serves 4

Tasty served with any seafood when entertaining out of doors.

1	**bag rotini noodles**	1/2	**teaspoon salt**
1	**cup mayonnaise**	1	**can black olives, sliced**
2	**tablespoons curry powder**		**Lettuce leaves**

- Cook noodles according to package directions. Cool under cold water.
- Mix together mayonnaise, curry powder and salt. Fold in the olives and rotini.
- Chill and serve on lettuce leaves.

CANNELLINI SALAD WITH CHICKEN

Serves 4

A favorite hot weather salad. Very colorful using a clear glass bowl and placing salad on a bed of fresh spinach or Bibb lettuce leaves.

1 pound fresh green beans, cut into 2-inch lengths
2 large red bell peppers, cut into 2-inch long strips
2 15-ounce cans cannellini beans, drained
1 pound chicken breast, cooked, cut into pieces
4 teaspoons Dijon mustard
2 teaspoons fresh tarragon
4 teaspoons Balsamic vinegar
6 tablespoons olive oil
Salt and pepper to taste
1 teaspoon orange peel, grated

- Place green beans in cold water and bring to a boil. Cook until tender but crisp. Immediately submerge them in ice water to stop the cooking; this will also help retain the color of the beans.
- Combine green beans, red pepper strips, drained cannellini and chicken.
- Mix mustard, tarragon and vinegar in small bowl. Gradually whisk in oil. Season with salt and pepper. Pour dressing over salad. Sprinkle with orange peel.

CRAB SALAD WITH PASTA SHELLS

Serves 4

Great luncheon dish on a warm day.

2 cups cooked Alaska king crab
1/2 pound pasta shells, cooked, cooled
1 cup frozen peas, uncooked
1/2 cup green onions, chopped
1/2 cup celery, chopped
2 eggs, hard-boiled
2 tomatoes, cut in wedges
Lettuce

- Combine all the ingredients and serve salad with Ginger Dressing.

GINGER DRESSING

1/2 cup mayonnaise
3 tablespoons ginger preserves
1 tablespoon fresh mint leaves, chopped

- Blend well and serve over crab salad.

BIBB SALAD DELUXE

Makes 1 1/2 cups

Nothing but fresh, clean leaves of Bibb lettuce under this dressing.

2 tablespoons whole sesame seeds
3 tablespoons fresh lime juice
1 cup salad oil
1/4 cup red wine vinegar
3 tablespoons clover honey

- Toast sesame seeds in a 300 degrees oven for about 8 minutes. Combine all other ingredients in blender or processor.
- Pour over lettuce leaves, and sprinkle with sesame seeds.

CHICKEN SALAD WITH CHUTNEY AND CURRY

Serves 4

3/4 cup mayonnaise
1/4 cup chutney
2 1/2 teaspoons curry powder
1/2 teaspoon salt
3 cups chicken, cooked and cubed
1 cup celery, diced
1 11-ounce can mandarin oranges
1/2 cup macadamia nuts
Lettuce leaves

- Mix mayonnaise, chutney, curry and salt for dressing. Fold in the chicken, celery, mandarin oranges and half of nuts.
- Serve on a bed of lettuce and sprinkle remaining nuts on top.

PASTA SALAD

Serves 4

A great way to use leftover pasta for a light lunch.

1/4 cup sesame oil
1/4 cup walnuts, broken up
1/2 teaspoon Hot Chinese Oil
2 tablespoons vinegar
3 tablespoons sugar
1/2 teaspoon soy sauce
3 tablespoons sesame seeds, toasted
1 pound pasta, cooked, cooled

- Mix all the ingredients except pasta and sesame seeds in sauce pan, heat until sugar dissolves. Pour over cold pasta while dressing is still warm. Sprinkle with sesame seeds.

FLORIDA ORANGE VINAIGRETTE

Makes 1 1/2 cups

We first tasted this zesty dressing in Florida, and it has been a favorite since.

1/4 cup fresh orange juice
2 tablespoons white wine vinegar
1 tablespoon tarragon flavored Dijon mustard
Salt and pepper to taste
1 cup mild olive oil

- With an electric beater mix all the ingredients and blend well until slightly thick.
- This is very good on fresh orange wedges.

HONEY LEMON DRESSING

One of our favorite dressings on fresh spinach.

1 cup mayonnaise
1/2 cup buttermilk
1 1/2 tablespoons lemon juice
4 tablespoons honey
Pinch of salt

- Mix mayonnaise with buttermilk slowly to blend well.
- Warm the lemon juice and honey and add salt. Blend with mayonnaise mixture.

HOMEMADE BÉARNAISE ESSENCE

Use this for making Béarnaise sauce.

2 bay leaves
4 sprigs fresh tarragon
2 sprigs of parsley
10 shallots, minced
10 peppercorns, crushed
1 cup dry white wine
1 cup plus 4 tablespoons tarragon vinegar
1/2 lemon, juice of

- Combine the first five ingredients and tie them inside a cheese cloth. Pour wine, vinegar and lemon juice into sauce pan and drop spice bag in. Cook until reduced to a third. Cool. This can be frozen, or kept in refrigerator for several months.
- It is very concentrated.

BÉARNAISE MAYONNAISE

Makes 2 cups

A classic sauce. Tasty served with cooked salmon, or any other fish.

2 egg yolks
2 tablespoons fresh lemon juice
2 tablespoons tarragon flavored mustard
1/2 cup oil
1/2 cup olive oil
Pinch of salt
1/4 teaspoon pepper
2 tablespoons béarnaise essence

- In a blender or food processor, blend egg yolks, lemon juice and mustard. Add the oils in a thin, steady stream until used up and mayonnaise is thick. Add salt and pepper. Fold in the béarnaise essence.

BALSAMIC VINAIGRETTE DRESSING

Makes 1 1/2 cups

A fantastic dressing on a mixture of lettuce, shredded cabbage and spinach leaves.

1/2 cup Balsamic vinegar
2 tablespoons Dijon mustard
2 teaspoons garlic, minced
1/2 teaspoon thyme, dried
1/2 teaspoon basil, dried
Salt and pepper to taste
1 1/2 cups olive oil

- Whisk first six ingredients together. Add olive oil in a steady stream. I use a food processor with it's cup holding the oil. A blender, will work, as well.

The Soup Tureen

THE SOUP TUREEN

HOT SOUPS

COLD SOUPS

CREAM OF SPINACH SOUP

Serves 6

We enjoy a garden full of fresh spinach, and we are always attempting new ways to prepare this healthful vegetable.

1/2 pound bacon
3 tablespoons butter
1 tablespoon oil
1 small onion, minced
3 pounds fresh spinach
2 tablespoons flour
2 tablespoons fresh lemon juice
2 cans chicken broth
1 cup whole milk
1 cup Half-and-Half
1/2 teaspoon pepper
1 cup sharp Cheddar cheese, grated
Pinch of nutmeg

- Fry bacon until crisp, set aside. Melt butter and oil in saucepan, add onion and sauté until transparent, set aside. Cook spinach for 6 minutes. Drain all liquid from spinach, set aside. Finely chop spinach, set aside.
- Return onion to saucepan and add flour, stir well, then add lemon juice and spinach and again stir well. Add liquid and broth and bring to a boil. Lower heat and let simmer for 10 minutes. Stir in milk, Half-and-Half and pepper and let simmer another 5 minutes.
- Ladle into warmed bowls. Top with cheese, crumbled bacon and a pinch of nutmeg.

CREAMY TOMATO SOUP

Serves 4

When the greenhouses are bursting with tomatoes, I can, with clear conscience, steal some for this tasty soup.

3 cups tomatoes, chopped
1 1/2 teaspoons salt
1/3 cup onion, chopped
1 6-ounce can tomato paste
2 teaspoons sugar
1 teaspoon fresh basil leaves
1/2 teaspoon fresh thyme
Pinch of white pepper
1/4 teaspoon soda
1 tablespoon butter
1 tablespoon flour
2 cups milk

- Combine, cover and cook all but last four ingredients for about 10 minutes. Cool slightly and run through a sieve or the food processor. Remove and discard tomato skin. Stir in soda and set aside.
- In a large heavy, saucepan melt butter; stir in flour until well blended. Add milk, stirring constantly for about 1 minute. Combine the tomato mixture to milk base and blend well. Cook until hot, do not boil.
- Serve warm with oyster crackers or croutons.

CREAMY CARROT SOUP

Serves 8

- 3 tablespoons butter
- 2 pounds carrots, chopped
- 2 large onions, chopped
- 2 potatoes, peeled, chopped
- 1 bay leaf
- 6 cups chicken broth
- 4 tablespoons butter
- 2 tablespoons flour
- 3/4 cup Half-and-Half
- Salt and pepper
- 1 teaspoon dill weed

- Melt butter in large saucepan over low heat. Add carrots and onions. Place a piece of waxed paper on top and let vegetables sweat about 6 minutes. When done, add potatoes and bay leaf. Stir in the broth and let simmer for 40 minutes.
- In a separate pan, melt butter and add flour. Slowly add the cream and stir well. When vegetable mixture has finished simmering, run it through the food processor or blender to make a smooth paste. Add this to the sauce base with butter, flour and cream and stir well. Discard bay leaf. Add salt and pepper and dill weed. Let simmer until it obtains desired temperature. Serve with your favorite crusty bread.

CREAMY BROCCOLI BISQUE

Serves 4

Nice creamy texture, always a hit at dinner parties.

- 3 tablespoons butter
- 1/3 cup leeks, diced
- 1/3 cup onions, diced
- 1/3 cup celery, diced
- 2 cups broccoli, in small pieces
- 3 tablespoons flour
- 3 cups chicken broth
- Salt and pepper to taste
- 1/4 teaspoon thyme
- 1/3 cup white wine
- 1/2 Maggi cube, chicken flavored
- 1 cup Half-and-Half

- Melt butter in saucepan with vegetables; place waxed paper on top and let this sweat over very low heat for 10 minutes. Blend in flour, add chicken broth slowly, stirring until smooth. Bring to a boil. Add salt and pepper, thyme, wine and Maggi. Lower heat and simmer for 20 minutes.
- Run it through food processor or blender until smooth. Return to low heat and blend in cream.

BARANOFF BEAN BISQUE

Serves 8

Baranoff or Baranov, was named for the first Governor of the Russian American colonies. Baranoff Warm Springs is a beautiful place to anchor your boat. The harbor overlooks a breathtaking waterfall. It also has, for a small fee, facilities for a natural hot spring bath.

- Soak 2 cups of Great Northern Beans overnight in 6 cups water. Next day, drain liquid.
- In a large soup kettle add the following to drained beans:

5 cups water
1 can beef consommé
1 large onion, cut up
1 carrot, sliced
1 stalk celery, cut up
5 peppercorns
2 whole cloves
1 whole clove of garlic
1 or 2 ham bones or 1 piece of ham

- Bring above ingredients to a boil and cook for 2 1/2 hours over low heat. Discard vegetables. Cut ham in small pieces and return to soup.
- Dice the following:

1 large onion
1 small green pepper
2 stalks celery
2 carrots
Bunch of parsley, chopped
1 cup mashed potatoes

- Add to soup and let simmer another 30 minutes.
- Add 1 cup cooked mashed potatoes to soup. This thickens it and gives it a nice texture.

CREAMY EDAM CHEESE BISQUE

Serves 4

4 cups chicken broth
1 Maggi cube, chicken flavored
5 eggs
1 1/2 cups Edam cheese, shredded
1/2 cup heavy cream
3/4 cup Virginia ham, chopped
4 tablespoons fresh dill
3 tablespoons Gordon's gin

- Bring the broth and Maggi cube to a boil in heavy pan. Remove and cool. Meanwhile, blend cheese and cream with beaten eggs. Slowly whisk the egg and cheese mixture into broth, stirring well. Add ham, gin and fresh dill. Return to heat and simmer for 5 minutes for flavors to blend.

OYSTER BISQUE

Serves 8

When in Virginia, I try to get my hands on as many oysters as possible. This is the very first thing gone from the buffet table.

1 quart oysters, reserve liquid
1 bay leaf
2 medium onions, chopped
2 stalks celery, chopped
1/2 cup butter
1/4 cup flour
1 pint Half-and-Half
1/2 teaspoon salt
1/2 teaspoon pepper
1/2 teaspoon paprika
1/3 cup parsley, chopped
1/4 cup dry sherry
Dash of Tabasco sauce

- Drain and chop oysters. Add enough water to oyster liquid to make one quart, add oysters, bay leaf, one onion and one stalk of celery. Simmer for 30 minutes. Remove from heat and set aside for one hour.
- Melt butter in heavy sauce pan and add the remaining onion and celery. Stir until limp. Add flour; do not brown. Stir while adding a little liquid from oysters at a time. This should be a nice, smooth sauce.
- Add the cream, salt and pepper and simmer 3 minutes.
- Finally, stir in the sherry. Garnish with paprika and parsley.
- Serve with Oyster Crackers.

TRADITIONAL TEE HARBOR CLAM CHOWDER

Serves 8

- **1 quart clams, steamed, chopped**
- **1/4 pound bacon**
- **1 large onion**
- **3 medium potatoes with peel, cubed**
- **2 cups cream**
- **1 cup milk**
- **1/2 cup water**
- **1 8-ounce bottle of clam juice**
- **1/4 teaspoon paprika**
- **Salt and pepper to taste**
- **1/2 stick butter**

- Steam clams in large pan; discard any that do not open.
- Chop bacon and fry until crisp. Cook onion in bacon grease until limp. Boil potato cubes in a separate pan for about 10 minutes. Drain potatoes into a 4-quart pan; add clams and cook until heated. Add cream, milk, water, clam juice, bacon, onion, potatoes, paprika, salt and pepper. Heat to desired temperature.
- Swirl in butter just before serving.

GERMAN BEER AND CHEESE SOUP

Serves 4

- **3 tablespoons butter**
- **3 tablespoons flour**
- **2 cups chicken broth**
- **1/2 cup onion, minced**
- **1/2 cup celery, minced**
- **1 bottle good-quality light beer**
- **Salt and pepper to taste**
- **1 cup sharp Cheddar cheese, shredded**
- **1/4 cup Parmesan cheese, grated**

- Make roux with butter and flour, stirring for 2 to 3 minutes. Pour broth in and stir well. Add onion and celery, cook until vegetables are tender, about 5 minutes. Add beer, salt and pepper. Fold in the cheeses, stir until they melt.
- Serve in warmed bowls.

SHELTER ISLAND CLAM CHOWDER

Serves 8

On a low tide, collect as many steamer clams as possible for this delicate clam chowder.

2 dozen steamer clams
1/4 cup water

- Steam clams until they open, discard any that fail to do so.
- Set clams aside. Strain broth through cheese cloth and set aside.

6 slices bacon, finely diced
1/4 cup butter
1 medium onion, finely chopped
1 cup celery, chopped
2 medium potatoes, chopped
2 large Maggi cubes, chicken flavored
1 quart chicken broth
1/4 cup parsley, chopped
1 tablespoon chervil, chopped
1/2 teaspoon white pepper
2 cups milk
1 cup Half-and-Half
Reserved broth from clams or use 1 cup commercial clam juice
1/4 teaspoon Hot Chinese Oil
2 cups mashed potatoes, to thicken bisque

- Sauté bacon until crisp, set aside, save drippings. Using a large soup pot, melt half of butter and drippings, sauté onions, celery and potatoes until limp, about 8 minutes. Crumble in the Maggi cubes, stir well until dissolved. Add broth, chervil, pepper, milk and parsley. Finally, blend in the clams, remaining butter and reserved liquid. Let simmer for 15 minutes. If the clams are large, I usually chop them into smaller pieces.
- Fold the mashed potatoes into soup and add cream. Stir in the parsley, let simmer over very low heat for 5 minutes. Turn off heat and stir in Chinese Oil. Sprinkle with crisp, crumbled bacon.

KLONDIKE CHEDDAR SOUP

Serves 6

Velvety smooth and filling.

- **1 cup onion, finely chopped**
- **4 tablespoons butter**
- **4 tablespoons flour**
- **1 teaspoon salt**
- **1 teaspoon white pepper**
- **3 cups milk**
- **1/2 cup water**
- **1 Knorr bouillon cube, chicken flavored**
- **2 1/2 cups extra sharp Cheddar cheese, shredded**
- **1/2 cup dry white wine**
- **3 tablespoons chives, chopped**
- **1 teaspoon paprika**

- Sauté onion in butter in a large sauce pan until limp, not brown. Add flour, salt and pepper. Stir well; add milk a little at a time until used up. Dissolve the bouillon cube in water and add to milk base. Keep stirring. Then add the shredded Cheddar cheese and stir until melted. Stir in the wine and finally the paprika and chives.
- Ladle into warmed soup bowls. Top with croutons or crisp bacon bits.

CHICHAGOF CHEDDAR CHOWDER

Serves 8

- **2 large onions, chopped**
- **1/2 cup celery, finely chopped**
- **6 tablespoons butter**
- **4 tablespoons flour**
- **5 cups chicken broth**
- **2 pounds sharp Cheddar cheese, shredded**
- **1 lemon, juice of**
- **2 sprigs fresh savory, or 1/2 teaspoon dried**
- **1 cup milk**
- **1 cup Half-and-Half**
- **1/4 teaspoon salt**
- **1/4 teaspoon white pepper**
- **1/2 cup chopped parsley**

- Sauté onions and celery in butter until limp. Add the flour, stirring until smooth. Slowly add the broth and cheese. Keep stirring. Add the savory and lemon juice and let simmer for 20 minutes over very low heat. Remove and run soup through food processor or blender until free of any bits of celery or onion. Return to heat, add milk and cream and heat to serving temperature. Season with salt and pepper. Garnish with chopped parsley.

BLACK BEAN SOUP

Serves 10

There is something special about a good soup. You will enjoy this terrific soup recipe that Tori Kleeschulte let me copy.

- Start by soaking 2 pounds of dried black beans in 4 quarts of cold water overnight. The next day, rinse the beans twice under cold water and add 4 quarts of water. Bring beans to a rapid boil; lower heat to medium and let them cook for 1 hour with a cover on.
- Sauté the following in 1 1/3 cups olive oil:

5 medium onions, sliced
12 cloves of garlic
12 sweet chili peppers, seeded, chopped

- Mash two cups of drained beans. Add to skillet with onions and fry a few minutes. Return all of the mixture to kettle with remaining beans. Cover and bring to a boil. Reduce heat and let simmer for 1 hour. After 1 hour of gentle simmering add:

8 teaspoons salt
1/2 tablespoon pepper, freshly ground
1/2 to 1 tablespoon whole dried oregano
4 bay leaves, crushed
1 teaspoon ground cumin
4 tablespoons white or red dry wine
3 tablespoons vinegar

- Cover and cook over low heat for another hour.
- Uncover and cook until soup thickens, about 1/2 hour.
- Serve with a thin slice of lemon and a dollop of sour cream.

FRESH MUSHROOM SOUP

Serves 6

A wonderful lemon-flavored soup. Chock-full of firm mushroom slices.

1 pound mushrooms, thickly sliced
2 tablespoons butter
4 teaspoons lemon juice
2 tablespoons flour
1 teaspoon salt
8 cups chicken broth
2 teaspoons sherry
4 egg yolks
2 teaspoons parsley, chopped

- Sauté mushrooms in butter until soft. Add lemon juice and stir well. Mix in the flour and salt. Add the chicken broth and bring to a boil. Lower heat and let simmer a few minutes. Blend sherry and egg yolks. Spoon a little of the warm soup into yolks, stir and return this to the soup.
- Sprinkle with parsley.

PLEASANT HARBOR PARSLEY SOUP

Serves 4

And you thought parsley was only for garnishing! Try this refreshing warm weather soup. Serve it with fresh croutons or a slice of lemon.

3 cups chicken broth
2 bunches parsley, stalks removed
1 tablespoon butter
1 tablespoon flour
1 1/4 cups Half-and-Half
Salt and pepper to taste
1 lemon, juice of

- In sauce pan, stir parsley into broth. Cook for 10 minutes.
- In the meantime, make the cream sauce.
- In a medium-sized sauce pan, melt butter and add flour. Blend well; stir constantly for about 2 minutes. Slowly add cream until nice and smooth.
- Run the parsley and broth mixture through food processor or use a blender until it's finely chopped. Return it to the pan with cream mixture and blend. Season with salt and pepper. Chill.
- Just before serving squeeze fresh lemon juice into each bowl.
- Looks attractive when garnished with a slice of lemon.

BRIE SOUP

Serves 6

This is a little more than a soup. I first had it in a restaurant in Seattle, and begged for the recipe. This is as close to it as I could come. It is heavenly and very rich.

1/4 stick butter
1/4 cup leeks, minced
1/4 cup green onion, minced
2 tablespoons flour
4 cups chicken broth, warm
1 pound Brie, with rind
1/4 cup Half and Half
Salt and pepper to taste

- Melt butter in heavy saucepan over low heat, as you don't want the butter to brown. Add the onions and leeks and cook until limp, about 5 minutes. Add flour and stir well. Whisk in the warm broth and let it simmer until reduced to 2 1/4 cups, about 15 minutes.
- Cut Brie into cubes, set aside a couple of pieces for each bowl when serving. Add to broth. Stir until melted. Add the cream, salt and pepper.
- Sprinkle freshly chopped chives on top. Serve warm, not piping hot.

MOOSE HUNTER'S OXTAIL SOUP

Serves 10

My absolute favorite of all soups to serve. The rich flavor cannot be described. When the hunters get ready for the moose hunt in October, I always make a huge pot of Oxtail Soup for them.

4 parsley sprigs
4 tops of celery
2 leeks
6 tablespoons butter
2 tablespoons vegetable oil
4 pounds oxtails, cut into 1-inch sections
2 carrots, thinly sliced
2 onions, thinly sliced
4 tablespoons flour
4 quarts consommé
1 cup carrots, diced
1 cup turnips, diced
4 tablespoons Madeira

BOUQUET GARNI:
2 teaspoons dried thyme
10 black peppercorns, tied inside cheese cloth

- Sauté parsley, celery tops and leeks in 2 tablespoons of butter, set aside.
- In a large soup pot, melt 2 tablespoons butter with oil over medium heat.
- Wipe oxtails with paper towels and drop into butter. Brown meat on all sides. Do this in sections, adding more butter as needed; don't crowd the pot. Set aside. Add a little more butter; now add carrots and onions, and sauté until brown. Add flour and stir well until flour has browned. Stir in the consommé a few cans at a time until all used. Bring to a rolling boil, whisking vigorously. Drop the cheesecloth with bouquet garni into soup with the sautéed parsley and leek mixture.
- Return the oxtails to soup pot and let simmer for 3 1/2 to 4 hours with loose-fitting lid.
- When done, set aside to cool. Remove oxtails with a slotted spoon, set aside to cool. In a small sauce pan, melt remaining butter and sauté carrots and turnips for a few minutes. Add to soup pot and simmer for 30 minutes.
- At this point, I set the pot of soup outside to cool so I can remove most of the fat from top.
- In the meantime, remove all meat from oxtails. Save bones for your favorite pet.
- Return meat to soup and heat to correct temperature.
- Add Madeira and stir.

TONGASS TOMATO SOUP

Serves 8

A good way to utilize the abundance of tomatoes from the garden or greenhouse.

- **4 pounds very ripe tomatoes**
- **2 medium onions**
- **2 carrots**
- **4 tablespoons butter**
- **4 tablespoons flour**
- **4 pints chicken broth**
- **1/2 teaspoon each:**
  - **parsley**
  - **thyme**
  - **basil, tied inside cheese cloth**
- **salt and freshly ground pepper**
- **4 tablespoons cream**
- **Port for each bowl**
- **Sour cream for each bowl**

- Dice tomatoes, onions and carrots. In a large saucepan melt butter and add vegetables; cover with a piece of waxed paper and let vegetables sweat for 10 minutes. Add flour, stir in broth, bouquet garni and salt and pepper. Simmer for 30 minutes over low heat.
- Remove bouquet garni and strain soup, or, what I do is run it through the food processor. Reheat and fold in cream, but do not boil or it will separate. Spoon in port and top with sour cream.
- This is also excellent cold.

CLASSIC VICHYSSOISE

Serves 6

We had 6 different versions of Vichyssoise submitted; this is the one we chose to use in the book. Velvety-smooth and delicious.

1 medium onion, diced
4 leeks, white part only, sliced
4 tablespoons butter
4 medium potatoes, sliced
1 quart chicken broth
1 large Maggi cube, chicken flavored
1 tablespoon salt
1/2 teaspoon white pepper
2 cups heavy cream
3 cups milk
1/4 cup chives, chopped

- Sauté onion and leeks in butter, do not brown. Add potatoes, chicken broth, Maggi, salt and pepper and let simmer for 35 minutes. Run the soup through food processor, blender or a fine strainer.
- Chill well. Add the cream and milk.
- Sprinkle with fresh chives.

GARDEN GAZPACHO

Serves 6

Most of these items can be picked in our garden during the summer. Choose fresh, ripe vegetables. This soup is perfect for hot weather.

4 large, ripe tomatoes, peeled and chopped
1 large cucumber, diced
1 medium onion, minced
1 green pepper, diced
1 cup tomato juice
1 can consommé
3 tablespoons olive oil
1 tablespoon wine vinegar
1 clove garlic, mashed
1 tablespoon paprika
1/4 teaspoon cayenne pepper
Salt and pepper to taste
1 tomato, chopped, for garnish
3 tablespoons green onions, chopped, for garnish

- Scald tomatoes quickly in hot water and peel. Combine all the ingredients in blender or food processor and pureé until smooth. Refrigerate until serving time.
- Serve in a chilled glass bowl; garnish with tomatoes and green onions.

MEXICAN AVOCADO SOPA

Serves 6

3	avocados	1/2	teaspoon salt
1 1/2	cups chicken broth	1 1/2	cups Half-and-Half
2	teaspoons lime juice	1	lime, sliced
1	clove garlic, minced	1	avocado for garnishing

- Make sure the avocados are ripe. Peel and slice. Pureé in food processor or blender with a little broth, lime juice, and garlic. Blend until smooth. Add the remaining broth, salt and cream. Chill thoroughly.
- Serve cold, garnished with thin lime slices and sliced wedges of avocado.

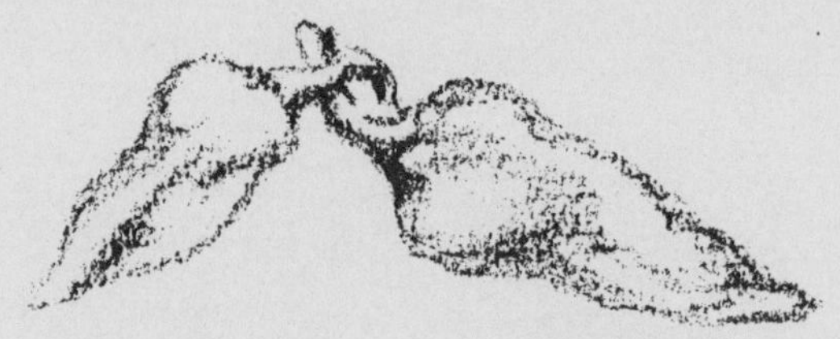

SPINACH AND LEEK SOUP

Serves 6

This is just as good served cold on a hot day, as it is served hot on a cold day.

4	cups red potatoes, sliced, with peel	2	cups white wine
1	large onion, sliced	1	cup Half-and-Half
1	small bunch spinach, chopped	1	tablespoon sherry
4	leeks, with part of greens		Salt and pepper to taste
1	quart chicken broth	1	tablespoon Tabasco sauce

- In a large soup pan, combine all vegetables, wine and broth. Simmer until soft. Run this through food processor or blender until smooth and without lumps. Add cream, sherry and seasonings. Warm until desired temperature.

SOUTH SHELTER SPINACH SOUP

Serves 8

It is almost a shame to use the wonderful fresh spinach in a soup, but this is worth it.

1 cup olive oil
9 yes 9, cloves garlic, minced
1 large onion, chopped
2 carrots, diced
2 stalks celery
4 teaspoons fresh basil, or 2 teaspoons dry
8 cups chicken broth
2 pounds fresh spinach, chopped
3 potatoes, finely diced
Parmesan cheese

- Heat olive oil in a large pan over medium heat. Stir together garlic, onion, carrots, celery and basil. Sauté for 5 minutes or until vegetables are limp. Do not brown garlic or it turns bitter. Add chicken broth, spinach and potatoes. Cook gently until potatoes are done. Garnish with Parmesan cheese.

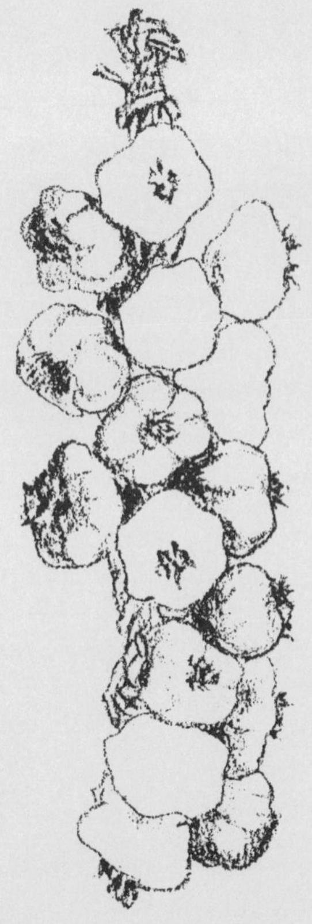

The Tide is Out...
The Table is Set...

THE TIDE IS OUT...THE TABLE IS SET

GUIDE TO SOME OF THE PACIFIC COAST FISH

- Albacore: Albacore is a tuna, rich in flavor, meaty and firm when cooked. It can be barbecued, broiled, poached or baked. It is usually available midsummer through October in the Northwest.
- Bass: Three common Pacific bass are Sea bass, grouper, and black sea bass. All are mild in flavor and have delicate white meat. Bass can be cooked as fillets, or is very good fried or used in stews or soups. These three types are available all year in Mexico and Southern California.
- Cod: Two good varieties of cod are available in Southeast Alaska, grey and black. The black cod is absolutely delicious when smoked, then lightly steamed. The grey cod has delicate white meat, a mild flavor, and is frequently used in stews and creamed dishes. Cod is prevalent all year in Northwestern waters.
- Halibut: Halibut comes in many sizes and are a great sport to catch when really big. The largest we have caught was 301 pounds. My favorite size is between 15 to 20 pounds, when the meat is delicate and sweet. It is very good deep fried, cooked in beer batter or in many stews. Halibut can be caught from May through September all along the Northwest coast.
- Salmon: Salmon, especially king salmon, is the most sought-after of all fish in Alaskan waters. King salmon grow to be very large, and have either red meat or white meat. Both are equally good eating. Some people prefer white, but the red looks pretty when used in lox or gravlax.

  Salmon tastes very good poached, broiled, fried, grilled or barbecued. The largest one caught on our boat was a 70 pound king salmon. It was a trophy fish and can be seen in the office of the Juneau Eye Clinic.

  Salmon can be found all year in Alaska; the best time to catch king salmon is from early April to late September.
- Silver Salmon: Cook silver salmon, or coho as you would king salmon. Silver salmon are smaller in size and most agree, it is equally as tasty as king salmon. They are fiesty and great fun to catch, and can be readily caught on bait, spinning gear or flies, and are available from mid-July to late September in Southeast Alaska.
- Red Snapper: Red snapper is a rock fish, and, like halibut live along the ocean floor. The flavor is mild and the meat is nice and flaky, white to pale pink in color. Snappers can taste good baked or broiled; you can sauté fillets in butter with lemon juice, barbecue them or use the traditional Vera-Cruz-style dish served all over Mexico. Red snapper can be found year round on the entire Pacific coast.
- Rockfish: Rockfish is also known as a rock cod or rosefish can be found year round in Alaska and is excellent prepared like any red snapper dish.

PROSPECTOR CRAB CAKES

Serves 4

When the crab is plentiful, we make a batch of these tasty cakes.

MAYONNAISE:

1	**egg**	**4**	**shakes Tabasco sauce**
1	**tablespoon Dijon mustard**	**1/4**	**teaspoon paprika**
2	**teaspoons lemon juice**	**1/2**	**cup oil**
2	**teaspoons red wine vinegar**	**1/4**	**cup olive oil**

- Combine egg, mustard, lemon juice, vinegar, Tabasco sauce and paprika in food processor or blender. Add oils in a slow steady stream with motor running. Set aside.

4	**cups bread crumbs**	**1**	**jar pimento, chopped**
1	**small green pepper, chopped**		**Above mayonnaise, or any other home-made, about 3/4 cup**
4	**tablespoons parsley, chopped**	**1 1/2**	**pounds crab meat**
1/4	**cup green onion, chopped**		**Butter for frying**
	Salt and pepper to taste		

- Mix half of bread crumbs, pepper, parsley, onion, and salt and pepper with mayonnaise and crab meat; add pimentos. Roll into 3-inch balls, then roll in remaining bread crumbs. Flatten balls. Fry in skillet with a small amount of butter, making sure not to crowd the pan. Fry until golden brown on both sides.

LENA POINT CRAB

Serves 6 crab lovers

With the crab pots outside our home across from Lena Point we often have more crab than we know what to do with. This is another donation from Diane Fraties. Try this treat.

2	**pounds crab meat, cooked**	**1/2**	**cup mayonnaise**
1	**cup celery, finely chopped**	**1 1/2**	**teaspoons dry mustard**
1	**cup green onion, sliced**	**1**	**teaspoon salt**
1/2	**cup parsley, minced**	**1**	**cup melted butter**
1	**green pepper, finely chopped**	**2 1/2**	**cups cracker crumbs**

- Mix all the above ingredients and spoon into buttered casserole, reserving a little for topping. Top with the reserved crumbs and drizzle a little butter on top of that.
- Bake at 350 degrees for 25-30 minutes.

FUNTER BAY CRAB CAKES

Serves 10

This dish is rich, all it needs is a salad and some crab lovers.

- **5 pounds crab meat, any kind**
- **1 1/2 onions, minced**
- **5 tablespoons Worcestershire sauce**
- **3 tablespoons Johnny's Seafood Seasoning**
- **1 tablespoon soy sauce**
- **1/4 teaspoon Tabasco sauce**
- **1 cup mayonnaise**
- **3/4 cup coarse-grained mustard**
- **5 eggs**
- **1/4 cup parsley, chopped**
- **1 sleeve Saltine crackers, crushed**

- In large bowl combine crab meat, onions, Worchestershire sauce, seafood seasoning, soy sauce and Tabasco sauce, mayonnaise and mustard; mix well. Beat eggs and fold into crab mixture. Add parsley. Form into 25-30 cakes. Roll cakes in crushed crackers.
- Heat electric frying pan to 350 degrees. Place as many cakes in pan as it will hold without crowding and fry for about 3 minutes on each side.
- No tartar sauce is necessary, but pass the lemon wedges.

ALASKA KING CRAB CASSEROLE

Serves 4

- **1/2 cup mayonnaise**
- **1/4 cup green pepper, chopped**
- **1 egg**
- **1 pimento, chopped**
- **1 tablespoon water**
- **1 teaspoon dry mustard**
- **1/2 teaspoon paprika**
- **1/2 teaspoon salt**
- **1/4 teaspoon pepper**
- **1 pound king crab meat, cooked**

- Combine all the ingredients except crab. Fold crab in gently, making sure it does not become too broken up.
- Butter a shallow casserole dish and fill with mixture. Top with a little mayonnaise applied with a pastry brush. Bake at 350 degrees for 10 minutes.

SITKA ABALONE

Serves 6

Abalone is the most delicate of all seafoods found in the Alaskan waters. There are lots off the coast of Sitka, and we plan our clinic trip around the tides when going into Sitka during the summer. When the tide is the lowest, the crew goes down, loaded with wetsuits and sharp knives and disappear for hours, returning with the limit of their shellfish.

Then the work begins. It takes hours to remove all the black stuff from the abalone, or so we had thought. Two summers ago, though, as we worked steadily, growing tired and beginning to wonder if it was worth the effort, Brownie Thompson rescued us from ourselves. Upon surveying our pile of abalone and inquiring how long we had been at it, a look of mild disbelief and horror crossed her face, and then she spoke. "Just freeze the abalone a little while and it all rubs off. After 16 years of grueling work, someone finally tells us. Guess we should have asked.

Now the fun part:

- Slice each abalone in half, making two medallions of abalone out of one. With a cleaver or hammer, pound the abalone a couple of times to relax the muscle.

15 abalones, cut into two pieces
1/4 cup flour
3 eggs, beaten
1 tablespoon milk
1/8 teaspoon salt
1 cup bread crumbs
1 teaspoon Johnny's Seafood Seasoning
1/4 cube butter
1/4 cup oil

- Dust abalone with seasoned flour. Dip abalone in beaten eggs mixed with salt and milk, then roll them in bread crumbs. Melt butter and oil in large skillet, let it get hot without burning. Working fast; fry each abalone in butter and oil for about 2 minutes on first side and 1 minutes on the other, sprinkle with seafood seasoning. Be careful not to crowd the pan, and add more butter to pan if needed.
- I like serving them with fresh lemon wedges and a homemade tartar sauce.

WINE STEAMED MUSSELS

Serves 4

We fell for some fantastic mussels in Virginia on a recent trip. This is how we enjoyed them.

1/4 cup white wine
1/4 cup white wine vinegar
1/2 tablespoon oregano
3 dozen mussels

LEMON BUTTER SAUCE
1/2 cup butter
1 lemon, juice of
1/4 teaspoon paprika
1/4 teaspoon tarragon
Salt and pepper to taste

- In a large pan bring wine, vinegar and oregano to a boil. Add mussels and cook until they open, about 7 minutes. Discard any that remain closed. In the meantime, heat butter, add lemon juice and seasonings. Cook for 2 minutes. Serve at once.

VIRGINIA OYSTER CASSEROLE

Serves 6

1/2 cup butter
1 medium onion, chopped
1 clove garlic, minced
1/2 green bell pepper, chopped
1/2 cup flour
1 1/2 teaspoons paprika
Dash cayenne pepper
1/2 teaspoon salt
1/4 teaspoon pepper
1 tablespoon lemon juice
2 teaspoons Worcestershire sauce
1 1/2 quarts fresh oysters, save liquid
1/4 cup cracker crumbs

- Grease a 2-guart casserole with butter, set aside.
- Melt butter, do not brown. Sauté onions, garlic and bell pepper until limp. Add the flour and stir well. Slowly add liquid from oysters. Add paprika, cayenne pepper, salt and pepper and stir well.
- Let simmer for 5 minutes. Add the lemon juice and Worcestershire sauce.
- Fold oysters into casserole and sprinkle with cracker crumbs. Bake for 40 minutes at 400 degrees.

VIOLET DAVIS'S SCALLOPED OYSTERS

Serves 4

1 pint select oysters, with liquid
1/2 cup light cream
3 cups oyster crackers, crushed
1/2 cup butter, melted
2 teaspoons celery seeds
1 teaspoon salt
1 teaspoon pepper
1/2 cup onions, thinly sliced, optional

- Heat oven to 375 degrees. Arrange oysters with liquid in greased 11 x 7-inch baking dish. Pour half of cream over oysters. Combine crumbs, butter, celery seeds, onions, salt and pepper, sprinkle. Pour remaining cream over mixture.
- Bake without cover for 30 to 40 minutes.

ROYAL SHRIMP IN TAMARI SAUCE

Serves 6

This is something real special. Have all the ingredients handy; this will only take minutes to cook.

1 1/2 pounds large shrimp
Flour for dredging
2 tablespoons olive oil
2 cloves garlic, sliced
4 cups fresh mushrooms, sliced
3 tablespoons Tamari (soy sauce)
4 tablespoons white wine
3 tablespoons fresh lemon juice
3 tablespoons chicken broth
1 1/2 cups fresh tomatoes, cubed
1/4 cup scallions, sliced

- Butterfly shrimp and dredge with flour; shake off as much as possible. In a large skillet heat olive oil; add garlic and shrimp and sauté over medium heat for about 2 minutes. Flip shrimp over and add mushrooms. Stir until mushrooms begin to darken, about 2 minutes. Remove shrimp and keep warm. Now add soy sauce, white wine, lemon juice and chicken broth, stir until sauce thickens. Add tomatoes and scallions, stir briefly, return shrimp for a quick warm-up. Serve immediately. I serve this with Pasta in Mint Pesto Sauce.

SHRIMP IN MUSTARD SAUCE

Serves 4

This dish is full of large firm shrimp. It has a very distinctive flavor of lemon and mustard.

2 tablespoons mild olive oil
2 shallots, sliced
24 large shrimp, shelled
1/4 cup dry vermouth
1/4 cup heavy cream, whipped
1/2 stick butter
1 1/2 tablespoons coarse mustard
2 tablespoons fresh lemon juice
Dash of salt and pepper

- Heat oil in large skillet. Sauté shallots 2 minutes. Add the shrimp and sauté for a total of about 4 minutes or until pink. Remove both shallots and shrimp.
- Add the vermouth to pan with oil and cook over high heat until volume is reduced to half. Lower temperature; add cream, butter and mustard and stir well. Return shrimp and shallots to pan. Coat well with sauce. At this point the sauce is slightly thick. Push shrimp to side and whisk in the lemon juice, salt and pepper. Serve at once. I usually serve plain buttered spinach pasta with this dish.

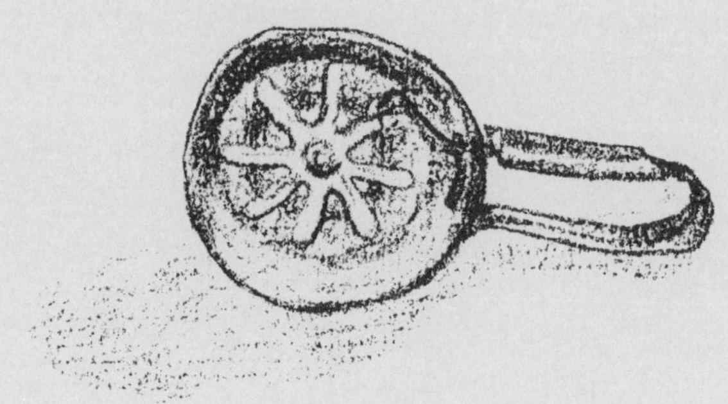

SOUTH END OF THE WRANGELL NARROWS

I wanted to call our meal that night something special. But the truth is, we were so busy, that I can't remember what we had for supper. What I do remember is this: The DamnYankee had one anchor out, as always. We were trying to get some sleep when the turbulence started up. Wind was blowing like never before, and every plank in the boat was trying to get in the last word about it. I remember clearly that our Old English Sheepdog, Hamlet, was so scared that he jumped directly on Bob's face, shaking as only a Shaggy Dog can.

We had a terrible time keeping our bodies on the bed, the boat rocked back and forth, things were falling from everywhere, and please let me add that bad weather is not one of my favorite parts of boating. The crew woke up, or, more truly, they were already awake like the rest of us. It was their job to secure the DamnYankee, we needed yet another anchor out. Our nephew Peter Jr. took charge. He has crewed for us for years, and knew what to do at all times. He was always the first one on the deck if we had any problems, and again, on this night, he was the first one up, securing the anchor and assuring all of us that things were safe, and they were. We finally enjoyed a good rest.

The next morning, the Boston Whaler was gone from it's usual place, roped to a cleat at the Yankee's stern. It was spotted not far from us, about a quarter of a mile towards the beach. We dressed Peter in his survival suit, and he jumped overboard to make a swim for it. He had just hit the water when a couple of friendly seals swam near him, whining like eager puppies. They thought they had someone to play with! Who could resist Peter in his bright International Orange outfit? The seals cruised around him making wild sounds, flapping their flippers, and acting like they knew he had been dumped there just to entertain them.

After some swimming, Peter returned with the boat. We entered this in our logbook as just another experience cruising Southeast Alaska. And I do remember this: we served the boy some sourdough pancakes with his favorite "chicken gravy".

SCANDINAVIAN RED SNAPPER

Serves 3-4

I have used this recipe on many other fish fillets like sole, dorado and cabrilla, and they all turn out terrific. Have plenty of fresh lemon wedges on hand for this crunchy on the outside, moist on the inside fish. Tie lemon wedges inside cheesecloth to catch seeds, it also keeps the fingers clean.

4 red snapper fillets
2 eggs, slightly beaten
3/4 cup bread crumbs
1/2 cube butter
1/2 teaspoon Johnny's Seafood Seasoning
1/4 teaspoon paprika
Lemon wedges
Fresh dill

- Wipe fish clean with paper towel. Dip each fish fillet in beaten eggs, then roll in bread crumbs. This can be done earlier in the day and kept in refrigerator until cooking time. In a pan large enough to hold fillets melt butter over moderate heat. Place fillets, sprinkle with seafood seasoning and paprika. Fry for 4 minutes on first side, turn and repeat on the other side.
- Garnish with lemon wedges and fresh dill.

TERIYAKI RED SNAPPER

Serves 8

Use only fresh fish. Flounder or any other firm, white fish works well.

4 cups water
2 cups soy sauce
6 cloves garlic
2 tablespoons fresh ginger, grated
2 teaspoons sugar
8 fish fillets

- Combine all the ingredients in a large, flat pan. Marinate fish for 2 to 4 hours.
- Grill fish over hot coals or on any grill until fish flakes, about 4 minutes per side depending on size.
- Do not overcook.

BATTER-FRIED SHRIMP

Serves 4

I use medium-sized shrimp for this meal. They puff up and are as light as a feather.

- **1 pound fresh shrimp, shelled**
- **2 teaspoons rice wine**
- **1 1/2 tablespoons cornstarch**
- **1/4 cup cornstarch**
- **1/3 cup cold water**
- **2 large eggs, separated**
- **1/4 teaspoon salt**
- **2 teaspoons baking powder**
- **3/4 cup flour**
- **2 teaspoons lard, melted**
- **5 cups oil for frying**

- Mix rice wine, 1 1/2 tablespoons cornstarch and shrimp in large bowl. Set aside for 1/2 hour.
- Mix cornstarch with water in a cup until smooth. Beat egg whites in a small bowl. Beat yolks in another bowl; to this add salt, baking powder, cornstarch mixture and flour to yolks and whisk until smooth.
- Fold in the whipped egg whites; whisk thoroughly.
- Warm a wok over high heat, about 350 degrees for a few seconds, then add oil and lard and bring up to temperature. Dip some of the shrimp into batter and place in wok. Fry, stirring gently for about 3 minutes. Shrimp will be evenly, lightly browned and cooked through. Remove with slotted spoon and drain on paper towel. Repeat with remaining shrimp.
- Fry shrimp a second time at 375 degrees. Do not dip in batter again; simply fry until golden, about 2 minutes.
- Serve with Sweet-and-Sour Sauce.

SWEET-AND-SOUR DIPPING AND DUNKING SAUCE

Makes 1 cup

- **4 tablespoons sugar**
- **1/2 teaspoon salt**
- **4 teaspoons cornstarch**
- **2/3 cup catsup**
- **4 tablespoons distilled vinegar**
- **2 tablespoons rice wine**
- **2 tablespoons soy sauce**

- Mix sugar, salt and cornstarch in small sauce pan. Add the remaining ingredients and heat until boiling. Lower heat and continue cooking for another 2 minutes, or until sauce thickens.

DEEP FRIED SQUID

Serves 4

More often than not, I hear how squid tastes like rubber bands. I wouldn't recommend buying them unless fresh. Check to make sure they are firm and creamy colored. This recipe guarantees very tender squid. The secret is not to overcook.

1 pound fresh, cleaned squid
1/4 cup flour
1/3 cup cornstarch
1/2 teaspoon salt
1/2 teaspoon baking powder
1 egg
1/3 cup water
1 1/2 tablespoons oil
4 cups oil for deep frying

- Cut each squid into four parts. Blend flour, cornstarch, salt and baking powder with egg and mix well. Add water and oil. Beat batter until smooth. Dip each piece of squid into batter to coat.
- Heat oil in a deep fryer or an electric frying pan to 375 degrees. Drop 3-4 pieces of squid at a time into hot oil; do not crowd. Fry for 5 minutes. Remove and drain on paper towel.

SOLE WITH TARRAGON

Serves 4

Perfect Friday night supper. We first had this served in a small casual seafood restaurant on Sanibel Island.

- **8 fillets of sole, skinned**
- **1/4 pint water**
- **1 stalk celery, chopped**
- **1 onion, sliced**
- **2 tablespoons tarragon vinegar**
- **1 bay leaf**
- **4 whole peppercorns**

- Preheat oven to 375 degrees. In a pan large enough to hold fillets, place rolled up sole in water with celery, onion, vinegar and spices, and bake for 10 minutes or until flaky. Pour off stock and reserve. Remove bay leaf, onion, celery and peppercorns.
- Combine stock and cream to measure 1 cup.

TARRAGON CREAM SAUCE

- **4 tablespoons butter**
- **5 tablespoons flour**
- **1 cup cream and above stock mixture**
- **4 teaspoons tarragon vinegar**
- **1/2 teaspoon salt**
- **1/4 teaspoon white pepper**
- **1 egg yolk**
- **1 cup whole seedless green grapes**

- Melt butter in sauce pan; add flour: stir and cook 2 minutes. Gradually add the stock/cream mixture and stir until smooth. Add vinegar, salt and white pepper. Beat egg yolk with a fork and add to sauce. Simmer 1 minute. Sprinkle the grapes on top. Serve over fillets of sole.

MAHI-MAHI

Serves 4

Linda Andrews serves this often to her family. It's very tasty and delicate.

5 tablespoons macadamia nuts, ground
4 fish fillets, Mahi-Mahi, flounder or sole
3 tablespoons butter, melted
Lemon wedges

- Spread 1/3 of nuts in shallow baking dish. Place fish on top. Spoon the remaining nuts on top and drizzle butter and lemon juice over. Bake at 350 degrees for 15-20 minutes.
- Serve at once, with fresh lemon wedges.

IRISH STYLE BAKED TROUT

Serves 4

4 green onions, sliced
1 green pepper
1/4 cup butter
1 cup bread crumbs
1/4 cup parsley
1 teaspoon lemon juice
4 cutthroat trout
1 teaspoon Johnny's Seafood Seasoning
Lemon wedges

- Sauté onions and green pepper a few minutes in half of butter; add bread crumbs, parsley and lemon juice.
- Rub cavities with seasoning and place 1/4 cup stuffing inside each fish. Grease a pan large enough to hold fish side by side, dot with butter and bake at 350 degrees for 20 minutes or less. Check fish and cook until it flakes, but not dry.
- Garnish with plenty of fresh lemon wedges.

SHRIMP IN BEER

Serves 6

There are many ways to cook shrimp; there is only one rule, never overcook them.

5 pounds large shrimp
3 cans flat beer
1 teaspoon Johnny's Seafood Seasoning

- Bring beer to boil, add the seasoning. Drop shrimp into beer and set timer for 3-4 minutes. Remove them before they start to curl up.
- Place shrimp in large bowl. Let everyone peel their own.
- Serve with Dipping Butter.

DIPPING BUTTER FOR SHRIMP

1 1/2 cubes butter
1/4 teaspoon salt
1/2 teaspoon paprika
1 lemon, juice of

- Melt butter and add salt, paprika and lemon juice. Serve with shrimp in small, separate bowl.

AUKE BAY SALMON SPREAD

Makes 2 1/2 cups

Best if made a couple of days ahead, kept cold in refrigerator and served on Pilot crackers.

2 cups cold, cooked salmon
3/4 cup mayonnaise
4 tablespoons prepared horseradish sauce
4 tablespoons sweet relish
3 tablespoons dried onion flakes
1/2 teaspoon Johnny's Seafood Seasoning

- Mix all the ingredients and store in jar with a tight fitting lid for several days.

SCANDINAVIAN STYLE FLOUNDER

Serves 6

This batter is also good with fillet of sole. Decrease cooking time according to thickness of fillets.

- **2 eggs**
- **3/4 cup bread crumbs**
- **1/2 teaspoon Johnny's Seafood Seasoning**
- **6 large flounder fillets**
- **2 tablespoons lemon juice**
- **1/4 stick butter**
- **1 teaspoon oil**
- **Fresh lemon wedges**

- Beat eggs lightly. Mix bread crumbs and seafood seasoning.
- Wipe fish and rub with lemon juice. Dip fillets first in eggs, then bread crumbs, making sure they have an even coating.
- Melt butter and oil in large frying pan. Check butter, don't let it burn or turn too dark. Add fish fillets and fry for 4 to 5 minutes on each side or until fish flakes.
- Serve with lemon wedges.

FRESH FISH FRIKADELLER

Serves 4

During the summer we always end up with a lot of halibut. After sharing with friends and relatives, we must come up with new ideas of how to prepare what we have left. This is a Danish recipe, it was my favorite as a child. We used cod instead, but it is delicious with halibut.

- **1 pound halibut**
- **1/2 onion, minced**
- **4 tablespoons potato flour**
- **1 egg**
- **1/2 pint milk**
- **1 teaspoon salt**
- **1/2 teaspoon white pepper**
- **3 tablespoons butter**
- **1/4 teaspoon oil**

- Start by grinding the fish or chopping it as finely as possible. It should be almost minced. Combine halibut with all other ingredients except butter and oil. Form into balls. Set aside and let it rest for 15 minutes. Heat water in a large pan and drop them into the water. Do not crowd them. Simmer for about 3 minutes. Remove and place on platter. Heat skillet and add butter. Fry fish balls for 5 minutes on each side. Serve hot.
- In Denmark it was served with fresh green peas and small new boiled parsley potatoes.

SITKOH BAY TROUT

Serves 1

We often end up hiding out in Sitkoh Bay waiting for the weather to calm down before crossing Chatham Strait on our way to Angoon. The crew hikes to a trout stream and returns with fresh cutthroat trout, and a healthy appetite.

1 trout per person
Flour to dredge with
Bacon grease to fry in
Johnny's Seafood Seasoning for flavoring

- Simply clean trout and remove heads and tails, to make more room in the pan. Roll in flour, heat bacon grease and fry trout until crisp, about 3 minutes on each side.
- I serve this with batter bread and lots of home-made jam.
- My reward is a quiet purr from the crew.

EAGLE BEACH TROUT

Serves 8

The very first place I ever caught a trout. In this case a Dolly Varden. Use this recipe with any trout, but it is best with a self-caught cutthroat or rainbow trout.

1 cup flour
1 teaspoon Johnny's Seafood Seasoning
8 whole trout with heads
1 1/2 sticks butter
3/4 cup pecans
3 tablespoons parsley, minced
1/3 cup fresh lemon juice
8 slices bacon, cooked until crisp
Lemon wedges

- Preheat oven to the lowest setting, or warm.
- Season flour with seafood seasoning. Dredge each trout in flour. Melt 3 tablespoons butter in heavy skillet and fry half of the fish about 4 minutes on each side, depending on the size. Meat should be pink and opaque.
- Place in oven to keep warm, repeat with the remaining trout, adding butter as needed. Add these to the batch to keep warm.
- Wipe skillet clean. Melt remaining butter, warm pecans in it for a few minutes; add parsley and lemon juice. Sprinkle on top of fish, garnish with crumbled bacon and wedges of fresh lemon.

BREN'S BARBECUED GINGER FISH

Serves 4

Use any white fish available. We use cabrilla or dorado when in Mexico, but I have made this with red snapper at home and it was terrific.

3 tablespoons butter
2 tablespoons Hoisin sauce
2 tablespoons soy sauce
2 cloves garlic, minced
3 tablespoons ginger root, sliced
1 1/2 pounds favorite fish
Oil for grill
Sprigs of parsley

- Mix all the ingredients except fish in a small pan and bring to a boil.
- Brush oil on grill to prevent fish from sticking. Place fish on grill, brush with Ginger Sauce. Grill to your liking, turn over and repeat on other side. Serve with those wonderful fresh limes.
- Garnish with sprigs of parsley.

GLACIER GRILLED SALMON

Serves 8

It wouldn't be fair to tell you how often we have this during the salmon season.

- **1 salmon fillet, about 10 pounds**
- **1/2 lemon, juice of**
- **1/2 teaspoon paprika**
- **1 1/2 teaspoons Johnny's Seafood Seasoning**
- **4 tablespoons butter**
- **2 teaspoons snipped fresh dill**
- **1/2 lemon, finely sliced**

- Wipe salmon clean. Pour lemon juice over and sprinkle with paprika and seafood seasoning. Cut butter into thin slices and place over salmon. Sprinkle the dill and finely sliced lemon on top.
- Place salmon on a piece of foil, fold edges up to keep juices from running. Grill fish for approximately 20 minutes over very hot coal or, if using gas grill, check the manual for cooking fish. Do not overcook, salmon is best when moist and delicate.
- Serve with homemade Remoulade Sauce.

REMOULADE SAUCE

Makes 1 cup sauce

- **1 cup mayonnaise**
- **4 tablespoons onion, finely minced**
- **2 tablespoons capers**
- **2 tablespoons sweet pickled relish**
- **1 tablespoon lemon juice**
- **1 teaspoon dried dill**
- **1 teaspoon paprika**
- **1/2 teaspoon dried mustard**

- Mix all the ingredients, let flavors blend and serve with any white fish or shell fish.
- This will last for weeks in refrigerator.

SALMON POACHED IN RASPBERRY SAUCE

Serves 4

First time we tasted this I was sure they had made a mistake — fish and raspberries? The restaurants call it Raspberry Beurre Blanc. We call it out of this world.

- **2 cups white wine**
- **1 stalk of celery, with top**
- **1 cup water**
- **6 peppercorns, whole**
- **1 bay leaf**
- **1 onion, cut up**
- **1/2 teaspoon salt**
- **3 parsley sprigs**
- **3 tablespoons lemon juice**
- **4 salmon steaks, 1 1/2 inches thick**

- Combine all the ingredients except salmon in a large frying pan or fish poacher. Bring to a boil, let simmer 5 minutes to allow flavors to blend. Lower heat to medium-low. Add the salmon steaks. Let them simmer for 8 minutes or until fish is flaky yet still moist; Making sure they do not boil.

RASPBERRY SAUCE

- **1/2 cup raspberry vinegar**
- **1/4 cup shallots, minced**
- **1 stick butter**
- **2 tablespoons raspberry jam or preserves.**

- In a small sauce pan combine vinegar and shallots; let simmer until reduced to 2 tablespoons. Cut butter into pieces. Whisk in a couple of slices of butter at a time, return pan to very low heat and add the remaining butter, keep whisking. The sauce should have the texture of thin mayonnaise.
- Finally add the raspberry jam, strained of any seeds.
- Place sauce on plate and arrange salmon steak on top.
- Garnish with a few raspberries or mint leaves.

POACHED SALMON IN LIME BUTTER

Serves 4

Colorful and delicate.

- Follow the same recipe for poaching salmon as for Poached Salmon in Raspberry Sauce.

LIME BUTTER SAUCE

1/2 cup white wine vinegar
3 tablespoons fresh lime juice
1/4 cup red onion, chopped
1 stick butter
1/4 cup heavy cream
1 lime, peel of
Lime slices
Parsley

- Combine wine, lime juice and onion. Cook until reduced to 2 tablespoons. Remove from heat. Add a couple of slices of butter, whisk. Return to low heat and whisk in the remaining butter. By now sauce should begin to thicken. Add cream and blend well. Stir in the lime peel.
- Serve over salmon steaks. Garnish with thin slices of lime and sprigs of parsley.

CURED SALMON IN OLIVE OIL

This was given to me years ago. It is another way of preparing the well known Gravlax often served in Scandinavian homes. It must be refrigerated, but it will last 2 to 3 weeks.

Remove skin from a 4 pound salmon fillet
6 tablespoons salt
4 tablespoons sugar
Olive oil

- Cover entire surface of salmon fillet with combined salt and sugar pressing it well into fish. Place in shallow dish about same size as fish, cover with plastic wrap and place heavy object on top, such as a big can. Refrigerate for 24 hours. When juices form, spoon them over salmon.
- Remove fillet from dish and wipe with paper towels. Cut salmon into very thin diagonal slices. Pack firmly into jars to within 1/2-inch of top. Drizzle olive oil over salmon to completely immerse it, slipping a knife down inside jar to remove air. Cover tightly and refrigerate at least one day before serving. Before serving press salmon between paper towels to remove excess oil. Serve on your favorite bagel.

BETTY'S SALMON STEAKS

Serves 4

This was given to me while we still lived in Oregon and didn't have Salmon as often as we do now. You will enjoy this easy-to-prepare meal.

1/2 cube butter
1 medium onion, chopped
4 salmon steaks
2 shakes of Tabasco sauce
Fresh dill

- Melt butter in electric frying pan, at 325 degrees or over moderately hot burner. Add the onion and sauté lightly. Add the soy sauce and Tabasco sauce and stir. Place salmon steaks on top, cover and let simmer until done, about 12 minutes, depending of the thickness of salmon. To overcook salmon is a crime. Garnish with dill.
- I enjoy serving this with steamed rice and Refreshing Cucumber Sauce.

SPICY SALMON STEAK

Szechwan peppercorns, one of my favorite spices is used in this version of barbecued salmon steaks.

1 cup bread crumbs
1 cup butter
6 salmon steaks, 6-8 ounces each
1/4 cup green onions, chopped
1/2 teaspoon Johnny's Seafood Seasoning
2 tablespoons Szechwan peppercorns
2 tablespoons black peppercorns, cracked
2 teaspoons garlic. minced

- Prepare the grill on high heat. Mix bread crumbs, butter, onions, garlic and both kinds of peppercorns. Season salmon with seafood seasoning. Brush salmon steaks with butter mixture, place on grill and barbecue for about 5 minutes on one side, turn and repeat brushing on other side. Grill for another 3 minutes or until opaque and crusty.
- Serve with Sour Cream Sauce.

HERRING ROE

Serves 6

I had tasted herring roe as a child in Denmark, but had never made it before that spring, the first year we moved to Alaska. With all the wonderful seafoods available to us, you might say, why bother with herring roe?

It started when we set herring nets in front of our home, hoping to get a few nice-size spring herring for some serious salmon fishing later on. In the very early morning we pulled the net, and we had more than just one herring in there. We had shrimp, a couple of Dolly Varden, and lots of hairy snails, not to mention what looked like a school of herring. We pulled and hauled, but both Bob and I couldn't keep up the bagging by ourselves, so we called friends for help. It was 4:30 on a Sunday morning. They all showed up, children too, as they liked fishing as well as any adult. After hours of work, I was sure no one would notice me slip into the warm kitchen. As I was preparing to get some fuel into the workers, the idea hit me: fried herring roe. Our friends had been good sports in the past, tasting my more unusual dishes. This concoction, however, was greeted with some blank stares, especially from the children who walked outside, thoroughly disgusted. All the adults tried it though, and shortly filled themselves. Soon, the youngsters started to drift into the kitchen where we were gathered and before I knew it, I could not keep up with demands from the junior crowd. It was a huge success.

24 herring
1/4 cup milk
1/2 cup flour
Butter for frying
1/2 teaspoon Johnny's Seafood Seasoning
Lots of fresh lemon wedges

- Remove roe from herring, rinse well. Dip roe in milk and roll in flour. Simply fry in browned butter for 1 1/2 minutes on each side, seasoning as you go, continue until all done. Serve with squeezed lemon juice.

THOMPSON'S PICKLED HERRING

Everyone has a secret way to prepare herring. Often, the secret is left out and the result is a royal flop. Jim Thompson let me in on his family's secret of preparing firm, delicious herring fillets.

- Start by catching herring. Fillet both sides from backbone and wash thoroughly in cold water. Remove all black coloring from meat. Place fillets in large container alternately with Morton's pickling salt. Cover container tightly and set aside for 20 days. Do not add any water, as the herring will produce it's own brine.
- When the pickling period is over, remove herring from brine and peel off skin. It will peel of easily if not rinsed first. Rinse and cut into bite-sized pieces. Soak 6 to 8 hours in cold water. After soaking, herring should be firm and salty to taste.
- If soaked too long herring will get soft and water will turn cloudy.
- Layer herring in gallon size jars alternately with sliced white onions and 4 bay leaves per jar until jar is 2/3 full. Place inside a piece of cheese cloth equal parts: whole peppercorns, whole cloves, and whole allspice, to total about 1 1/2 ounces. Tie off and pound a few times with meat mallet. Place in jars and continue layering herring and onions to fill jars.
- Combine 4 cups of vinegar with 1 1/2 cups sugar, stirring to dissolve sugar. Pour into jars and close lids. Store in a cool dark place for 4 to 5 days. When serving, cut fillets into bite-size pieces. Remove pickled onions and replace with thin slices of red or white onions. This keeps up to one months in refrigerator.

HALIBUT FINGERS

Serves 6

This is not new to Alaskans, but it is worth passing on.

- **1 can flat Heineken beer**
- **1 1/2 cups Bisquick mix**
- **1/2 teaspoon paprika**
- **1/2 teaspoon salt**
- **1/2 teaspoon white pepper**
- **4 pounds halibut cut into fingers or sticks**
- **4 tablespoons butter**
- **4 tablespoons oil**
- **1 tablespoon Johnny's Seafood Seasoning**

- Combine beer, Bisquick, paprika, whisk to make a nice smooth, not-too thick batter. Fold in the halibut, and season batter with salt and pepper.
- Fry halibut fingers in butter and oil for about 7 minutes per side, depending on their thickness. Sprinkle both sides with seafood seasoning. Make sure the heat is high enough to brown the fish and form a crust.
- Serve with wedges of fresh lemon.

FRESH BAKED ALASKA HALIBUT

Serves 6 hungry fishermen

This can be assembled earlier in the day and kept cold until baking time.

- **4 pounds halibut fillets**
- **1/2 cup dry white wine**
- **3/4 cup dry bread crumbs**
- **1/2 cup parsley, chopped**
- **1 cup sour cream**
- **1 cup mayonnaise**
- **1 teaspoon paprika**
- **1 teaspoon salt**
- **1/2 teaspoon white pepper**
- **2 tablespoons lemon juice**

- Rinse halibut fillets, wipe and dry. Soak in wine for 1/2 hour. Mix the bread crumbs and parsley, set aside for topping. Blend sour cream and mayonnaise with paprika, salt, white pepper and lemon juice.
- Place halibut fillets in a shallow roasting pan in a single layer. Pour sauce over and top with parsley and bread crumbs mixture.
- Bake for 30 minutes in a 400 degree oven.

HALIBUT STEAKS

Serves 4

This is quite plain, but an excellent way to get the full flavor of the delicate white meat of halibut.

4 halibut steaks
1/4 cup lemon juice
1/2 cup olive oil
1 clove garlic, minced
Pinch of crumbled dried oregano leaves
1/2 teaspoon lemon peel
1/2 teaspoon Johnny's Seafood Seasoning

- Combine all the ingredients except seafood seasoning and pour over fish. Let marinate for 1 hour. Heat grill. Brush a little oil on the grill to prevent fish from sticking.
- Grill over medium heat for about 5 minutes on each side, sprinkling with Johnny's Seafood Seasoning. Be sure to turn fish gently to keep it from crumbling, as it is so delicate. Placing steaks in a metal hamburger rack works well.
- Serve with wedges of lemon.

AUKE LAKE HALIBUT LOGS

Serves 4

1 cup white wine
1 cup Cornflake crumbs
1/2 cup Parmesan cheese
1/2 teaspoon garlic powder
1 pound halibut

- Preheat oven to 350 degrees. Marinate halibut in wine for 1/2 hour. Remove and pat dry and cut into logs the size of your finger. Mix Cornflake crumbs, Parmesan cheese and garlic powder. Roll halibut in crumbs. Place on cookie sheet.
- Bake at 350 degrees for 10 minutes, or test for desired consistency.
- Taste good served with home-made tartar sauce.

BETH'S HALIBUT STICKS

Serves 4

These great fish sticks are baked in the oven. They come out crunchy on the outside and moist on the inside. A terrific way to avoid heavy frying in butter.

1 pound halibut
1/2 cup oil
3/4 teaspoon garlic powder
A few shakes of Johnny's Doc, or other seafood seasoning
3/4 cup Cornflake Crumbs
3/4 cup Parmesan cheese

- Cut halibut into 1 1/2 x 4-inch strips. Marinate in oil and garlic powder for 30 minutes or longer. Remove from oil, season with seafood seasoning to taste. Dip sticks in mixture of Cornflake crumbs and Parmesan cheese.
- Place side by side in shallow baking dish; lining the pan first with foil makes clean up easier. Bake for 30 minutes at 375 degrees. Check by inserting a knife point into the thickest part of halibut. It should be firm and opaque.

BROILED HALIBUT LOGS

Serves 4

From Diane Howell's files. This is very moist and tender, and the children love it.

1 1/2 pounds halibut, cut into finger-sized logs
1/2 cube butter or margarine, melted
1 cup cracker crumbs
1 lemon, juice of
1/4 cup mayonnaise
Johnny's Seafood Seasoning

- Preheat oven to broil.
- Roll the halibut logs in melted butter or margarine, then dip in cracker crumbs. Place logs flat in baking pan. Spread a little mayonnaise on top of each. Sprinkle with lemon juice and seafood seasoning and place under broiler for 10 minutes. Turn logs; spread again with mayonnaise, sprinkle lemon juice and seasoning over. Return halibut to oven and broil another 10 minutes.

BARBECUED WRANGELL SHRIMP

Serves 6

Last time Terry Buness came for a visit he did the cooking of the shrimp. When I asked him how he did it, he laughed and said "the minute they hit the grill, consider them done". He was right, 60 to 90 seconds on each side barely gives you time to turn them.

1 cube melted butter
3 garlic cloves, minced
1 lemon, juice of
2 shakes of Tabasco sauce
5 pounds shrimps, spots
Johnny's Seafood Seasonings
Dash of paprika

- Melt butter, add garlic, lemon juice and a touch of paprika. Shell the shrimp, leaving tails on.
- Brush shrimp with melted butter mixture. Place on hot grill. Turn at once and remove. Sprinkle with a little seasoning salt if desired.

JOANN'S DIPPING SAUCE

Makes 3 cups

Serve with cooked shrimp, crab or other seafoods.

8 ounces catsup
7 ounces chili sauce
3 tablespoons mayonnaise
1 white onion, minced
1/2 lemon, juice of
2 teaspoons horseradish sauce
Dash of Worchestershire sauce
Dash of Tabasco sauce
Salt and pepper to taste

- Mix all the ingredients. Refrigerate until serving time.

MEXICAN STYLE FISH

Serves 4

In the winter when we head south to do a different kind of fishing, we eat fish 5 times a week and never seem to grow tired of the endless ways to prepare it.

2 pounds fresh white fish, halibut, cabrilla, or dorado
4 tablespoons butter
1 teaspoon Johnny's Seafood Seasoning
1/4 cup medium-hot Mexican salsa sauce
1 lime, juice of
1 cup black olives, drained
Limes

- Heat oven or grill to 450 degrees.
- Place fish on cookie sheet, cover with foil and let bake for 10 minutes. Pull foil away and drizzle fish with butter. Sprinkle with seasoning and pour the salsa, lime juice and olives over. Let bake for another 15 minutes or until done.
- Serve with those juicy Mexican limes.

MARINADE FOR SALMON STEAK

This outstanding way to grill your salmon comes from Jim Thompson in Wrangell.

2 parts olive oil
1 part red wine vinegar
Dash of lemon juice
3 liberal shakes of Season-All Seasoning salt
3 liberal shakes of Johnny's Seafood Seasoning
Dash of lemon pepper

- Heat grill; it should be very hot. Stir together all ingredients except lemon pepper. Let steaks marinate for 5 minutes. Baste steak with marinade, sprinkle with lemon pepper. Brush oil on grill to prevent meat from sticking. Place salmon steaks, basted side down, and grill for 4 to 6 minutes depending on thickness of steak. Baste and grill on other side. Salmon should be golden brown on the outside, moist and flaky on the inside.

Poultry Plus

POULTRY PLUS

DRUNKEN CHICKEN

Serves 8

A simple, yet elegant main course. This goes well with pasta.

4 whole chicken breasts
2 tablespoons butter
2 tablespoons olive oil
2 carrots, sliced
6 green onions, chopped
1/4 cup brandy
1 cup white wine
2 teaspoons tarragon, dried
1/2 teaspoon chervil, dried
1/2 teaspoon salt
1/4 teaspoon pepper
1 tablespoon flour
1 cup cream
1 egg yolk
1/4 pound mushrooms
2 tablespoons butter
1/4 teaspoon paprika

- Remove skin and bones from chicken breasts. Do not cut into smaller pieces.
- In large skillet or sauce pan, sauté chicken in butter and oil, turning on all sides until brown. Remove chicken from pan and set aside.
- Add carrots and onions to drippings and stir a few minutes or until golden. Return chicken to pan.
- When hot, heat brandy in ladle over gas flame, ignite. Pour over chicken. Add the wine, tarragon, chervil, salt and pepper. Bring to a boil, lower temperature and let simmer for 40 minutes.
- Remove chicken and keep warm. Strain the drippings and discard the vegetables. Return drippings and add flour; stir well, add the cream and egg yolk. Keep stirring until sauce it's smooth.
- Sauté mushrooms in small sauce pan of butter until golden. Stir into sauce. Slice chicken and pour sauce over. If sauce is too thick, add a little wine.
- Sprinkle with a bit of tarragon and paprika.
- This is especially good with any wild rice casserole.

PEACHY CHICKEN

Serves 4

Don't let the long list of ingredients scare you; once this has been assembled, it's a breeze.

2 whole chicken breasts, split
1/2 teaspoon salt
1/4 cup green onions
2 cloves garlic, minced
1/4 cup butter
1 teaspoon paprika
1 pound fresh broccoli, cut into small bouquets
1/2 cup sour cream
1/2 cup yoghurt
1/4 cup mayonnaise
1/2 cup Parmesan cheese
4 peach halves, canned
2 tablespoons almonds, chopped

- Sprinkle chicken with salt. Sauté onions and garlic in butter for a couple of minutes. Add the paprika. Now add the chicken, making sure it gets coated completely with sauce. Place chicken in ovenproof casserole and bake in oven for 30 minutes at 375 degrees. Lower temperature to 350 degrees and cover the pan with foil or a lid. Bake for another 20 minutes.
- Cook broccoli, drain and keep warm. Blend sour cream, yoghurt and mayonnaise. Place chicken on a bed of broccoli and spoon sauce over chicken breasts. Sprinkle with Parmesan cheese. Turn oven to broil. Place under broiler until chicken turns light brown and bubbly.
- Garnish platter with peach halves, sprinkled with almond slivers.

SPICY CHICKEN THIGHS

Serves 4

Another simple way of serving a tasty meal.

3 tablespoons Dijon mustard
8 chicken thighs or breasts
1/2 cup brown sugar
1/2 cup white wine
1/2 cup soy sauce
2 tablespoons Szechuan sauce
2 tablespoons Teriyaki sauce
4 green onions, chopped

- Start by preheating oven to 350 degrees. Spread mustard all over chicken.
- Combine everything else and pour over chicken.
- Bake for 45 minutes, basting often. Lower heat and bake for another 45 minutes.
- We often serve this with rice and a fresh salad.

JAPANESE CHICKEN CASSEROLE

Serves 4-6

Several years ago a delightful lady, Midori Buzzell, taught several of us some very tasty Japanese recipes. This one is easy and very good.

2 1/2 pounds chicken pieces, cut up
4 tablespoons flour
1/2 teaspoon ginger root, grated
4 tablespoons butter
1/4 cup soy sauce
1/4 cup brown sugar
1/2 cup water
2 tablespoons red wine vinegar
1 20 1/2-ounce can crushed pineapple, drained

- Dust chicken with flour, then rub with ginger. Heat an electric skillet to 375 degrees. Melt butter and brown chicken on all sides. Set aside. Drain skillet of any fat, wipe clean. Return chicken to skillet. Mix soy sauce, brown sugar, water and vinegar and pour over chicken, coating it well. Add the pineapple and lower heat to 325 degrees.
- Cook covered for 1 hour or until tender.
- Spoon over hot rice and serve.

CREAM SHERRY CHICKEN

Serves 6

Easy to do for entertaining, it can be prepared ahead and popped in the oven in no-time.

6 large chicken breasts, halved
2 tablespoons butter
1 teaspoon salt
1 teaspoon curry powder
1/2 cup plum jam
1/4 cup cream sherry
1 can pitted plums, for garnishing

- Brown chicken breasts in butter. Season with salt. Remove and set aside. Stir curry into the pan juices; add jam and sherry. Place chicken in oven proof pan and pour sauce over. Cover and bake in oven at 350 degrees for 40 minutes. Remove chicken and keep warm. Let pan juices come to a boil, keep boiling until sauce is reduced to half.
- Place chicken on heated platter; and top with sauce and plums.
- I serve this with plain steamed rice.

CHICKEN-ASPARAGUS CASSEROLE

Serves 4

Given to me years ago by Wanda White in Sitka. This has been one of my most used dishes to assemble on short notice for company.

- **3 whole chicken breasts, skinned and boned**
- **1 1/2 teaspoons msg**
- **1/4 teaspoon pepper**
- **3 tablespoons vegetable oil**
- **2 packages fresh or frozen asparagus**
- **1 can cream of mushroom soup, concentrated**
- **1/4 cup mayonnaise**
- **4 tablespoons white wine**
- **2 teaspoons lemon juice**
- **1 tablespoon or more curry powder**
- **1/2 cup Cheddar cheese, shredded**

- Cut chicken into 2″ by 4″ pieces.
- Sprinkle with msg and pepper. In skillet, sauté chicken pieces in oil for about 6 minutes or until opaque. Drain. Cook asparagus for 5 minutes. Drain. Arrange asparagus in a 9 x 9 x 2-inch pan. Place chicken on top. Mix soup, mayonnaise, wine and lemon juice with curry. Pour over chicken and asparagus. Top with shredded cheese. Cover with foil and bake for 45 minutes at 375 degrees.
- I usually serve this with rice and top it with chutney.

STICKY CHICKEN

Serves 4

Wrangell, Alaska is full of good cooks. Clara Thompson shared this with me, and it is outstanding and easy.

- **1/2 cup sake**
- **1/2 cup soy sauce**
- **1/2 cup sugar**
- **8 chicken thighs**

- Simply mix sake, soy sauce and sugar until sugar is dissolved. Pour over chicken and bake for 45 minutes at 350 degrees. Lower temperature to 300 degrees and bake another 45 minutes.
- The secret to a nice glaze is basting often during the cooking period.

FRUIT AND CHICKEN SALAD

Serves 4

Donated by Vi Davis. This is a lovely luncheon dish. Serve it with a tall glass of iced tea. Garnish tea with mint leaves.

1 whole cooked chicken breast
1 bag almond slivers, 1/2 cup
3 tablespoons sugar
Any fresh lettuce, I use Bibb or spinach
1/2 cantaloupe, diced
1 cup grapes
1 stalk celery, diced
2 green onions, finely chopped
Avocado, slivered
Red onion rings for garnish
Poppy seed dressing

- Prepare greens. Remove skin from chicken, cut into slivers. Toast almonds in sugar; cool and set aside. Arrange lettuce on individual salad plates. Place cantaloupe, grapes, celery, onions and chicken on top of greens. Garnish with avocado, almonds, and red onion rings.
- Pour poppy seed dressing over salad.

POPPY SEED DRESSING

Makes 2 pints

1 1/2 cups sugar
2 teaspoons dry mustard
1 1/2 teaspoons salt
1/2 tablespoon onion juice
3 tablespoons poppy seeds
2/3 cup vinegar
2 cups vegetable oil

- Mix sugar, mustard, salt, onion juice and poppy seeds with vinegar. Slowly add oil and blend well. Refrigerate.
- Keeps well.

CHICKEN BREAST IN PARSLEY PESTO SAUCE

Serves 6

Share this tasty dish with some good friends and a bottle of your favorite wine.

CHICKEN:

6	**chicken breasts, boned and skinned**	**2**	**eggs, beaten, for wash**
	Pesto Sauce	**1**	**cup bread crumbs**
	flour for dredging		**Oil for frying**

- Remove bones and skin from chicken. With a meat hammer, pound chicken flat. Cover one side with Pesto. Roll up and secure with toothpicks or kitchen twine. Dust with flour and dip in egg wash. Roll in bread crumbs. Refrigerate for 1/2 hour.
- In skillet heat 1 inch of oil and brown chicken breast on all sides. Remove and place in oven preheated to 400 degrees. Bake for 30 minutes.

PARSLEY PESTO SAUCE

1	**cup fresh parsley, chopped**	**1/2**	**cup grated Parmesan cheese**
1	**clove garlic**	**1/4**	**teaspoon salt**
1	**cup fresh basil, chopped**		**Freshly ground pepper**
1/2	**cup olive oil**		**Parsley sprigs.**
1	**tablespoon butter, melted**		

- Chop parsley, garlic and basil in food processor; add oil and melted butter until thick and smooth. Add cheese, salt and pepper. Pour a little sauce on serving platter, place chicken breasts on top, drizzle additional sauce over chicken and garnish with parsley sprigs.

POT ROASTED CHICKEN

Serves 4

The Danes cook chicken on top of the stove. I only recall pork roast, goose, bread and cookies being cooked in the oven. Almost everything else was done in a heavy pot.

1	**chicken, about 3 pounds**	1	**bunch parsley**
1 1/2	**teaspoons salt**	1	**cup chicken broth**
1/2	**teaspoon paprika**	1	**cup Half-and-Half**
	Pinch of pepper	4	**tablespoons red currant jelly**
1/4	**cube butter**	3	**tablespoons flour**

- Clean and dry chicken; sprinkle inside with salt, paprika and pepper. Place 1 tablespoon butter in cavity with a bunch of parsley. Melt remaining butter in heavy pan. Carefully sear chicken on all sides until nice and brown. Add broth to pot and cook, covered, for 45 minutes over low, gentle heat.
- Remove chicken and keep warm. Combine Half-and Half and red currant jelly in bowl with flour; stir really well, you want no lumps here. Stir in any juices from chicken, heat and stir sauce until thick. Check seasoning, adjust before serving.
- Arrange chicken on platter and serve with sauce.

CHICKEN WITH MARSALA

Serves 4

There are as many ways to prepare Chicken Marsala as there are ways to fry a chicken. This one is full of wonderful flavors.

4	**chicken breasts, skinned and boned**	1	**tablespoon parsley, minced**
2	**tablespoons butter**	1	**clove garlic, minced**
1	**tablespoon olive oil**		**Salt and pepper to taste**
12	**capers, drained**	2/3	**cup heavy cream**
4	**anchovies**	4	**tablespoons Marsala**
4	**slices Mozzarella cheese**		

- Pound chicken flat. Melt butter with oil over medium-high heat, sauté chicken for about 5 minutes. Remove from heat. Place 3 capers and 1 anchovy on each piece of chicken, then top with a slice of cheese. Return pan to stove and sprinkle cheese-topped chicken with parsley. Cover and let cook until cheese has melted.
- Remove chicken from pan and keep warm. Add garlic to pan drippings and sauté for 30 seconds; sprinkle garlic with salt and pepper. Add cream and Marsala. Cook and stir gently until thick, about 3 minutes.
- Spoon over chicken and serve at once.

ROTISSERIE CHICKEN

Serves 4

Juicy golden chicken stuffed full of vitamins.

1 chicken, 3 1/2 to 4 pounds
Salt and pepper to taste
1 lime, cut in half
1 large bunch parsley
Seasoning salt for poultry
Paprika
1 sprig fresh rosemary

- Wash and dry chicken. Season inside with salt and pepper.
- Stuff with lime halves and parsley. Tie legs together with kitchen twine and place chicken on spit. Season skin-side well with a poultry seasoning and plenty of paprika.
- Throw rosemary sprig on hot coals. Roast chicken for 2 hours over low heat.

CHICKEN IN MUSHROOMS AND CREAM

Serves 4

4 chicken breasts
Flour for dredging
1/4 to 1/2 pound butter
1/2 pound mushrooms, sliced
1/4 cup cream sherry
1/2 teaspoon tarragon, fresh
1/2 pint heavy cream

- Remove skin and bones from chicken. Dredge in flour. Brown in half of butter. Place in casserole and bake at 300 degrees for 1 hour.
- Sauté mushrooms in remaining butter, add sherry, tarragon and cream. Simmer until you have obtained a medium-thick gravy, about 10 minutes. Remove chicken from oven.
- Place on a bed of cooked rice. Spoon sauce over.

CHICKEN BREAST DELIGHT

Serves 4

A one-dish meal full of surprises.

2 whole chicken breasts, split
1/2 teaspoon salt
1 teaspoon lemon pepper, granulated
1/2 cup green onions, chopped
1/4 cup butter
1 teaspoon sweet paprika
1 bunch fresh spinach, about 1 pound
6 canned apricot halves
1/4 cup cream
1 cup sour cream
1/4 cup Romano cheese
3 tablespoons pine nuts, chopped

- Season chicken with salt and lemon pepper. Sauté green onions in butter for a few minutes; stir in paprika. Dip chicken in this melted butter mixture to coat evenly. Place in a shallow baking dish, and cover loosely with foil. Bake at 375 degrees for about 30 minutes.
- Cook spinach until tender. Drain, set aside and keep warm until chicken is done.
- Arrange apricots and spinach beside chicken. Combine cream and sour cream and spoon over chicken. Sprinkle with Romano cheese and chopped pine nuts. Place chicken on lower rack of oven and broil for about 5 minutes or until richly browned.

CHUTNEY GAME HENS

Serves 4

Just a hint of something tropical flavors these plump game hens.

1 20-ounce can pineapple chunks, drained, save syrup
1/2 cup chutney
1 teaspoon tarragon
4 Cornish game hens
Salt and pepper to taste
1 large onion, chopped
1 large bunch parsley, stems removed

- Stir together 4 tablespoons pineapple juice, chutney and tarragon. Season the inside of hens with salt and pepper. Stuff hens with pineapple, onion and parsley.
- Heat oven to 350 degrees. Place hens in shallow pan and brush with chutney mixture. Cover pan with foil and roast for 1/2 hour. Remove foil and roast for another 45 minutes, brushing often with chutney glaze.
- Steamed rice tastes very good with this.

ROASTED DOMESTIC GOOSE

Serves 10

Writing this recipe makes me think of Christmas in Denmark. This was served as often as beautiful pork roasts with crisp crackling were. Nothing dry about this bird, the prunes and apples prevent that.

1	**8-ounce package prunes**
1	**goose, about 9 pounds**
1	**tablespoon salt**
1/4	**teaspoon pepper**
2	**tart apples**
1	**tablespoon sugar**
2	**cups boiling chicken broth**
4	**tablespoons flour**
2	**tablespoons currant jelly, optional**
1	**tablespoon Kitchen Bouquet**

- Soak prunes in water the night before. Wash and wipe goose, inside and out. Combine salt and pepper and season cavity. Peel apples and slice. Sprinkle apples and prunes with sugar, place inside. Secure the cavity with skewers. Rub a little salt on the outside. Place in a 375 degree oven and roast for about 20 minutes, to brown. Lower temperature to 325 degrees, roast for another 2 hours. Turn bird over and roast for another hour. Thirty minutes before roasting time is up, remove drippings to a sauce pan and set aside. To get a real crunchy skin, turn oven to 425 degrees, for the last 10 minutes, make sure to watch goose carefully. Total roasting time is about 3 1/2 hours.
- Strain meat juices. Cool them a little to let fat rise and skim it off. Add flour to 2 cups of meat juice, and stir well for a smooth gravy. Let it come to a boil for 4 minutes. Test for seasonings, correct if nessesary.
- I usually add a couple of tablespoons of currant jelly to gravy. Color sauce with Kitchen Bouquet.
- Arrange goose on platter with apples and prunes around it.
- We serve the traditional Caramelized Potatoes and Red Cabbage with this festive bird..

On the Meat Block

ON THE MEAT BLOCK

OXTAIL STEW IN THE OVEN

Serves 4

The oxtails cook so slowly and so long, all you really need to do at supper time is make sure everyone has a good appetite and a wet washcloth for a napkin.

1/2	**cup olive oil**
6	**pounds oxtail, trimmed of any fat**
1/2	**teaspoon salt**
1/4	**teaspoon pepper**
2/3	**cup flour**
3	**cloves garlic, minced**
1	**stalk celery, chopped**
1	**green pepper, chopped**
1	**onion, chopped**
2	**tablespoons dark brown sugar**
2	**tablespoons red wine vinegar**
2	**teaspoons Worcestershire sauce**
4	**shakes Maggi liquid sauce, optional**
2	**teaspoons hot paprika**
2	**bay leaves**
1	**8-ounce can whole tomatoes**
2	**teaspoons thyme, dried**
1/4	**cup Madeira**

- Heat olive oil in a large pot with a tight fitting lid, like a roasting pan. Season oxtails with salt and pepper. Dredge oxtails in flour. Cook in small batches on all sides until crusty and brown. Remove meat from pan, drain all but 2 tablespoons of oil. Sauté garlic, celery, pepper and onion for about 8 minutes over medium heat. Add the brown sugar, vinegar, Worchestershire and Maggi; stir well. Blend in paprika, bay leaves, tomatoes and thyme and cook for another 10 minutes.
- Return oxtails to pot; blend all of the ingredients. Cover and place in oven at 325 degrees for 3 to 4 hours, or until meat falls off bones. Let sit to cool for 20 minutes, then remove bones and skim off any fat. Remove meat from sauce and keep warm. Let pot come to a boil and reduce sauce to half, add 1/4 cup Madeira, simmer 5 minutes.
- Best served with small new potatoes, cucumber salad and small carrots.
- Save bones for man's best friend.

STUFFED FLANK STEAK SUPREME

Serves 4

Thanks to Gary Cooper, who is known as an outstanding cook, we have made this dish many times, and let me tell you, "it is out of this world". His mother Shirley, a friend of mine, read the recipe over the phone to me, this is how we timed and cooked it. The sauce makes this dish soooo wonderful.

- **1 beef flank steak, about 1 1/2 pounds**
- **1/2 cup crab meat**
- **1/2 cup sharp Cheddar cheese, shredded**
- **Salt and pepper to taste**

- Butterfly steak, do not cut all the way through on one end. Mix crab and cheese. Lay steak open and flat; place crab and cheese mixture inside. Close meat with kitchen twine or tooth picks. Season with salt and pepper.
- Place in a preheated oven at 375 degrees. Bake until meat thermometer reaches 140 degrees for medium-rare, about 25 minutes.

BÉARNAISE SAUCE:

- **2 cubes butter**
- **1 shallot, minced**
- **1/3 cup tarragon vinegar**
- **3 egg yolks**
- **2 tablespoons fresh tarragon or 1 tablespoon dry**

- Cut butter into portions, 2 tablespoons each, as this is how it's added.
- Cook shallots in vinegar until liquid is reduced to half. Add egg yolks and whisk, add tarragon, keep whisking; it should start getting thick at this point. Now start adding butter, making sure you blend and whisk all the time. Keep adding until all butter is used. Now it's smooth. I keep it warm over hot water in a double boiler, not allowing saucepan to touch water in double boiler.
- Pour over meat and serve at once.

SITKA STUFFED STEAK

Serves 6

4	tablespoons butter
6	tablespoons olive oil
1	very large onion, chopped
3	cloves garlic, minced
1	4 1/2-ounce jar stuffed green olives
1/2	cup cooked ham, chopped
1/2	cup sharp Cheddar cheese, shredded
1	teaspoon thyme
1	teaspoon salt
1	teaspoon black pepper, freshly ground
2	tablespoons parsley, minced
2	egg yolks, beaten lightly
2 1/2	pounds flank steak
1 1/2	tablespoons butter
2	cans beef consommé

- Start by melting butter with olive oil in large pan. Sauté onions and garlic until limp. Add olives, ham, cheese, thyme, salt and pepper, stir to blend. Remove from heat. Add parsley and beaten eggs.
- Butterfly steak. Spread with stuffing and roll up. Secure with kitchen twine.
- Melt 1 1/2 tablespoons butter in Dutch oven and brown meat on all sides. Add consommé and braise in oven for 2 hours. Remove meat from pan and keep warm. Pour meat juices into a smaller saucepan and boil down until thick and smooth.
- Pour over sliced meat.

PEPPER STEAK FLAMBÉ

Serves 4

4	thick porterhouse steaks
3	tablespoons green peppercorns in brine, mashed
3	tablespoons butter
	Salt to taste
4	tablespoons brandy
1/2	cup heavy cream

- Heat a heavy pan until nice and hot. Place trimmed steaks in dry pan and fry for 1 minute on each side to seal in juices. Divide peppercorns, mash them and spread 1/2 tablespoon on each side. Add butter to pan; fry for 4 minutes, turn over and fry another 3 minutes for rare steaks. Season with salt. Remove steaks and keep warm in oven.
- Return pan to heat and spoon in the brandy and ignite. Let flame die down. Add cream and stir until thick.
- Pour sauce over steaks and serve at once.

CRUNCHY CORNED BEEF SALAD LOAF

Serves 8

This dish was served at a party Clara Thompson attended recently in Wrangell celebrating her friend's 70th birthday. Very unusual, festive looking, and extremely tasty.

- **1 envelope unflavored gelatin**
- **3/4 cup water**
- **1 can beef consommé**
- **4 tablespoons white wine vinegar**
- **1 tablespoon sugar**
- **1/4 teaspoon pepper**
- **1/2 cup mayonnaise**
- **1 15-ounce can corned beef, finely diced**
- **1 15-ounce can sauerkraut, drained**
- **1/2 cup celery, finely chopped**
- **1/2 cup green pepper, finely chopped**
- **1/4 cup carrots, shredded**
- **1/4 cup green onions, sliced**
- **Lettuce leaves, for garnish**
- **Egg, sliced for garnish**

- Soften gelatin in water, then stir over direct heat to dissolve. Combine gelatin with consommé, vinegar, sugar and pepper.
- Chill until the mixture reaches consistency of unbeaten egg whites, about 45 minutes.
- Stir in the mayonnaise until smooth. Mix in corned beef, sauerkraut, celery, green pepper, carrots and onions.
- Pour into a 5 x 9-inch loaf pan. Cover and chill until set, about 4 hours or overnight.
- Unmold salad onto a lettuce-lined serving platter. Garnish with sliced egg. Cut into 1-inch thick slices.

BARTLETT BEEF STROGANOFF

Serves 4

The aroma of this dish cooking is wonderful.

- **1 pound beef sirloin, cut into 1/4-inch strips**
- **1 tablespoon flour, for dredging**
- **4 tablespoons butter, melted**
- **1/2 cup onion, chopped**
- **1 clove garlic, minced**
- **1 cup mushrooms, sliced**
- **3 tablespoons flour**
- **1 tablespoon tomato paste**
- **1 1/4 cups beef consommé**
- **1 cup sour cream**
- **2 tablespoons sherry**
- **Salt and pepper to taste**

- Dredge meat in flour. Brown quickly in 1 tablespoon melted butter. Add onion, garlic and mushrooms, and cook until tender, about 8 minutes. Remove meat and vegetables from skillet. Add remaining butter to pan drippings, blend in flour. Add tomato paste and consommé. Whisk sauce until it is thick and smooth. Return meat mixture to pan. Stir in sour cream and sherry. Add salt and pepper to taste.
- Serve over steamed rice or tender cooked noodles.

SPINACH LASAGNE WITH SAVORY

Serves 12

This moist dish reheats well. Bake ahead of time, then when ready to serve, cover with foil and bake for 30 minutes at 350 degrees. The list is long, but do use all the ingredients for correct flavor.

1 8-ounce package lasagne noodles
1 1/2 pounds ground moose or beef
1 cup onion, chopped
1 cup green pepper, chopped
1 12-ounce can tomato paste
2 1/3 cups hot water
1 cup Burgundy wine
1 large Maggi cube, beef flavored
3 tablespoons parsley, chopped
3 tablespoons fresh savory
1 1/2 tablespoons garlic, minced
1 teaspoon salt
1 teaspoon oregano
1 teaspoon basil
1/2 teaspoon pepper
3 eggs, slightly beaten
4 cups Ricotta or cottage cheese
1 package frozen spinach, thawed, drained
6 ounces Mozzarella cheese, sliced
1 6-ounce can tomato paste
1 15 1/2-ounce jar spaghetti sauce
1/2 cup Romano cheese, grated

- Cook noodles in boiling water with a little salt until tender but firm, about 10 minutes. Drain and set aside.
- Brown meat with onion and pepper in skillet over low heat. Drain off excess fat. In a large sauce pan, blend in large can of tomato paste, water, wine, Maggi cube, parsley, savory, garlic, salt, oregano, basil, pepper and bring to a boil. Add meat and cook 15 minutes.
- Blend eggs and Ricotta in bowl with the small can of tomato paste. Using half of the meat sauce, noodles, Ricotta mixture, spinach and Mozzarella cheese, alternatly layer ingredients in a 13 x 9 x 2-inch lasagne pan, ending with meat. Pour spaghetti sauce over entire surface; sprinkle with Romano cheese.
- Bake at 350 degrees for 45 minutes.

DELILAH'S LUMPIA

Makes 24

This recipe deserves a special note. We have enjoyed these outstanding rolls for years when visiting Petersburg where the master of lumpia lives. I'll describe them as an egg roll, but they are so much lighter, and much better tasting.

1 pound ground beef
1/2 pound ground sausage
1/2 cup onions, chopped
2 cloves garlic, minced
1 small cabbage, thinly sliced
5 carrots, shredded
1 10-ounce package French-style green beans
Garlic salt to taste
Onion salt to taste
Pepper to taste
Few shakes of msg
24 lumpia wrappers
Oil for frying
Egg yolk

- Brown beef and sausage in large pan with onion and garlic. Remove most of grease.
- Add cabbage, carrots and beans and stir constantly, about 5 minutes. Season with garlic salt, onion salt, pepper and msg. Don't overcook vegetables. They should be slightly crunchy.
- Remove from heat and drain. Set aside to cool.
- Separate lumpia wrappers. Place 1 1/2 tablespoons of meat and vegetable mixture inside each wrapper.
- Roll like an egg roll. Dip fingers in a little egg yolk and seal edges. The yolk works like glue and prevents the filling from escaping.
- Fry lumpia in medium-hot oil. If using an electric frying pan, about 375 degrees. Fry until golden brown.

UNCLE ROBERT SMITH'S LASAGNE

Serves 6

Our friend Robert Smith was loved by everyone who ever met him. He was known to all of his friends as "Uncle Robert". Southeast Alaska was a better place when he was with us.

First Part:

1	**16-ounce package lasagne noodles**
1 1/2	**pounds ground meat, beef or game**
1	**tablespoon olive oil**
1	**large clove garlic, minced**
1	**large green pepper**
2	**medium onions**
	Salt and pepper to taste
2	**tablespoons oregano**

Second Part:

1	**14 1/2-ounce can tomatoes**
1/2	**cup red wine**
1	**8-ounce cans tomato sauce**

Third Part:

1	**pound cottage cheese**
1	**pound Mozzarella cheese**
1/2	**cup Parmesan cheese**

- Cook lasagne noodles according to directions, minus 2 minutes. Drain and set aside. In a large skillet, brown meat in oil with onions, garlic and green pepper. Stir until brown and crumbly. Blend in salt, pepper and oregano. Combine tomatoes, wine and tomato sauce, stir well. Let simmer for 20 minutes.
- Grease lasagne pan with oil or butter.
- Layer some of the meat mixture in bottom of pan and top with noodles, cottage cheese and Mozzarella cheese. Continue in this fashion until all used, ending up with a little meat mixture on top. Finally cover dish with Mozzarella and sprinkle on the Parmesan cheese.
- Bake at 350 degrees for 40 minutes.

MEXICALI COP-OUT CASSEROLE

Serves 6

This dish is a favorite in our daughters home. This is easy and very tasty. You can prepare this dish in 20 minutes, pop it in the oven and have a great meal, with little effort. Serve with cool Mexican Corona beer with a wedge of lime.

2 pounds ground meat, either beef or moose
3 tablespoons olive oil
Salt and pepper to taste
1 large onion, chopped
1 large green pepper, chopped
2 cloves garlic, minced
1 10-ounce can hot enchilada sauce
1 10-ounce can mild enchilada sauce
2 15 1/2-ounce cans refried beans with sausage
1 12-count package flour tortillas, torn into 1-inch pieces
1 pound sharp Cheddar cheese, shredded
1 16-ounce can black olives, drained, cut in half

- Brown meat in olive oil with salt, pepper, onion, green pepper and garlic. Drain off fat. Add enchilada sauce and refried beans.
- Layer mixture in ovenproof casserole with torn pieces of tortilla, ending with meat mixture. Top with shredded cheese. Decorate with olives, round side up. Bake at 350 degrees for 45 minutes.
- Pass condiments of chopped green pepper and tomato, sour cream, olives and salsa sauce.

DANISH MEATBALLS (Frikadeller)

Makes 1 dozen, depending on size formed

In over 1 1/2 million homes in Denmark, the housewife serves frikadeller at least once a week. Some use all pork meat, some veal, and some using half of each. I prefer to use the following:

1/2 pound moose meat, ground
1/2 pound veal, ground
1/2 pound lean pork, ground
1 large onion, chopped
1 pint milk
1/4 cup flour
1/2 teaspoon salt
1/2 teaspoon pepper
2 eggs
1/2 can club soda
Butter or margarine for frying

- Ask your butcher to grind the meat 3 times, or do it yourself.
- The secret to the light, fluffy frikadeller you might have tasted is stirring, stirring and more stirring. With the help of a mixer it can be done with little effort.
- Place the meat in mixer with onion, salt and pepper, milk and flour and start the stirring. Break in the eggs one at a time, letting the motor run for another 3-4 minutes.
- Set in a cool place and let rest for 1/2 hour.
- Stir again, now adding the club soda to meat mixture.
- Melt butter and/or margerine. Dip a spoon into butter and then into meat mixture; this permits the ball to run off the spoon without sticking. Form balls and fry in melted shortening until brown, about 8 minutes on each side.
- The frikadeller will be crisp on the outside and juicy inside.

PORK CHOPS (Koteletter)

Serves 6

Another Danish favorite. A typical Sunday supper dish.

- **6 pork chops**
- **1/4 cube butter**
- **4 onions, diced**
- **4 tart apples, diced**
- **1 1/2 tablespoons curry powder**
- **3 tablespoons flour**
- **1 1/2 cups beef broth**
- **1 lemon, juice of**
- **2 tablespoons chutney**
- **1/4 teaspoon sugar**
- **Salt and pepper to taste**

- Brown chops in butter on both sides to seal in the juices.
- Transfer to an oven-proof dish. In the same frying pan, gently fry onions and apples for 3 minutes. Add curry powder and flour, stirring well, then slowly pour in stock and lemon juice. Add chutney and seasonings.
- Pour sauce over chops, cover with foil, and bake at 400 degrees for 30 minutes.
- Pile on top of some steamed rice.

BURNING LOVE

Serves 4

Crazy name for this dish. I remember having it as a child in Denmark, and loving it. During and after the war there was a ration on many things, among them meat. Although this has side pork in it, I believe we used bacon. It's your choice. If you use side pork, remember that it needs salt.

- **1 pound side pork, cut into strips and cubed**
- **3 tablespoons butter**
- **2 large onions, in rings**
- **2 pounds mashed potatoes (about 6)**
- **Parsley, chopped**
- **Salt and pepper to taste**

- Fry pork gently in butter over low heat until the fat begins to run, then increase heat and cook until crisp. Remove and fry onion rings in bacon drippings, season with salt and pepper.
- Make a mountain of the mashed potatoes on a large platter. Place meat strips on top with some of the drippings.
- Garnish with parsley.

DANISH SIDE PORK

Serves 4

When I return to Denmark after absences of several years, this is always the very first thing I ask to have for dinner.

1 pound lean side pork
Flour to dredge meat in
2 eggs, beaten with fork
1 cup bread crumbs
2 tablespoons butter
Salt and pepper to taste

- Have side pork rather thickly sliced. Cut rind with sharp knife to prevent it from curling. Pound the meat a little with a meat hammer. Dust with flour. Dip meat into beaten eggs, then into bread crumbs.
- Melt butter in large skillet over medium high heat; add the pork and fry on both sides until golden and crisp. Season with salt and pepper.
- This is usually served with Parsley Sauce, small new potatoes and green peas.

BIKSEMAD

Serves 4

This is what most Danish housewives make with the left over pork roast. As far as this family is concerned, it is as good or better than the original roast.

1 pound leftover roast
2 medium onions, chopped
1 pound cooked, firm potatoes
2 tablespoons bacon grease
1 cup green peas
2 tablespoons Worchestershire sauce
Any leftover gravy, or 1 cup consommé
5 tablespoons Gerkins, sliced thin

- Dice meat, onions and potatoes. Fry onions until limp. Add meat and potatoes. Stir in the peas, Worchestershire sauce, and gravy, or, if you use consommé add 1 1/2 tablespoons flour to meat mixture. Stir in consommé to make gravy. Heat until desired temperature. Fold in sliced Gerkins.
- The traditional way of serving this is to top each serving with a fried egg, or shakes of Tabasco sauce.

ROASTED PORK LOIN WITH GRAVY

Serves 6

This is the most well known pork recipe in all of Denmark. It is usually served at Christmas time, but we eat it all year round. It's terrific, especially the cracklings. Ask for a roast with the rind on.

4 pound pork loin roast
1 teaspoon salt
1/4 teaspoon pepper
1 bay leaf
1 cup pitted prunes
1 cup chopped apples

- Heat oven to 425 degrees.
- With a sharp knife, finely score the rind cutting through it but not into the meat.
- Boil some water, then pour it into a shallow roasting pan and place in oven. Lay roast with rind down in water and cook for 20 minutes. Remove meat from oven and rub it with salt, pepper and crumbled bay leaf. Return to oven rind side up. Reduce heat to 325 degrees and roast for another 1 1/2 hours. Add prunes and apple chunks to pan; cook for another 30 minutes or until roast is done. Drain pan of all juices and set them aside. Return roast to oven at 450 degrees. Watch carefully and remove when rind (cracklings) begin to bubble. Or, place under broiler long enough for cracklings to get crisp.

GRAVY:

1 1/2 cups pan juice
5 tablespoons flour
4 tablespoons currant jelly
Salt and pepper to taste
Pinch of sugar
1/2 tablespoon Kitchen Bouquet for coloring

- Pour 1/4 of pan juices in sauce pan, add flour and make a sauce by adding pan juices a little at a time, stirring until smooth. Add seasonings and jelly. Finally add the gravy coloring. Taste and correct seasoning.

ROASTED MUSTARD PORK

Serves 6

A perfect Sunday supper with the family. I suggest the Red Cabbage and Caramelized Potatoes with this.

4 pounds pork loin roast
1/2 teaspoon salt
1/2 teaspoon pepper
4 tablespoons dry mustard

- Rub roast all over with salt and pepper. Spread mustard over the entire top.
- Roast at 350 degrees for 2 hours.

BARBECUED PORK SPARERIBS

Serves 4

We cook this on the spit when weather permits. It is also good cooked inside, but remember to line the bottom of oven with foil, as the sauce can make a terrible, sticky mess. This marinade is also used for basting.

4 racks of spareribs
1 lemon, juice of
1/2 cup clover honey
1/2 cup apricot preserves
1/2 cup soy sauce
4 shakes of Maggi liquid
1 tablespoon fresh ginger, grated
1 clove garlic, minced

- Mix all the ingredients, except ribs. Place spareribs and marinade in a pan small enough to allow marinade to cover racks of meat. Set aside for 1 hour. Barbecue for 1 1/2 hours or according to your grill's directions.
- If cooking inside, bake in 350 degree oven for 1 1/2 hour. Baste often.

GRANDMA FOX'S TAMALE PIE

Serves 6

My sister-in-law, Donna, let me copy her Mother's favorite Tamale Pie recipe.

1 pound lean pork steak
4 tablespoons olive oil
1 clove garlic, sliced
1 onion, chopped
1 cup cornmeal
1 teaspoon salt
1/2 teaspoon pepper
1 tablespoon chili powder
1 cup milk
1 16-ounce can whole corn
1 28-ounce can whole tomatoes, with juice
1 16-ounce can black olives

- Cut pork into small pieces and sauté in oil until brown. Add garlic and onion and cook for 15 minutes. Stir in the cornmeal, salt, pepper, chili powder and milk. Then add corn and tomatoes and let simmer with cover for 30 minutes. Add the drained olives.
- Grease baking dish, pour in the mixture and bake in a 350 degree oven for 30 minutes.

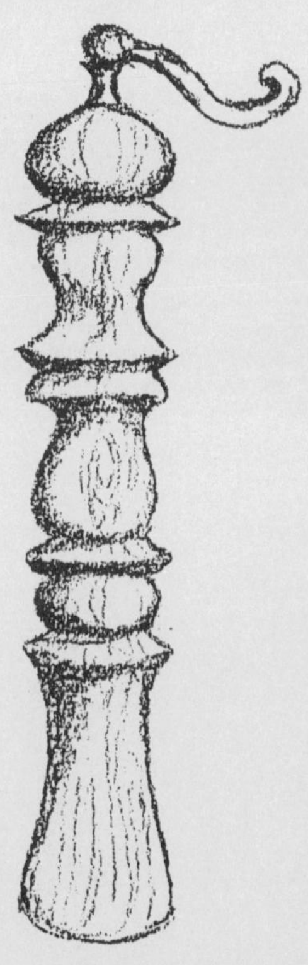

PORK TENDERLOIN MEDALLIONS

Serves 4

The sauce makes this dish outstanding.

1 1/2	**pounds lean pork loin**	**4**	**shallots, sliced**
	Flour for dredging	**8**	**large mushrooms, sliced**
8	**tablespoons butter**	**1**	**cup Marsala wine**
	Salt and pepper to taste	**1/2**	**cup chicken broth**

- Cut loin into 1-inch thick pieces. Pound these lightly with meat hammer until they are 1/2 inch thick. Dredge in flour, shaking off excess. Melt 2 tablespoons butter in large skillet. Fry medallions 1 1/2 minutes on each side, browning them evenly. Season them with salt and pepper. Remove and keep warm. Discard grease and wipe pan clean.
- Melt 2 tablespoons butter and sauté shallots and mushrooms for 1 1/2 minutes. set aside and keep warm. Combine Marsala and broth in pan and bring to a boil. Reduce heat to medium-low and cook until sauce is halved. Swirl in remaining butter and stir until thick, about 3 minutes.
- Arrange pork medallions on platter; top with mushroom/shallot mixture and pour sauce over. Serve immediately with plain buttered pasta; with this sauce you will want no other flavors interfering.

MARINATED PORK ROAST

Serves 8

Marinate the roast one day ahead for best results.

1	**5 pound boned, rolled pork loin roast**	**2**	**cloves garlic, minced**
1/2	**cup soy sauce**	**1**	**tablespoon dry mustard**
1/2	**cup dry sherry**	**1**	**teaspoon ginger, grated**
1/2	**cup Lingonberry preserves**	**1**	**teaspoon thyme**

- Combine all the ingredients except roast. Mix well. Place meat inside a plastic bag in a deep bowl. Pour in marinade and close bag. Set in refrigerator overnight, turning meat occasionally.
- Remove meat and place on rack in shallow roasting pan. Roast uncovered at 325 degrees for 3 hours, or until meat thermometer reaches 175 degrees.
- Baste often with marinade during last hour of roasting.

ROASTED RACK OF SPRING LAMB

Serves 4

This is an elegant dish. We serve this often and are complimented every time. Count on 2 people sharing 1 rack of lamb.

- **2 racks of lamb**
- **3 tablespoons olive oil**
- **1/2 teaspoon salt**
- **1/4 teaspoon black pepper, freshly ground**
- **3 cloves garlic, minced**
- **3 tablespoons Dijon Mustard**
- **1/2 cup parsley, chopped**
- **1/2 cup fresh bread crumbs**
- **3 tablespoons filberts, crushed**
- **4 tablespoons butter, melted**

- Heat oven to 500 degrees.
- Start by opening the flaps on rack. Rub meat with olive oil and season inside flap with salt, pepper and half of garlic. Place lamb meat-side down in roasting pan. Roast for 10 minutes. Remove and turn meat-side up. Spread mustard on top of racks. Mix the parsley and bread crumbs, nuts and remaining garlic, spread this on top of mustard, to make bread crumb mixture stick to lamb.
- Drizzle butter, entirely over racks. Return to oven and roast for 15 more minutes for rare meat, 20 minutes for medium.
- Carve between each rib.

PERRY STREET CASSOULET

Serves 4

We have made cassoulet with so many combinations you won't beleive it. This is our very favorite and also the absolute quickest way possible to have brother Frank's tasty treat.

- **1 large onion, chopped**
- **4 cloves garlic, minced**
- **2 tablespoons butter**
- **1 pound lamb, ground**
- **1/2 pound Italian bulk sausage**
- **1 beef flavored boullion cube**
- **1 cup water**
- **2 15-ounce cans cannelline (white kidney beans)**
- **1/3 cup tomato juice**
- **3/4 cup dry vermouth**
- **1/2 teaspoon thyme**
- **1/2 cup parsley, chopped**
- **Salt and pepper to taste**
- **1/2 pound Kilbasse sausage, sliced**

- Sauté onion and garlic in butter until limp. Add ground lamb and Italian sausage and cook for 10 minutes, or until meat is no longer red. Dissolve boullion cube in water and add to meat. Drain one can of cannellini; add to meat mixture. Add second can of beans, undrained. Blend in tomato juice and vermouth. Season with thyme, parsley, salt and pepper. Stir in sausage slices. Pour into ovenproof casserole pan. Bake at 350 degrees for 40 minutes.

LUXURY LEG OF LAMB

Serves 6

We happen to use leg of venison, but I use the same recipe. It's moist, tender and full of flavor, due to the slow cooking method.

1-4 to 6 pound leg of lamb
1/3 cup olive oil
1/4 cup white wine
1 tablespoon peanut butter
1/2 teaspoon Dijon mustard
1 tablespoon honey
1 tablespoon tarragon vinegar
1 tablespoon soy sauce
1 clove garlic, minced
2 teaspoons curry powder
1 lime, juice of
1/2 cup ginger ale

- Heat oven to 325 degrees.
- Warm and blend all the ingredients except ginger ale.
- Have leg of lamb at room temperature. Pour the entire marinade over lamb. Place in a preheated oven for 2 hours.
- The secret to a moist piece of meat is constant basting, as often as every 20 minutes.
- Add the ginger ale to pan and baste with it for the last 15 minutes of roasting time. Check meat with meat thermometer for accuracy.

SALTIMBOCCA

Serves 4

A traditional Italian dish, and a snap to prepare.

3 tablespoons flour
1/2 teaspoon freshly ground pepper
1 pound veal scallops, 1/4-inch thick
2 tablespoons olive oil
8 thin slices Prosciutto, cut into 1/2-inch squares
1 cup sherry
2 tablespoons beef stock
2 cups precooked spinach
1/4 pound Gruyère cheese, shredded

- Combine the flour and pepper in a plastic bag with the veal and shake to coat well. Place large skillet over high heat until quite hot. Coat bottom of pan with olive oil. Fry veal for 2 minutes or until golden brown, repeat on other side. Add Prosciutto and fry for 30 seconds.
- Add sherry and stock and fry for another 30 seconds. Remove from heat and place on a bed of spinach. Top with shredded cheese.

OSSO BUCCO

Serves 4

I have been told by friends that this is their favorite meal served in our home. It might sound complicated, but it is in fact very easy, and it's worth every minute you spend preparing it.

4 veal shanks (about 3 pounds in all)
Salt and pepper to taste
1/4 cup flour
1/4 stick butter
4 tablespoons olive oil
1 1/2 cups onions, chopped
1 cup celery, chopped
1 cup carrots, chopped
5 cloves garlic, minced
1/2 cup dry white wine
1 1/2 pounds tomatoes, seeded and chopped
1 can consommé or more
1 tablespoon tomato paste
3 sprigs parsley
Bouquet Garni: 1 teaspoon each, thyme, basil and bay leaf

- Wipe veal shanks dry; sprinkle both sides with salt and pepper. Dust with flour. Melt butter in skillet or Dutch oven and brown shanks on all sides to seal in juices. Remove and keep warm. Add olive oil to same pan, and sauté onions, celery and carrots with garlic until tender, about 5 minutes. Remove vegetables. Try to scrape off browned bits as you stir. Tie thyme, basil, and bay leaf inside cheesecloth. Add wine to skillet or dutch oven and reduce to half.
- Return shanks to pan. Add tomatoes and consommé to shanks. Add the browned vegetable and spices. Place in a 350 degree oven and bake for 1 1/2 hour or until shanks are tender.
- Remove shanks from Dutch oven and keep warm. Discard vegetables and bouqet garni. Over high heat bring pan juices to a boil with tomato paste and parsley, now reduce to 2 cups, stirring constantly. Cover and let simmer until sauce is thick. It is traditional to top this with Gremolata.

GREMOLATA

1 clove garlic, minced
3 tablespoons parsley, chopped
1 teaspoon lemon peel, grated

- Mix ingredients. Sprinkle over shanks and sauce. Cover for 2 minutes. Serve immediately.

VEAL FLORENTINE

Serves 4

My favorite veal dish. Given to me by a chef in San Fransisco on Blue Moon Alley.

1	**bunch fresh spinach**
6	**tablespoons butter**
1	**16-ounce can whole tomatoes**
3	**cloves garlic, minced**
1/2	**cup white wine**
1/4	**cup water**
1	**tablespoon tomato paste**
1/2	**teaspoon sugar**
3/4	**teaspoon salt**
1/2	**teaspoon white pepper**
1/4	**cup flour**
4	**veal cutlets, 1-inch thick**
1	**tablespoon olive oil**
4	**slices Mozzarella cheese, 1 ounce each**

- Rinse spinach. Remove large stalks and cut spinach into coarse shreds. Steam in covered pan for 5 minutes, shaking pan to prevent burning. Add 2 tablespoons of butter and keep shaking pan until butter is absorbed. Set aside.
- Remove skin from tomatoes and press through sieve; discard seeds and set aside.
- Heat 2 tablespoons butter in sauce pan; add garlic and sauté for 30 seconds. Add tomatoes, wine, water and tomato paste. Stir well. Blend in sugar, salt and pepper. Let it come to a boil. Cook uncovered for 10 minutes. Set aside.
- Mix flour and a little salt in a small bag. Pound veal cutlets to 1/4-inch thick. Shake one piece at a time in flour to coat evenly. Heat oil and the remaining butter over medium heat in skillet.
- Add veal to skillet; cook, turning once, until light brown, about 2 minutes on each side. Remove from heat. Divide spinach on veal and top with a slice of cheese. Pour tomato mixture into skillet without it touching cheese. Lift edges to let sauce flow under meat. Cook until sauce bubbles. Reduce to very low heat. Simmer 5 minutes.

FRIKADELLER OF VEAL IN CAPER SAUCE

Serves 6

With love from Denmark.

1 1/2 pounds lean veal, chopped
1 cup onions, minced
1 cup club soda
3 tablespoons flour
2 tablespoons fresh basil, or 1 dried
1 teaspoon salt
1/2 teaspoon pepper
3 tablespoons butter
1 tablespoon oil

- Blend first seven ingredients using a mixer and letting lots of air into meat while blending, this makes the meat balls lighter.
- Form into small oval-shaped balls and fry in butter and oil over medium-high heat for 10 minutes on each side. Remove and keep warm.
- Discard all but 2 tablespoons of pan drippings.

CAPER SAUCE

2 tablespoons flour
2 tablespoons pan drippings
1 cup chicken broth
1 egg yolk
1/2 cup cream
2 tablespoons capers, drained and chopped
1/2 tablespoon lemon juice
2 tablespoons parsley, chopped
1 teaspoon salt
1/4 teaspoon cayenne pepper

- Blend the flour and drippings, mix thoroughly. Over medium heat, add broth a little at a time, stirring well between each addition. Bring to a boil. Lower temperature and simmer for 2 minutes. Blend egg yolk and cream together.
- Combine with sauce by removing 3 tablespoons of hot sauce and adding it to cream mixture while stirring well. Pour back into pan with sauce, stirring constantly; bring this back to a boil. Remove from heat immediatly upon boiling. Add capers, lemon juice, parsley, salt and cayenne pepper.
- Pour over cooked frikadeller and pass the remaining sauce in a bowl.

SCALOPPINE VENISON LOIN

Serves 4

You can substitute with pork loin or veal.

1 1/2 pounds venison loin
1/2 teaspoon salt
1/2 teaspoon freshly ground pepper
1 teaspoon sweet paprika
1/2 cup flour
4 tablespoons butter
1/4 cup Marsala wine
1 1/2 tablespoons Dijon mustard
1/2 cup beef consommé
1/2 cup parsley, chopped

- Remove any trace of fat from loin. Slice into medallions about 1 1/2-inches thick. Place between two pieces of plastic and pound with a meat hammer or the wide part of a meat cleaver, until 1/2-inch thick.
- Season with salt, pepper and paprika. Dredge in flour to seal in the juices.
- Heat large skillet, melt butter and place medallions in skillet. Cook for about 1 1/2 minutes on each side. Remove and keep warm under foil, not in oven.
- Pour the wine into pan, raise heat and cook until liquid is almost gone. Try to remove all the brown particles from the pan and stir well. Add consommé and boil for 1/2 minute. Remove from heat and add mustard. Arrange medallions on serving platter and pour sauce over.
- Garnish with chopped parsley.

VENISON CHOPS WITH MARMALADE

Serves 4

4 tablespoons butter
2 tablespoons oil
4 venison chops
Salt and pepper to taste
1/2 cup chopped onion
1/3 cup dry sherry
1/2 cup chicken broth
3 tablespoons lemon marmalade
1/4 cup Half-and-Half

- Melt butter in hot skillet with oil. Add chops and sear both sides to seal in juices. Season with salt and pepper. Lower heat and cook meat for a total of about 9 minutes. Remove chops and keep warm.
- In the same skillet, cook onion until tender, about 10 minutes. Add sherry, broth and marmalade. Bring sauce to a boil, keep stirring until sauce is reduced by one-third. Lower temperature and whisk in cream. Simmer 10 minutes.
- Place chops on platter, top with sauce. Serve remaining sauce at the table.
- We enjoy this with Oven Roasted Baby Potatoes.

VENISON LOIN IN MADEIRA

Serves 4

1	**loin of venison**	8	**mushrooms, sliced thick**
	Flour for dredging	1/2	**cup Madeira**
3/4	**cube butter**	1/2	**cup sour cream**
1	**onion, sliced into rings**		

- Cut medallions of deer loin into 1-inch thick pieces. Place between two pieces of plastic and pound with meat hammer until 1/2-inch thick. Lightly dredge in flour. Melt 2 tablespoons of butter in skillet; brown meat on both sides for a total of 2 1/2 minutes. Remove and keep warm. Sauté onion for 2 minutes. Add mushrooms and sauté just until tender, about 1 minute. Add half of Madeira, bring to a boil, reduce to half. Stir in the remaining wine, swirl in rest of butter butter. Fold in the sour cream and stir until thick.
- Place meat on platter and serve with sauce.

ORIENTAL VENISON STEAKS

Serves 4

The best advice I can give about cooking venison is never overcook, as it will become tough and stringy. Marinating the meat for a few hours is one way to tenderize any tough cuts.

4	**venison steaks**	1	**tablespoon juniper berries, crushed**
1/4	**cup soy sauce**	3	**cloves garlic, minced**
1/4	**cup dry sherry**	2	**teaspoons ginger root, freshly grated**
2	**tablespoons peanut oil**		

- Trim meat of any trace of fat, not doing so can spoil an otherwise perfectly good steak. Combine all the ingredients and marinate meat for 3 to 4 hours, turning often.
- Grill 7 minutes per side for juicy, medium-rare steaks.

TORTILLA CASSEROLE

Serves 8

A teen-age favorite. It's quick to put together and the taste is great.

1 1/2 pounds ground moose meat or beef
1 large onion, chopped
1 1-pound can tomatoes, chopped
1 8-ounce can tomato sauce
1 4-ounce can green chilies, drained, chopped
1 red hot chili pepper, seeded, crushed
1 1 1/2-ounce envelope powdered spaghetti sauce mix
1/2 cup water
1 teaspoon salt
4 shakes Tabasco sauce
1 pound ricotta or cottage cheese
2 eggs, beaten
8 corn or flour tortillas
1 pound Jack cheese, shredded

- Preheat oven to 350 degrees.
- Brown meat and onion in large skillet with a little grease, if using moose meat. Add tomatoes, tomato sauce, chilies, red chili pepper, spaghetti sauce mix, water, salt and Tabasco sauce. Stir well. Let simmer for 15 minutes.
- Blend cheese with beaten eggs in bowl.
- In a flat 12 x 8 x 2-inch baking dish, like a lasagne pan spread 1 cup meat mixture, top first with 2 tortillas, then with ricotta mixture and finally with Jack cheese. Continue building in this manner to form 2 stacks of 4 tortillas each, until all mixture is used. Complete with a layer of Jack cheese.
- Bake for 30 minutes. Slice like a pie.

DANISH MOOSE BURGERS IN HUNTER SAUCE

Serves 4

You can use ground beef in this dish. We use moose and find it very tasty.

1 1/2 pounds ground moose meat
1 large onion, chopped
4 shakes of Maggi liquid
1/2 teaspoon salt
1/4 teaspoon pepper
4 tablespoons flour
4 tablespoons bacon grease or butter

- Combine meat, onion, and Maggi. Shape 4 mooseburger's, making them 3/4-inch thick. Mix flour, salt and pepper. Dust meat well in flour with seasonings. Coat with as much flour as possible.
- Heat a skillet, add bacon grease. Fry burgers 4 to 6 minutes on each side. Remove and keep warm.

HUNTER SAUCE:

1 large onion, sliced
1 green pepper, in chunks
10 mushrooms, sliced
2 tablespoons bacon grease
4 tablespoons flour
1 teaspoon dry mustard
1 can beef consommé
2 tablespoons lemon juice
1 tablespoon Kitchen Bouquet

- Sauté onion, pepper and mushrooms in bacon grease until limp. Remove vegetables and keep warm.
- Add flour and mustard to skillet and blend with pan juices. Slowly add the consommé and stir until nice and smooth. Add lemon juice and Kitchen Bouquet. Return onion mixture to sauce. Pour over burgers and serve.

CURRIED MOOSE STROGANOFF

Serves 3-4

This comes from a Japanese cooking class I attended. This is spicy hot; just pile some chutney on top to cool it down.

1 onion, chopped
1 clove garlic, minced
1/2 cube butter
1 pound ground moose meat, or beef
Dash of msg
2 tablespoons curry powder
1/2 teaspoon salt
2 teaspoons sugar
1 tablespoon soy sauce
4 tablespoons sour cream

- Sauté onion and garlic in butter until limp. Add meat and fry for 7 minutes. Shake msg. and curry powder on meat mixture. Add salt and sugar, stir in soy sauce. Let simmer for 10 minutes. Fold in sour cream and heat to correct temperature.
- Serve over cooked rice.

MOOSE MOUSSAKA

Serves 6

Wonderful for a crowd. Just double ingredients.

1	**large eggplant**
1/2	**teaspoon salt**
1	**pound ground moose meat, or lamb**
1/2	**pound sausage meat**
2	**medium onions, chopped**
2	**cloves garlic, minced**
1	**cup tomatoes, canned**
1/2	**cup white wine**
1/4	**cup parsley, minced**
1	**teaspoon salt**
1/2	**teaspoon oregano, crumbled**
1/2	**teaspoon thyme**
1/4	**teaspoon nutmeg**
2	**eggs, separated**
1/2	**cup bread crumbs**
1/4	**cup olive oil**

- Cut egg plant into 1/2-inch slices, sprinkle with salt and set aside to ripen for 1/2 hour, then rinse and dry.
- Brown meats with onion and garlic. Drain off fat. Add tomatoes, wine, parsley, salt, oregano, thyme and nutmeg. Cover and simmer for 30 minutes.
- Mix in unbeaten egg whites and half of crumbs. Brown eggplant slices in olive oil for 5 minutes. Spread remaining bread crumbs in casserole dish. Place eggplant on bread crumbs, spoon meat mixture on top; set aside.

SAUCE:

3	**tablespoons butter**
3	**tablespoons flour**
1 1/2	**cups milk**
2	**egg yolks**
1/2	**teaspoon salt**
1/4	**teaspoon pepper**
6	**teaspoons Parmesan cheese**

- Melt butter, but do not brown. Add flour slowly, stirring constantly. Remove from heat. Gradually stir in milk. Return to heat and cook until sauce thickens. Add egg yolks, salt and pepper and blend well.
- Pour sauce over Moose Moussaka and sprinkle with Parmesan cheese. Bake at 350 degrees for 45 minutes

QUAIL FOR DINNER

Serves 4

8	**quail**
	Salt and pepper to taste
1 1/2	**cup Madeira**
1/2	**cup raisins**
4	**cloves**
1	**cup cooked rice**
1/4	**teaspoon powdered ginger**
1	**tablespoon orange peel, grated**
1	**tablespoon butter, melted**
1/2	**cup pecans**
1	**orange, juice of**
1/2	**cup butter, melted**
1/2	**cup warmed cognac**

- Wash and dry quail. Sprinkle inside and out with salt and pepper. Heat oven to 450 degrees. Combine Madeira and cloves in sauce pan. Bring to a boil, reduce heat and simmer for 5 minutes. Strain the mixture, discard cloves.
- Combine rice, ginger, orange peel, one tablespoon melted butter, raisins and pecans in a mixing bowl. Mix well and stuff the quail.
- Place birds on a rack in a shallow roasting pan and brush with butter. Bake 5 minutes. Reduce temperature to 300 degrees and bake for another 25 minutes. Baste often with the remaining combination of butter, Madeira and orange juice. Pour pan juices over the quail. To serve pour warmed cognac over the birds and ignite.

From the Vegetable Garden

FROM THE VEGETABLE GARDEN

BRENDA'S ZUCCHINI JACK CASSEROLE

Serves 10

This can all be prepared ahead and baked while you do other things. Very tasty.

2 pounds zucchini
4 eggs
1/2 cup milk
1 teaspoon salt
2 teaspoons baking powder
3 tablespoons flour
1/4 cup chopped parsley
1 7-ounce can green chilies
1 onion, chopped
1 glove garlic, minced
3/4 pound Jack cheese, shredded
1 cup croutons, seasoned
3 tablespoons butter

- Slice zucchini into 1/4-inch thick rounds. In a large bowl, beat together eggs, milk, salt, baking powder and flour until smooth. Stir in parsley, chilies, garlic, onion, cheese and zucchini. Spoon into greased 9 x 13-inch baking pan. Toss croutons with melted butter, then sprinkle on top.
- Bake in a 350 degree oven for 35 to 40 minutes, or until set in the middle. Let stand 10 minutes before serving.

CORN PUDDING

Serves 6-8

Corn is not an often used vegetable in Europe. I had never tasted it in a "pudding" before a friend served this one out of her mother's great recipe collection.

4 tablespoons cornstarch
2 cups milk
1 16-ounce can whole kernel corn
4 eggs, beaten
1/2 stick butter, melted
1 teaspoon salt
2-3 tablespoons sugar
Dash of paprika

- Make a smooth paste of cornstarch and a little of the milk.
- Combine with remaining ingredients. Turn the mixture into a 2-quart greased casserole and dot with additional butter and a little paprika.
- Bake in oven at 375 degrees for 45 minuets to an hour, or until a knife comes out wet but not milky. Brown the top lightly under broiler.

QUICK CORN PUDDING

Serves 4-6

A different version of Corn Pudding from Brenda's files.

1/2	**cup sugar**
2	**tablespoons cornstarch**
2	**eggs**
1	**16-ounce can cream-style corn**
1	**13-ounce can evaporated milk**
	Butter

- Lightly grease a 1 1/2-quart baking dish. Combine sugar and cornstarch in a medium bowl. Add eggs, corn and milk. Mix well. Turn into baking dish and dot with butter.
- Bake at 350 degrees for about 1 hour or until center is firm.

COPPER PENNIES

Marinated and served either hot or cold. I had five recipes submitted under the same name; this is the one we chose.

5	**pounds carrots, sliced, semi-cooked until barely tender**
1	**cup onions, chopped**
1	**cup green peppers, chopped**
2	**cups salad oil**
1	**cup cider vinegar**
2	**cups tomato juice**
1 1/2	**cups sugar**
1	**tablespoon Worchestershire sauce**
1	**tablespoon Dijon mustard**

- In a large glass bowl, toss the semi-cooked carrots with the uncooked onions and green peppers.
- Combine all other ingredients in blender or processor. Pour over vegetables and let marinate at least overnight.
- The vegetables get better the longer they marinate and they will last for a week in the refrigerator.

CARROTS HOLLANDAISE

Serves 4

A luxurious, but easy dish.

1	**pound long thin carrots, cut into 2 inch pieces**	2	**egg yolks**
1	**cup water**	3	**tablespoons heavy cream**
1	**cup chicken broth**	2	**tablespoons parsley, chopped**
1/2	**cube butter**	1/2	**teaspoon salt**
2	**teaspoons sugar**		**Fresh ground pepper**

- Cook carrots in advance, re-heat in butter and add to egg sauce just before serving.
- Cook cleaned carrots in water and broth for 8 to 10 minutes, do not overcook. While carrots are cooking, heat a sauce pan and melt butter. When carrots are tender, add to butter, sprinkle with sugar. Cook over very low heat for 3 minutes or until carrots are fully cooked. Beat yolks with cream, add parsley and stir gently: season with salt and pepper. Add egg mixture to carrots and stir gently until sauce has thickened.

GLAZED CARROTS

Serves 4

When our niece came home for a visit from Africa recently, we were surprised that her young son, Eddie, ate these with gusto. Make plenty — they disappear fast.

2	**pounds small carrots**	3	**tablespoons Dijon mustard**
3	**tablespoons butter**	1/4	**cup parsley, chopped**
1/4	**cup brown sugar**	1/2	**teaspoon nutmeg, grated**

- Cook carrots in salted boiling water until tender. Drain well.
- Melt butter in sauce pan; add sugar and mustard. Cook until syrupy, about 3 minutes.
- Add carrots, stirring to coat, for another 4 minutes. Sprinkle with parsley and nutmeg.

SOUTHEAST ALASKA LIMA BEANS

Serves 8

- 4 cups dried Lima beans
- 1 pound thickly sliced bacon, uncooked, diced
- 6 tablespoons brown sugar
- 1 tablespoon dry mustard
- 1 tablespoon salt
- 1 teaspoon freshly ground pepper
- 1 teaspoon ground ginger
- 1 1/4 cups boiling water
- 6 tablespoons molasses

- Soak beans in water overnight. Drain well. Cover again with cold water and bring to a boil. Lower temperature and let simmer for 45 minutes. Drain well.
- Preheat oven to 250 degrees. Transfer beans to a 3-quart casserole. Add bacon, brown sugar, mustard, salt, pepper and ginger. Stir gently to prevent beans from breaking up. Add 1/4 cup boiling water, stir gently. Add molasses and the remaining 1 cup boiling water. Cover and let cook for 4 hours. Check the water frequently and add more if beans seem too dry.
- Increase oven temperature to 300 degrees and bake uncovered for another 30 minutes or until top is light brown.

GREEN BEANS AND PINE NUTS

Serves 6

Blanching the green beans by plunging them into ice water immediately after cooking keeps them nice, green and crunchy.

- 1 1/2 cups green beans
- 3 tablespoons butter
- 1/2 cup pine nuts
- 1/4 cup parsley
- 3/4 teaspoon salt
- 1/2 teaspoon pepper

- Bring large saucepan of water to a boil with a little salt. Cook beans for 4 to 5 minutes or until tender; do not overcook. Drain beans and place them a bowl of water and ice.
- Melt butter in pan with nuts, parsley, salt and pepper. Stir in the green beans. Keep warm until serving time.

CALICO BAKED BEANS

Serves 8-10

Our friend Romer Derr let me use his family recipe. It was served often in Carole and Romer's home.

2 28-ounce cans baked beans
2 15-ounce cans butter beans
2 15 1/4-ounce cans red kidney beans
2 16-ounce cans green baby Limas, drained
2 medium onions, chopped
1 cup catsup
3/4 cup brown sugar
2 tablespoons molasses
2 tablespoons dry mustard
1 pound bacon, uncooked, diced

- Simply combine all the ingredients and bake at 350 degrees for 2 hours.
- Please note: the only beans that are drained are the baby Limas.

GOURMET POTATOES

Serves 4

These are twice-baked and stuffed.

- **2 large Idaho potatoes**
- **4 strips bacon**
- **1/4 cup green onions, chopped**
- **1/2 cup sour cream**
- **1/2 teaspoon salt**
- **1/2 teaspoon pepper**
- **Pinch of paprika**
- **4 tablespoons Parmesan cheese**

- Scrub potatoes and bake in oven at 400 degrees for 1 hour. Fry bacon until crisp and crumble it up. Cut potatoes in half and scoop meat out into bowl. Add green onions, sour cream, salt, pepper and paprika to potato meat and blend well in mixer. Fold in the bacon.
- Stuff mixture into potato skins. Sprinkle tops with Parmesan cheese and a little more paprika for coloring.
- Bake at 350 degrees for 20 minutes.

GERMAN POTATO SALAD

Serves 6

There is a tangy flavor to this dish. I like serving it with Bratwurst or other sausage.

- **3 tablespoons butter**
- **1 large onion, sliced**
- **3 tablespoons vinegar**
- **1 teaspoon salt**
- **1 teaspoon freshly ground pepper**
- **1 tablespoon sugar**
- **3 tablespoons cream or water**
- **3 cups potatoes, boiled, diced**

- Melt butter but do not brown. In heavy kettle over low heat, cook onions in butter until limp. Add vinegar, salt and pepper. Stir well. Add the sugar and cream. Finally, add the diced potatoes. Simmer for 15 minutes. Shake pan instead of stirring, so the potatoes become shiny. Serve warm.

FRENCH POTATOES GRATIN

Serves 6

Of the many fine French potato dishes, this one is our favorite. It goes with any meat or poultry dinner.

2 pounds potatoes
1/2 pint milk
1/2 pint heavy cream
1 clove garlic, minced
Salt and pepper to taste
1/2 cup Emmenthal cheese, shredded

- Preheat oven to 400 degrees. Grease a shallow baking dish, about 9-inch square, with butter. Peel potatoes and slice into 1/4-inch thick pieces. Place potatoes in a large saucepan with milk, cream, garlic, salt and pepper. Bring to a boil, lower to simmer, and cook for 3 minutes.
- Pour the contents into the greased dish. Sprinkle with cheese; bake for 40 minutes. Let rest 10 minutes before serving.

OVEN ROASTED BABY POTATOES

Serves 6

We often have a battle about the potatoes growing in the garden. ''He'' wants to see how big they can get, and ''she'' wants to pick them small. This is a ''she'' potato recipe.

2 pounds small potatoes, uniformly sized
2 tablespoons olive oil
6 cloves garlic, minced
1/4 teaspoon pepper
1 sprig fresh rosemary, or 1/4 teaspoon dried
Sea salt or coarse salt

- Heat oven to 450 degrees.
- Wipe potatoes clean, do not peel. Combine olive oil with garlic, pepper and rosemary. Pour over the ''she'' potatoes. Roast in a preheated oven for 45 minutes, turning once or twice. Remove and sprinkle with sea salt.

POTATOES CHANTILLY

Serves 4-6

Your friends will flip over this great dish given to me years ago from a member of the Portland Garden Club.

4 medium potatoes
1 onion, cut into rings
Salt and pepper to taste
4 tablespoons parsley, chopped
3 tablespoons butter
Dash of Tabasco sauce
Dash of Worchestershire sauce
1/2 cup cream
3/4 cup Cheddar cheese

- Line a 9 x 13-inch pan with foil, making sure edges are sealed so they won't leak.
- Cut potatoes French-fry style and place in bottom of pan. Add onion, salt, pepper and parsley. Dot with butter. Shake Tabasco sauce and Worchestershire on top. Pour cream over and add cheese. Fold edges of foil together so dish is sealed.
- Bake at 425 degrees for 40 minutes.

POMMES ST. GERMAIN

Serves 6

These potato chips can be tricky to make. Keeping track of the oil temperature is the crucial part, then I promise they will taste great, no matter what.

2 pounds red potatoes, with skin
Oil to fill deep fat fryer 3/4 full, or an electric frying pan with temperature setting
Coarse salt

- The potatoes will need to be fried twice for that special texture.
- Cut cleaned potatoes paper-thin, do not rinse. For the first frying, heat oil to 275 degrees. Fry potatoes briefly, until they are soft, but not colored. For the second frying, heat oil to 475 degrees.
- The minute the potatoes hit the hot oil they should puff up and turn golden brown. Remove potatoes quickly and sprinkle them with coarse salt or sea salt.
- Serve at room temperature.

SWISS POTATO PANCAKES

Serves 3-4

A favorite in this family. Cooking potatoes in a non-stick pan makes them slip out really easily.

4 slices bacon, diced
1 pound potatoes
1 medium onion
1/8 teaspoon salt
1/8 teaspoon pepper
2 tablespoons butter or bacon fat
1 tablespoon flour, to bind

- With the help of a food processor or a husband, coarsely shred both onion and potatoes.
- Cook bacon until crisp. Drain on paper towel and set aside.
- Wash potatoes twice in cold water. Drain and pat dry. In the same frying pan heat bacon grease. In a bowl, mix flour, potatoes, onion, bacon, salt and pepper. Pour potato mixture into pan making sure the potatoes cover the whole pan bottom. Fry potatoes without stirring over medium heat for 10 minutes. Check often to see if it's brown and crisp, and shake pan frequently to avoid sticking.
- Turn over and fry on other side. Add a little more grease to pan so it will brown and become crispy. Cook another 5 to 6 minutes.

CARAMEL POTATOES

Serves 6

This goes hand in hand with the Pork Roast and the Red Cabbage.

- Start by boiling 12 small red or new potatoes. Cool and peel.

1/2 cup sugar
6 tablespoons butter
1 tablespoon water

- Melt sugar and let it cook until golden. Watch it carefully as it burns easily. Add butter. Stir potatoes and water into pan. Keep turning, or shake the pan to make potatoes nice and shiny.

DIJON POTATOES

Serves 4

Just love these easy-to-make potatoes.

2 tablespoons butter
2 tablespoons olive oil
2 cloves garlic, minced
4 red potatoes, with skin, sliced
1 onion, sliced
Salt and pepper to taste
2 green onions, sliced
2 1/2 tablespoons Dijon mustard
1/4 teaspoon paprika

- Preheat a frying pan large enough to hold all the potatoes. Melt butter and olive oil, and sauté garlic until soft, not brown. Add the potatoes, fry on all sides. Remove potatoes and set aside. Sauté onions in the same pan until limp. Drain all oil and butter and return potatoes to pan with onions. Season with salt and pepper. Add the green onions and mustard. Stir to coat potatoes.
- Sprinkle with paprika.

SOUTH SEA POTATOES

Serves 6

6 medium-sized russet potatoes
1/4 cup onions, grated
3/4 cup cream
1 cup Swiss cheese, shredded
1/2 cup macadamia nuts, chopped

- Bake potatoes at 350 degrees for 1 hour. Cut potatoes in half lengthwise; remove potato meat and mix in onions, cream and 1/2 cup cheese. Add 1/4 cup nuts, stir to blend well.
- Return mixture to potato shells and sprinkle the remaining nuts and cheese on top of potatoes and bake for 10 minutes.

CHILIES RELLENO LARAINE

Serves 8

- **4 4-ounce cans green chilies, sliced and seeded**
- **1 cup Jack cheese, shredded**
- **1 cup Cheddar cheese, shredded**
- **1/2 teaspoon salt**
- **1/4 teaspoon pepper**
- **Cumin to taste**
- **8 eggs, well beaten**

- Place chilies in casserole. Pile cheeses on top. Mix salt, pepper and cumin with beaten eggs; slowly pour egg mixture over cheese-topped chilies. Bake in a 325 degree oven for 30 minutes.
- Serve as a side dish with Mexican food.

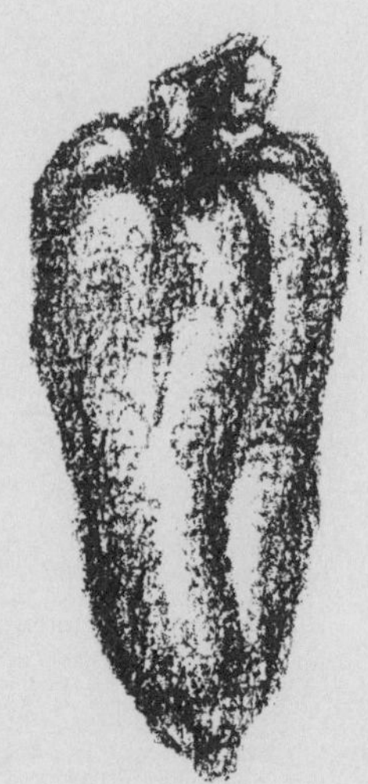

PARMESAN ONIONS

Serves 4

- **3 tablespoons butter**
- **1 teaspoon sugar**
- **1/2 teaspoon salt**
- **12 small onions, peeled**
- **4 tablespoons chicken broth**
- **1/4 cup sherry**
- **6 tablespoons Parmesan cheese, grated**

- Melt butter in skillet with a lid. Stir in sugar and peeled onions. Shake to coat evenly with sugar; this will caramelize them. Add salt, broth, and sherry, cover and let simmer for 30 minutes. Do not overcook.
- Serve with the juices and sprinkle with Parmesan cheese.

SESAME BROCCOLI

Serves 4

This is particularly good when served with barbecued chicken. This broccoli dish can be prepared earlier in the day and kept at room temperature until serving time.

1 pound broccoli
2 teaspoons sesame oil
1/2 cup sesame seeds
1/4 cup sake
1 1/2 tablespoons soy sauce
2 teaspoons honey

- Cook fresh broccoli until done, but still crisp.
- Toast sesame seeds under moderate heat until golden. Cool.
- Mix remaining ingredients and then add the sesame seeds. Pour mixture over cooked broccoli. Served at room temperature.

RED CABBAGE

Serves 8

This tasty vegetable is too good to be ignored. We eat it year round. Especially good served with chicken or pork roast.

1 head red cabbage, 3 pounds
4 tablespoons cider vinegar
1/4 cup butter
1/4 cup sugar
1 teaspoon salt
1 apple, cubed
1/2 to 3/4 cup red currant jelly

- Finely chop the cabbage and sprinkle with a little vinegar, to prevent it from turning dark.
- Melt butter in large kettle. Add the sugar and stir until dissolved. Add the cabbage and salt. Let cook for 20 minutes under a tight lid. Add the chopped apple, vinegar and currant jelly and simmer for 2 hours.

SOUTHEAST ALASKA SPINACH DISH

Serves 4

Another idea from the Japanese cooking class I enjoyed. This is a nice change from plain spinach. This recipe calls for frozen spinach, but we have a garden full of vegetables every year, and fresh spinach is always the best.

2 pounds spinach, cooked
2 tablespoons poppy seeds
4 tablespoons soy sauce
3 tablespoons sugar
3 tablespoons vinegar
1 tablespoon butter

- Cook spinach in large pot of water with a little salt until tender, about 10 minutes. Drain well and keep warm.
- Blend all the sauce ingredients. Pour over the cooked spinach.

CHILLED ASPARAGUS

With all the steamers I have in the kitchen cabinets, you would think I steamed my asparagus. I was told of this outstanding method of preparing it and I will never, ever use a steamer for asparagus again.

1 large pot boiling water
Salt as desired
2 bunches asparagus
1 large bowl of ice-cold water with some ice cubes
1 pair of tongs for fishing out the asparagus

- Bring water and salt to a boil. Add asparagus; cook for 4 to 5 minutes depending on size, I suggest you check them often. They must remain firm when tested with a sharp knife.
- Remove from boiling water and immediately place them in the ice water. They will have a bright green color since the cold water stops the cooking.
- They are delicious cold, but if you want to serve them warm, let stand in water only long enough to stop the cooking. Place inside towel and keep warm until serving time.
- In Europe, vegetables are kept warm by placing them in a covered dish, inside a down comforter.

PARSLEY BAKED ONIONS

Serves 4

These can also be made in the microwave oven. A nice change from baked potatoes.

4 medium onions
2 teaspoons sherry
3 tablespoons butter
1/4 teaspoon paprika
1/3 teaspoon salt
Dash of pepper on each onion

- Mix the following:

1/2 cup bread crumbs
1/4 cup parsley, chopped
2 tablespoons Parmesan cheese
2 teaspoons olive oil
Butter

- Combine all the ingredients except onions and bread crumb mixture. Peel onions, cut bottom so they can stand upright in a small baking dish. Make deep slashes on tops, spread sherry mixture over onions, and cover with foil, not too tightly. Place in a preheated oven and bake at 350 degrees for 45 minutes. Spread the bread crumb mixture over cooked onions, dot with butter and return to oven. Broil for 3 to 4 minutes or until golden brown.

LEEKS WITH CHEESE SAUCE

Serves 4

Most people use leeks for soup. In Denmark they are used in many casseroles, as well. They are, in fact, delicious just steamed.

2 pounds leeks, white part only
3 tablespoons butter
2 tablespoons flour
1 cup cream
5 tablespoons Cheddar cheese, grated
1 tablespoon Dijon mustard
1 tablespoon lemon juice
1/2 teaspoon salt
1/4 teaspoon white pepper

- Clean leeks well under running water. Boil them in salted water until tender, for about 15 minutes. Drain and reserve 1/2 cup of water. Set leeks aside to drip free of liquid. Melt butter in sauce pan, alternately add flour, cream and 1/2 cup reserved liquid until all used. Make sure there is no hint of a floury taste; if there is, add a little more leek water. Blend in cheese and mustard, reserving 1 tablespoon cheese. Stir well; add lemon juice, salt and pepper.
- Place leeks in slightly greased ovenproof dish. Pour cheese sauce over and sprinkle with remaining cheese. Cook for 10 minutes in oven set at 400 degrees.

CREAMED KALE

Serves 4

We have fresh, green, curly kale growing all the way into the fall. I did not plan on using my recipe for kale in this book since my husband, growing up in Virginia despised it as a child. As a matter of fact, he didn't even want it to take up space in the garden for it. Now he can't get enough of it. This is the way I serve fresh kale.

- Cook 2 pounds of kale, stalks removed in salted water for about 15 minutes, or until done. Drain all water from kale in a salad spinner or colander. Set aside.

SAUCE:

3	**tablespoons butter**	**1/2**	**teaspoon sugar**
3	**tablespoons flour**		**Salt and pepper to taste**
3/4	**cup whole milk**	**1**	**egg yolk**
1	**lemon, juice of**		

- Melt butter, add flour and slowly add milk until you have a smooth sauce. Blend in the lemon juice, sugar, salt and pepper.
- Chop kale into fine pieces in a food processor or with a sharp knife, as you would spinach.
- Combine kale and sauce, stir well. Finally, blend in the egg yolk. Serve warm.

FRITTATA

Serves 4

Just perfect for lunch. This classic Italian omelette is chock-full of fresh vegetables, and it tastes as good cold as it does warm.

1/4	**cup olive oil**	**1/2**	**teaspoon basil, dried**
2	**medium onions, thinly sliced**	**1/2**	**teaspoon marjoram, dried**
2	**green onions, chopped**	**1/4**	**teaspoon salt**
1	**14 1/2 ounce can tomatoes, peeled**	**1/4**	**teaspoon pepper**
1/4	**pound ham, chopped**	**6**	**large eggs**
1/4	**cup Parmesan cheese, grated**	**2**	**tablespoons butter**
4	**tablespoons parsley, minced**		

- Heat oil in a medium-sized frying pan. Add onion and sauté until limp, about 6 minutes. Add tomatoes and stir for another 4 minutes. With slotted spoon, transfer onions and tomatoes to a bowl. Set aside to cool. Discard drippings.
- Add ham, cheese, parsley, basil, marjoram, salt and pepper to the cooled tomato/onion mixture and blend well. Beat eggs seperately, then stir well into other ingredients.
- Heat butter in a frittata pan or any skillet with a flame-proof handle. Pour in mixture.
- Cook without stirring over very low heat until all but the top is set, about 10 minutes. You can test it by shaking pan. Heat broiler and place skillet under heat for 1 to 2 minutes, just enough to set the frittata but not brown it.

BRANN'S ONION PIE

Serves 6

If awards were passed out for onion pies, this would win. Thanks to talented Kathy Brann of North Carolina. When available, try this with Vidalia or Walla Walla Sweet onions.

1 sleeve Saltine crackers, crushed
1 stick butter, room temperature
5 medium onions, sliced

- Mix crackers and butter. Press into pie dish. Slice onions into 1/4-inch rings and steam until wilted, about 5 minutes.
- Place onions on top of pie crust. Set aside while preparing sauce.

SAUCE:

1/2 stick butter
2 1/2 tablespoons flour
1 1/2 cups milk
Salt and pepper to taste
1 egg, beaten
8 ounces Swiss cheese, shredded

- Melt butter, add flour and stir well. Slowly add milk, stirring to make a smooth sauce. Add salt and pepper to taste.
- Bring sauce to a slow boil. Remove a little of the sauce, and stir into egg and add this to pot; this prevents the egg from separating once it has been added to the hot sauce. Pour over onion rings. Top with cheese and bake for 25 minutes at 400 degrees. Let stand for 10 minutes before cutting into wedges.

SPICED BAKED ONIONS

Serves 8

Spending a good part of the summer on the boat, I find it hard to keep fresh vegetables all the time. Onions last long and we have learned to enjoy them many ways. This is fit for company.

4 large Spanish onions, about 2 pounds
2 tablespoons butter
1/2 cup chicken broth
1/2 cup dry white wine
2 teaspoons sugar
1 teaspoon lemon rind, grated
Pinch of cinnamon
Pinch of cloves
Salt and pepper to taste
1/4 cup pine nuts, crushed

- Preheat oven to 350 degrees.
- Peel onions and cut in half crosswise. Arrange halves cut-side up in a baking dish just large enough to hold them. In a medium saucepan combine 1 tablespoon butter with all remaining ingredients except pine nuts.
- Bring liquid to a simmer. Pour over onions, cover dish with foil and bake for 45 minutes. Melt remaining butter and pour over onions. Continue baking for another 15 minutes of until nuts are golden brown.

International Flavours

INTERNATIONAL DISHES

INTERNATIONAL DISHES

I am very fortunate to have lived in or visited many different countries over the years. This selection of international recipes is based on dishes I have enjoyed in restaurants or in homes. Some are borrowed, some revised and some copied. I hope, here, to inspire my readers to try some fun new ways of preparing international dishes. Since spices and ingredients in most other countries differ from those we commonly use, you may not have them on hand. I have found, however, that most items in these recipes can easily be obtained at the local supermarket.

ARMENIA
GARBANZO BEANS AND SPINACH (Nivik)

Serves 6

1 1/2 pounds garbanzo beans
1 large onion, chopped
1/4 cup olive oil
1/4 cup tomato paste
1/4 cup pine nuts
1/2 cup red pepper, minced
2 teaspoons salt
1 teaspoon sugar
1 1/2 pounds spinach

- Soak beans overnight in 5 cups of water. Reserve water.
- Clean and finely chop spinach. Set aside.
- Bring beans and water to a boil and simmer for 2 hours or until tender. Drain beans and set aside.
- In a skillet, fry onion in olive oil until limp. Add tomato paste, pine nuts, salt, pepper and sugar. Stir well.
- Add both the beans and spinach to skillet and let simmer for 30 minutes.
- The dish must be moist. If necessary, add more liquid.

AUSTRALIA

DUNDEE'S LEG OF LAMB

Serves 8

- **1 6-7 pound leg of lamb**
- **1/2 cup Dijon mustard**
- **2 teaspoons fresh rosemary**
- **1 clove garlic, minced**
- **1/3 cup parsley, chopped**
- **1/4 cup olive oil**
- **1/2 cup fresh bread crumbs**

- Combine mustard, rosemary, garlic and parsley in bowl.
- Mix in olive oil. Pour mixture over lamb and let marinate for 3 hours. Preheat oven to 325 degrees. Place lamb on a rack in roasting pan. Cover meat with bread crumbs. Drizzle some of the marinade over meat and roast it for 1 hour and 45 minutes, or done to your liking.
- We usually enjoy pasta with this dish.

AUSTRIA

WIENER SCHNITZEL

Serves 4

- **4 veal cutlets**
- **1/2 teaspoon salt**
- **Pepper to taste**
- **2 tablespoons flour**
- **1 egg, beaten**
- **1/2 cup bread crumbs**
- **Oil for frying**
- **4 lemon slices**
- **4 Anchovy fillets**

- Pound meat with meat hammer until about 1/4-inch thick.
- Season with salt and pepper. Coat with flour. Dip each cutlet in beaten egg, then coat with bread crumbs.
- Place in refrigerator for 1/2 hour. This will help the crumbs to adhere.
- Heat an electric frying pan to 375 degrees. Heat 1/4-inch of oil. Fry cutlets 3 minutes on each side. They should be crisp and brown.
- Arrange on platter and garnish each cutlet with a slice of lemon and a rolled anchovy fillet.

BELGIUM
CHICORY SALAD

Serves 4

2 tomatoes
1 pound endive
1/2 pound Swiss cheese
4 eggs, cooked
3 tablespoons vinegar
1 tablespoon lemon juice
3 tablespoons olive oil
1 teaspoon mustard, dry
1/2 teaspoon sugar
Salt and pepper to taste

- Divide endive into eight pieces, and place in lukewarm water for 15 minutes to remove bitter taste. Cut eggs and tomatoes into wedges.
- Arrange endive with eggs and tomatoes in bowl.
- Blend vinegar, lemon juice, olive oil and seasonings and pour over salad. Chill 1/2 hour before serving.
- Very attractive when served in a see-through salad bowl.

CANADA
ROYAL CANADIAN WILD GOOSE

Serves 6

1 5 pound goose
1/2 pound mushrooms, chopped
2 stalks celery, chopped
2 carrots, chopped
1 large onion, chopped
2 cloves garlic, chopped
1/4 stick butter
2 teaspoons fresh thyme
1 bay leaf
Dash of Tabasco sauce
2 cups chicken stock
1/2 teaspoon salt
1/4 teaspoon pepper
1/2 cup parsley, chopped
1 Granny Smith apple, cut up
5 slices bacon
1 cup port

- Sauté mushrooms, celery, carrots, onion and garlic in butter. Place a piece of waxed paper on top, lower temperature and let vegetables sweat for 5 minutes. Add thyme, bay leaf, Tabasco sauce and chicken stock to vegetables. Let simmer a couple of minutes.
- Sprinkle the cavity with salt and pepper. Place parsley and apple inside bird. Stuff bird with one half of vegetable mixture. Secure bacon on top of bird.
- Heat oven to 450 degrees and roast goose for 30 minutes. Add port to remaining vegetables and surround goose with them.
- Lower temperature to 350 degrees and continue roasting, for about 20 minutes per pound.
- Remove bacon and serve goose with pan drippings and vegetables.

DENMARK
FRIED HERRING (Stegt Sild)

Serves 5

- 9 large, fat herring
- 2 tablespoons flour
- 1/4 teaspoon pepper
- 1/2 teaspoon salt
- 3 tablespoons butter
- 6 medium tomatoes, sliced
- 1 cup parsley, chopped
- 1/2 tablespoon sugar
- Salt and pepper to taste

- Clean herring. Remove heads and bones. You can remove bones by placing your thumb by the head and working your way down the spine.
- Dust herring with seasoned flour and fry in butter on both sides until crisp, about 4 minutes per side. Remove and keep warm. In the same skillet fry the tomatoes and parsley. Sprinkle with salt, pepper and sugar. Mash tomatoes as you cook; serve them on top of fried herring. Serve with small new boiled potatoes.

ENGLAND
CUMBERLAND SAUCE

Makes 3/4 cup

Perfect with any game meal.

- 3/4 cup red currant jelly
- 3 tablespoons red wine
- 1 teaspoon dry mustard
- 3 tablespoons lemon juice
- 1 orange, peel of, slivered

- Combine currant jelly and wine with orange peel and simmer for 15 minutes. Blend in the other ingredients. Serve with any game meat, roast chicken, baked ham or as we often use it for, pork roast.

FRANCE
FRENCH ONION SOUP

Serves 8

This recipe was given to me by the chef at the Mark Hopkins Hotel in San Fransisco.

12	**onions, sliced**
4	**tablespoons butter**
1/2	**tablespoon sugar**
1	**teaspoon Kitchen Bouquet**
1 1/2	**teaspoons salt**
1/2	**teaspoon pepper**
1	**teaspoon Worchestershire sauce**
1/2	**teaspoon Tabasco sauce**
6	**cans beef broth**
1/2	**cup dry wine**
6	**cans consommé**
	Jack cheese
	Toasted French bread, sliced
	Mozzarella cheese

- Sauté onions in butter in a large soup kettle until limp. Stir in Kitchen Bouquet, sugar, salt and pepper. Blend well. Add Worchestershire sauce and Tabasco sauce. Add broth, wine and consommé and let simmer for 3 hours.
- Shred jack cheese and place some in bottom of each serving bowl. Ladle soup into bowls, place one piece of toast in each bowl and 2 thin slices of Mozzarella on top of that.
- Heat under the broiler long enough for cheese to melt.

GREECE

SPINACH PIE (Spanakopita)

Serves 8

2 pounds spinach
1 medium onion, chopped
1/2 cup olive oil
1 cup green onions, chopped
1/2 cup parsley, chopped
2 teaspoons dill, dried
1/4 teaspoon nutmeg, ground
1/2 teaspoon salt
1/4 teaspoon pepper, freshly ground
4 eggs, beaten
1/2 cup cottage cheese
1/4 cup Parmesan cheese, finely grated
1 cup Feta cheese, crumbled
1/4 cup pine nuts
1/2 cup melted butter
10 sheets Fillo pastry

- Wash spinach and cook 8 minutes. Drain well in colander or salad spinner. Fry onion in olive oil. Place cooked spinach in large bowl, add cooked onion and oil along with green onion, parsley and seasonings. Mix in the eggs, cheeses and nuts.
- Brush a 10 x 12-inch baking dish with butter. Line with 1 sheet of Fillo, brush with butter and add more sheets of pastry, brushing with butter between each layer as you go. Use five sheets of Fillo on bottom, spread filling and five on top, still brushing with butter.
- To prevent Fillo from drying out, place it under a damp towel while preparing the dish. End up brushing butter on top of final sheet.
- Sprinkle a little water on top to prevent pastry from curling.
- Bake at 350 degrees for 45 minutes or until puffed and golden.
- Cut and serve warm.

HUNGARY

HUNGARIAN CHRISTMAS BREAD

Makes 2 loaves

2	**packages dry yeast**	**1/4**	**cup oil**
5	**cups flour**	**2**	**teaspoons salt**
1/2	**cup milk**	**3**	**eggs**
1/2	**cup sugar**	**1**	**can Solo poppy cake filling**
1/4	**cup water**	**1**	**cup raisins**
1/4	**cup dark rum, plus 1 tablespoon**		**Poppy seeds**

- Sift together yeast and 2 cups flour. Heat milk. Add sugar, water, rum, oil and salt to milk. This should be very warm to the touch. Mix milk mixture with flour and yeast. Beat until smooth. Blend in 2 eggs and another cup flour, beat 1 minute. Add the remaining flour to make a moderately stiff dough. Knead until light and satiny, about 5 minutes. Cover with towel and let rest 30 minutes. Divide dough in half. Roll each half into a 10 x 12-inch rectangle.
- Combine Solo filling with 1 tablespoon rum and spread over dough. Sprinkle with raisins. Roll up like a jelly roll. Seal bottom and ends.
- Brush with the remaining beaten egg and sprinkle with poppy seeds. Make shallow slashes on top of bread.
- Set aside and let rise in warm place until doubled, about 1 hour.
- Bake in a preheated oven at 350 degrees for 40 minutes.

ITALY

CAPPELLETTI PESTO

Makes 1 1/3 cups

- **8 ounces Cappelletti pasta**
- **2 tablespoons olive oil**
- **1 clove garlic, pressed**
- **2 tablespoons white wine vinegar**
- **1/2 red pepper, finely chopped**
- **2 green onions, chopped**
- **1/4 cup pine nuts**
- **1/3 cup Pesto Sauce, see below**

- Cook pasta in large kettle of salted water until tender, yet firm. Drain, rinse with cold water; drain again.
- In a large bowl combine cooled pasta with olive oil, garlic, vinegar, red pepper, green onion and pine nuts to cooled pasta. Toss gently. Add pesto sauce. Mix well and chill for at least 1 hour.

PESTO SAUCE

- **2 cups packed fresh basil leaves, washed and dried**
- **1 cup Parmesan cheese**
- **1/2 cup olive oil**
- **1/2 teaspoon salt**
- **4 cloves garlic, minced**

- Place all the ingredients in food processor and blend until smooth. This keeps well in refrigerator. Freeze for longer storage. Pour a little olive oil on top of pesto before freezing.

INDIA

SWEET RICE

Serves 4

- **2 1/2 tablespoons oil**
- **4 whole cloves**
- **4 cardamom pods**
- **4 whole black peppercorns**
- **1 bay leaf**
- **1 onion, thinly sliced**
- **2 cups long grain rice**
- **1 tablespoon coriander**
- **1/2 teaspoon cinnamon, ground**
- **1/4 teaspoon nutmeg, ground**
- **3 cups beef broth**
- **1/2 teaspoon salt**
- **1 tablespoon brown sugar**
- **1/2 cup raisins**
- **1/2 cup almonds, slivered**
- **1/4 cup peanuts**

- Heat oil in heavy pot. Fry cloves, cardamom pods, pepper and bay leaf just a few seconds. Add onion rings and fry for 3 minutes. Add rice, coriander, cinnamon and nutmeg, stir for 4 minutes. Add broth and salt and over low heat and let rice cook for 15 minutes, stirring often.
- Add brown sugar and let simmer for another 20 minutes.
- Sprinkle with peanuts, raisins and slivered almond.

IRELAND
IRISH COFFEE

1	cup steaming coffee
1 1/2	ounces Irish Mist Liqueur
	Whipped cream for topping

IRELAND
IRISH MIST AND SODA

1 1/2	ounces Irish Mist Liqueur
4	ounces Club Soda

- Served over ice and a wedge of lime in tall glass.

ISRAEL
AVOCADO WITH HONEY SAUCE

Serves 4

1	red onion, chopped
1	teaspoon Dijon mustard
1/4	cup clove honey
1/4	cup fresh lemon juice, plus 1 tablespoon
1/3	cup olive oil
	Lettuce leaves
1	grapefruit, in wedges
3	avocados, chilled

- Chop onion in blender and add mustard, honey and lemon juice. Blend until smooth; slowly add olive oil. Place in refrigerator and chill until serving time.
- Cut avocados into wedges. Brush with lemon juice to preserve color. Arrange on lettuce leaves with grapefruit wedges. Pour dressing over and serve immediately.

KOREA

BEEF AND MUSHROOMS ON SKEWERS (Sanjuck)

Serves 4

- 1/2 pound beef, top round
- 1/4 pound mushrooms, small
- 2 tablespoons sesame oil
- 2 tablespoons soy sauce
- 1 teaspoons sesame seeds, toasted
- 1 clove garlic, minced
- 1/2 teaspoon sugar
- Pinch of pepper
- 2 bunches green onions
- 3 eggs, beaten
- 3 tablespoons flour
- Oil for frying

- Toast sesame seeds in oven for 15 minutes on low. set aside.
- Cut meat into 1-inch cubes. Toss meat with mushrooms, sesame oil, soy sauce and toasted sesame seeds. Add sugar, garlic and pepper. Set aside.
- Cut onions into 2 inch lengths.
- On short skewers alternate meat, onions and mushrooms until all used up. Dip skewers in beaten eggs and roll in or dust with flour. Let rest 5 minutes. Cover bottom of large frying pan with oil; heat until medium hot. Fry skewers with meat and vegetables until brown and crusty, about 15 minutes.

MEXICO

SOFT DINNER ROLLS (Bolillos)

Makes 1 dozen

The best Bolillos we have ever had were from a tiny backyard bakery on the Pacific coast on the Baja Peninsula. The following recipe is as close as we could come to the original.

We think it is outstanding.

2	**cups warm water, about 105 degrees**	**4 1/2**	**cups flour**
2	**packages yeast**	**1**	**tablespoon cornstarch**
2	**teaspoons salt**	**1/3**	**cup cold water**
1/4	**cup sugar**		

- In a large bowl, stir together water, yeast, salt, and sugar. Add 2 cups of flour, mix well. Stir in 1 1/2 cups more to make a firm dough. Place dough in mixer or on flour board and knead for 6 minutes. Knead in the remaining flour. Place in greased bowl and cover, let rise in a warm place until doubled in size, about 2 hours.
- Preheat oven to 450 degrees.
- Punch dough down and divide into 12 even pieces. Roll each piece into a ball, then pull each end to form am oblong shape. Place on greased cookie sheet and, with a sharp knife that has been dipped into ice water, make a slash in each roll. Mix cornstarch and water. Brush each roll.
- Place rolls in oven. Set another baking pan with boiling water in oven one shelf below. This will give the rolls a nice crust.
- Bake for 10 minutes. Lower heat to 375 degrees and bake for another 20 minutes, or until golden brown.

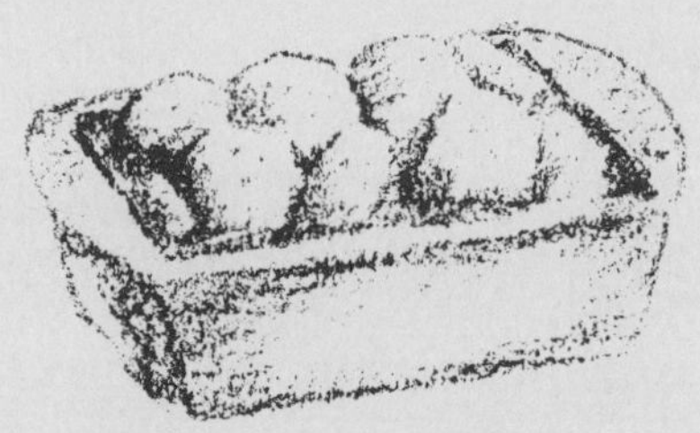

NETHERLANDS
SPLIT PEA SOUP (Erwtensoep)

Serves 8

I lived with a family from Holland years ago, this dish was on their menu at least twice a month.

- **1 pound green split peas**
- **2 large pigs feet, or ham hock**
- **1/2 pound salt pork, rind removed**
- **1 1/2 pounds potatoes, peeled and chopped**
- **2 carrots, finely chopped**
- **4 large leeks**
- **1 medium celery root, peeled and chopped**
- **2 celery stalks, leaves of**
- **2 Knorr Bouillon cubes, beef flavored**
- **1/2 pound Kielbasa, sliced**
- **1/2 teaspoon fresh savory**
- **1/2 teaspoon fresh thyme**
- **1/4 teaspoon pepper, freshly ground**

- Combine peas, pigs feet, salt pork and 4 quarts water in large soup pot. Bring to boil over high heat, skimming off any foam. Reduce heat and keep skimming. Simmer for 3 hours. Skim again. Add chopped potatoes, carrots, leeks, celery root and celery leaves, and simmer for 30 minutes more.
- Remove pork and pigs feet from soup pot. Remove all skin and bones, and cut meat into small cubes. Add 2 bouillon cubes, stir to dissolve. Return meat with sliced sausage to pot. Season with savory, thyme, pepper and cook for 10 minutes or until sausage is warm.

NORWAY
RIKKA'S FISH CAKES

Serves 6

Thanks to the Roy Otness family in Petersburg you can now enjoy one of the most popular standby dishes served in Norway.

- **5 cups fresh halibut**
- **4 tablespoons cornstarch**
- **3 cups ice cold fish stock**
- **1/4 teaspoon mace or nutmeg**
- **2 teaspoon pepper**
- **2 teaspoons onion powder**
- **2 eggs**
- **2 teaspoons salt**
- **Oil and butter for frying**

- Make fish stock and keep very cold. In a pinch, Knorr's Seafood Bouillon works fine for this.
- Grind halibut very thoroughly at least 3 times in meat grinder.
- Be sure fish is ice cold. Beat fish in mixer for 10 minutes. Add cornstarch and beat 5 minutes more. Pour stock in slowly, while beating hard. Add mace, pepper, onion powder and eggs. Lastly, add salt. Beat really hard. The salt makes the mixture come together. Use cold water on hands to form balls. Fry fish cakes in hot fat consisting of half vegetable oil and half butter. Fry until light brown, turning once. Serve warm.

POLAND
SAUEREKRAUT SALAD
(Surowska z Kiszonej Kapusty)

Serves 6

1/4	**cup vegetable oil**	**1**	**pound fresh sauerkraut**
1	**teaspoon caraway seeds**	**1**	**tart Granny Smith apple, shredded**
1	**teaspoon sugar**	**2**	**carrots, coarsely grated**
1/2	**teaspoon salt**		

- Combine oil, caraway seeds, sugar and salt. Stir to dissolve salt and sugar. Drain sauerkraut and wash under running water. Let soak in fresh water for 15 minutes. Drain and squeeze completely dry, chop into fine pieces.
- Combine sauerkraut, apple and carrots with oil mixture and blend well. Refrigerate until serving time.

RUSSIA
KULICH (Easter Bread)

Makes 3 loaves

We never celebrate Easter without my sister-in-law, Donna, making this bread. We enjoy it even better toasted.

1	**yeast cake**	**2**	**eggs, beaten**
2 1/2	**cups milk**	**1/2**	**cup raisins**
1	**cup sugar**	**3**	**yolks, beaten**
1/3	**cup butter**	**1/2**	**cup almonds**
1/3	**teaspoon salt**	**1**	**teaspoon lemon extract**
8	**cups flour**		

- Soften yeast in 1/3 cup milk. Scald remaining milk. Add butter, salt and sugar to milk, cool until tepid. Blend yeast mixture with half of flour. Set aside and let rest for 2 hours.
- Add beaten eggs, yolks, raisins, almonds, lemon extract and the remaining flour, knead really well. Set aside and let rise until double in bulk.
- Divide dough into 3 parts. Grease three 1 pound coffee cans. Fill cans 1/3 to 1/2 full. Bake at 350 degrees for 40 minutes or longer. Glaze bread with powdered sugar icing.
- Decorate each with a candied cherry.

SWEDEN

SWEDISH PANCAKES (Tunna Pannkagor)

Serves 6

Almost like delicate crepes. Serve them with lingonberry preserves.

1/2 cup flour
1 tablespoon sugar
1/2 teaspoon salt
2 eggs, slightly beaten
1 cup Half-and-Half
2 1/2 tablespoons water
Melted butter, for frying
Powdered sugar, for topping
Lingonberry preserves or jam

- Mix flour, sugar and salt in bowl. Beat eggs with cream and water. Combine the two mixtures.
- Melt butter, do not brown. Pour enough batter into omelet pan to cover bottom, about 3 tablespoons. When pancake is dry on top run a long-bladed spatula under it and turn to brown on other side.
- Remove pancake from pan and continue with the remaining batter. Dust each pancake with powdered sugar and keep warm in oven.
- Roll each cake and arrange on heated platter.
- Serve with the traditional lingonberry preserves.

THAILAND
PEPPERY PORK

Serves 4

This is best if cooked in a wok or electric frying pan so the heat can be controlled.

- **1 pound lean pork**
- **1/2 cup peanut oil**
- **1 cup roasted peanuts**
- **1 teaspoon sesame oil**
- **2 cloves garlic, minced**
- **1 teaspoon ginger, grated**
- **2 red hot peppers, seeded and minced**
- **1 red bell pepper, strips**
- **1 green bell pepper, strips**
- **2 tablespoons hot chili sauce**
- **3 tablespoons sake**
- **1 tablespoon cornstarch**

- Cut pork into bite-size cubes. Set aside. Heat peanut oil to 350 degrees or medium high, and place peanuts in metal sieve in hot oil, turning until light brown and crisp. Remove peanuts, set aside. Fry pork in same oil at 400 degrees or high, for about 1 minute, stirring well. Remove and set aside.
- Add sesame oil to remaining oil. Add garlic and fresh ginger with the red hot peppers, and stir for 30 seconds. Add bell peppers, wok for 45 seconds. Add chili sauce, pork and peanuts, wok for 1 minute longer.
- Make paste of cornstarch and sake; pour over dish and turn to coat meat.

YUGOSLAVIA

STUFFED CABBAGE LEAVES (Sarmale)

Serves 6

This dish is called by several names. Among them are Sarmale, Sarmi or Sarma; most of us know it as Stuffed Cabbage Leaves. It originated in Yugoslavia and is still served in all the Balkan countries.

1 head cabbage
3 tablespoons butter
2 onions, chopped
1 clove garlic, minced
1 1/2 pounds lamb, ground
1 1/2 cups cooked rice
1/2 cup raisins
1 teaspoon salt
1/4 teaspoon pepper
1 egg, beaten
4 tablespoons parsley, chopped
1 cup tomato sauce or stewed tomatoes
5 tablespoons bread crumbs

- Remove 8 to 10 leaves from cabbage; cook these until tender in salted water. Or, if you like, cook the whole cabbage until tender and then remove leaves.
- In a large frying pan sauté onions, garlic and meat in butter until meat is browned. Add rice, raisins, salt and pepper. Blend well. Set aside to cool. Stir in egg and parsley. Spread mixture over leaves and roll up. Transfer to heatproof dish. Cover with tomato sauce.
- Bake in a 350 degree oven for 20 minutes.
- Sprinkle cabbage rolls with bread crumbs and set under broiler to brown crumbs.

In the Sauce Bowl

IN THE SAUCE BOWL

PARSLEY SAUCE

Makes 2 cups

Terrific served with pork dishes.

2 ounces butter
2 ounces flour
1 cup milk
1 cup Half-and-Half
1 tablespoon lemon juice
4 tablespoons parsley, chopped
Salt and pepper to taste

- In a medium saucepan melt butter, stir in the flour and cook for 2 minutes, stirring constantly without browning the roux. Remove from heat and gradually add milk and Half-and-Half, stirring until smooth. Return to heat and bring to a boil: never stop stirring. When sauce is thick, boil for another 2 minutes. Add lemon juice and parsley and season with salt and pepper.

RED PEPPER SAUCE FOR PASTA

Serves 2

A colorful festive looking dish.

6 tablespoons butter
1/2 green pepper, chopped
4 green onions, chopped
3 cloves garlic, minced
1/2 red pepper, chopped
3 small red hot peppers, minced
1/2 pound spaghetti
1 tablespoon oil
1/2 cup Parmesan cheese
3 tablespoons parsley, chopped
1/2 teaspoon salt
1/4 teaspoon pepper

- In a large skillet heat butter over medium heat. Sauté peppers, green onion, garlic and red peppers 2 minutes. Boil spaghetti in large pot with salt and 1 tablespoon oil for 8 minutes. Drain well.
- Add spaghetti to peppers in skillet, toss well. Add the cheese, parsley, salt and pepper. Serve immediately.

CUMBERLAND SAUCE

- 3 shallots, finely chopped
- 1 orange
- 1 lemon
- 1/2 teaspoon sugar
- 1/4 teaspoon cayenne pepper
- 5 tablespoons port wine
- 1 teaspoon Dijon mustard
- 6 tablespoons melted currant jelly

- Boil shallots in a little water for 3 minutes.
- Remove zest from both lemon and orange and cut into fine slivers. Boil in water for 10 minutes. Drain and combine with the drained shallots. Squeeze juice from half of lemon and from whole orange; add to zest. Blend in the port, mustard and currant jelly. Heat to desired temperature. Serve with boiled ham or roasted chicken.

DILL SAUCE

Makes 1/2 cup

A quick light sauce to serve with any seafood.

- 1 egg
- 2 lemons, juice of
- 2 tablespoons olive oil
- 2 tablespoons dill, chopped
- Salt and pepper to taste

- Combine all the ingredients in blender or food processor and process until thickened, about 3 minutes.

BLUEBERRY CUMBERLAND SAUCE

Makes 1 1/2 cups

- **1 cup blueberry jam**
- **3 tablespoons prepared mustard**
- **1 tablespoon onion, minced**
- **2 tablespoons orange rind**
- **1/2 cup orange juice**
- **2 tablespoons lemon juice**
- **1/2 cup port wine**
- **2 tablespoons cornstarch**

- Combine all the ingredients except port wine and cornstarch. Cook over low heat, stirring frequently, until jelly is melted. Mix wine and cornstarch, and stir into jelly mixture. Cook over low heat until sauce thickens.
- Serve with any meat, poultry or ham.

MINT SAUCE FOR LAMB

- **1 cup white wine vinegar**
- **1/4 cup sugar**
- **Pinch of salt**
- **Pinch of pepper**
- **1/4 cup fresh mint, minced**

- Mix all the ingredients and bring to a boil. Let simmer for a few minutes.
- Pour over sliced lamb.

SPINACH PESTO SAUCE

Makes 2 1/2 cups

Serve over steaming Fettuccini. Top with some Romano cheese, a handful of walnuts and you have a great meal.

- **2 1/2 cups fresh spinach**
- **2 1/2 cups fresh basil**
- **5 cloves garlic**
- **1/4 cup olive oil**
- **3/4 cup walnut oil**
- **2 cups Parmesan cheese**
- **1 lemon, juice of**
- **Salt and fresh ground pepper to taste**

- Place garlic, spinach and basil in food processor with steel blade and process to a pulp. With motor running add olive oil, walnut oil and Parmesan cheese. Process until blended.
- Add lemon juice, salt and pepper.

SOUR CREAM SAUCE

Serves 6

- **2** **cups sour cream**
- **1/2** **cup vermouth**
- **1/4** **teaspoon salt**
- **1/2** **teaspoon dried dill, or 1 tablespoon fresh**
- **6** **tablespoons lime or lemon juice**
- **Dash of pepper**

• Mix all ingredients well. Store in refrigerator until serving time.

REFRESHING CUCUMBER SAUCE

This sauce is especially good with seafood recipes.

- **3** **cucumbers, peeled**
- **2** **teaspoons salt**
- **1** **cup sour cream**
- **1** **tablespoon fresh dill**

• Peel and split cucumbers and remove seeds. Finely chop; sprinkle with salt; set aside for at least 2 hours in refrigerator. Drain well and mix with sour cream and dill.

TERRIFIC TERIYAKI STEAK SAUCE

Makes 2 1/4 cups

Use this marinade on your favorite steak. Reserve any leftover for later use. This will keep in your refrigerator for several months.

- **1 1/4** **cups brown sugar, packed**
- **1** **cup soy sauce**
- **1** **1/4-inch piece ginger, freshly grated**
- **1** **clove garlic, minced**
- **1/4** **teaspoon sesame oil**

• Pour this mixture over your steaks and refrigerate for 3 to 4 hours.

• Grill, barbecue or broil steaks to your liking.

COPENHAGEN SUNSHINE SAUCE

Makes 1 cup

Tasty on top of fresh green beans, cauliflower and other cooked vegetables.

3 tablespoons butter
1 teaspoon curry powder
2 tablespoons flour
1 cup Half-and-Half
6 tablespoons water
1 Maggi bouillon cube, chicken flavored
1 tablespoon white vine vinegar
1 teaspoon French's mustard
Pinch turmeric
1/4 teaspoon white pepper
Salt to taste

- Melt butter with curry. Blend in flour. Add Half-and-Half a little at a time, keep stirring. Add water and Maggi cube, blend well. Let simmer for 5 minutes so flavors will blend. Add vinegar, mustard, turmeric, salt and pepper. Simmer 3 minutes.
- This sauce is also good on sliced ham.

SAUCE DIABLO

Makes 3/4 cup

Good served on any meat or seafood dish.

2 tablespoons butter
1 tablespoon oil
1 medium onion, chopped
2 tablespoons flour
1/2 cup water
2 small Maggi cubes, any flavor
1 teaspoon paprika
1/4 teaspoon cayenne pepper
1 teaspoon vinegar
1 tablespoon parsley, chopped

- Melt butter and oil and sauté onions until limp. In a jar, blend flour and a couple of tablespoons of water, shake well; add to onion mixture. Stir to blend. Dissolve Maggi cubes in remaining water, and add to mixture. Bring to a boil. Add paprika, cayenne pepper and vinegar. Lower heat and let simmer 5 minutes.
- Finally fold in the parsley.

MINT BÉARNAISE SAUCE

Makes 3/4 cup

2 tablespoons shallots, finely chopped
2 tablespoons white wine vinegar
3 tablespoons fresh mint leaves
1/2 cup butter
1 large egg
2 teaspoons lime juice

- Combine shallots, vinegar and mint in small sauce pan and place over medium heat. Simmer until most of liquid has evaporated, about 1 tablespoon left. Reduce temperature to the lowest setting. Add butter and continue to heat until butter is melted.
- Combine egg and lime juice in food processor or blender. With motor running, add warm butter mixture in a slow steady stream. Sauce will thicken.
- Serve at room temperature.

BASIC TARTAR SAUCE

Makes 1 1/2 cups

This is always on our table when serving seafood. Even if you don't care for tartar sauce, this one you will like.

1 egg yolk
1 tablespoon fresh lemon juice
1 teaspoon tarragon vinegar
1 teaspoon Dijon mustard
1 cup mayonnaise
1 teaspoon paprika
1 teaspoon green onion, chopped
1 tablespoon capers, drained and chopped
2 tablespoons parsley, chopped
1/2 teaspoon salt
Pinch white pepper

- Blend all the ingredients and refrigerate with cover until ready to serve.

COLD BÉARNAISE SAUCE

Use the Béarnaise Essence in this book or purchase a bottle in the gourmet department of your local supermarket.

- **2 egg yolks**
- **1/4 teaspoon salt**
- **1 teaspoon onion powder**
- **1 tablespoon salad oil**
- **1/4 pound butter, melted**
- **1 tablespoon Béarnaise Essence**
- **1 teaspoon parsley, chopped**

- Place yolks, salt and onion powder in food processor or bowl and beat, adding oil very slowly. When mixture has thickened, add the melted butter one tablespoon at a time and continue beating until all butter is used.
- Add Béarnaise Essence and chopped parsley.
- Keep in refrigerator until needed.

REMOULADE SAUCE

This is one of my favorite seafood sauces, and very easy to prepare.

- **1 cup mayonnaise**
- **3 tablespoons piccalilli**
- **3 tablespoons parsley, chopped**

- Simply mix well and let flavors blend. Use on top of fillets of fish, on fish burgers, or as a condiment for any poached fish.

HOMEMADE MAYONNAISE

Makes 2 1/4 cups

My mother-in-law made this mayonnaise for her children for years. I have copied the recipe down, word for word. For some reason or other it never quite comes out the same. Could it be that you must live in Virginia to obtain the same taste?

- **1 egg**
- **2 egg yolks**
- **3/4 teaspoon salt**
- **1/4 teaspoon white pepper**
- **1/4 teaspoon dry mustard**
- **1 cup olive oil**
- **1 cup salad oil**
- **2 tablespoons white wine vinegar, or lemon juice**

- This can be prepared in a blender or a mixer, or in my case the food processor.
- Break into the blender or food processor the egg and egg yolks; add salt, pepper and mustard. With the motor running add the oils and vinegar very slowly. Once in awhile scrape the oil from sides into mixture. Keep mixing until it is stiff and all oil has been used.
- Store in refrigerator.

MOCK TARTAR SAUCE

I serve this with seafood when in a hurry.

- **1 cup mayonnaise**
- **1 tablespoon soy sauce**

- Mix and serve with any white fish.

The Pasta Party

THE PASTA PARTY

RICE

SPINACH PESTO AND PASTA

Serves 6-8

Another delightful way of utilizing fresh produce. The sauce freezes well; just pour a thin layer of olive oil on top and it will last for months.

SPINACH PESTO:

2 1/2 cups fresh spinach
2 1/2 cups fresh basil
3/4 cup walnut oil
3/4 cup olive oil
1 lemon, juice of
5 cloves garlic, minced
1 3/4 cups Parmesan cheese, grated
Salt and freshly ground pepper, to taste

- Place spinach and basil in blender or food processor and chop to a pulp. With machine running, drizzle walnut and olive oil over. Add lemon juice, garlic and cheese. Process until blended. Add salt and pepper. Serve over hot pasta.
- Makes 2 cups sauce.

PASTA:

2 pounds pasta
1 yellow pepper, diced
1/2 red pepper, diced
1 cup walnuts, chopped

- Cook pasta; drain in colander. Rinse with cool water and place in a large bowl. Combine pasta with 1 cup Spinach Pesto, yellow and red peppers and walnuts. Toss gently with pasta. Serve immediately.

PETERSBURG PANCIT

Serves 4

A touch of Phillipine flavor from Delilah in Petersburg, Alaska.

4 lean pork chops
1 tablespoon oil
1 clove garlic, minced
1 small onion
2 carrots, cut into strips
1 cup cabbage, thinly sliced
1/2 cup chicken broth
Dash msg
1/2 pound shrimp, cooked
Salt and pepper to taste
4 tablespoons soy sauce
3 cups Chinese noodles

- Cut pork chops into bite size-pieces. Brown well in oil. Add garlic and onion and saute' until limp. Add carrots, cabbage and broth; sprinkle with msg and let simmer 5 minutes.
- Stir shrimp in gently, so that they remain whole.
- Add salt and pepper, sprinkle with soy sauce.
- Cook Chinese noodles according to package directions.
- Toss noodles together with meat and vegetables.

WALNUT-SPINACH AND MARUZZE PASTA

Serves 4-6

WALNUT AND SPINACH PESTO:

- **2 cups fresh spinach leaves**
- **2 tablespoons dried basil**
- **1/2 cup walnuts, chopped**
- **3 cloves garlic, minced**
- **3/4 cup olive oil**
- **1/4 cup walnut oil**
- **1/2 teaspoon salt**
- **2 tablespoons fresh lemon juice**
- **1/2 cup Parmesan cheese**
- **1/4 cup Romano cheese**

PASTA:

- **1 1/2 pounds Maruzze (seashell pasta)**
- **2 tablespoons olive oil**
- **1/4 teaspoon salt**

- Using a food processor to grind spinach, basil, nuts and garlic makes this easy.
- Add olive oil and walnut oil in a slow stream. Blend in salt and lemon juice. Finally, add cheeses and blend until smooth.
- Cook pasta shells in large pot of rapidly boiling water with salt and a little olive oil until tender, but still firm to the bite. Drain and transfer to serving bowl. Toss with Walnut and Spinach Pesto to coat.
- This is also good with small, precooked shrimp, blanched broccoli and cubed zucchini.

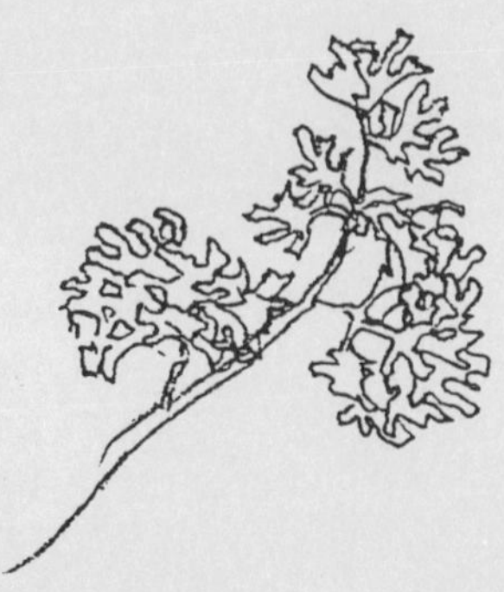

CHINESE SESAME PASTA

Serves 8

I like using the fine, thin Chinese egg noodles.

SESAME MAYONNAISE:

1	**egg**	**3**	**tablespoons Dijon mustard**
2	**yolks**	**1/4**	**cup sesame oil**
2 1/2	**tablespoons rice vinegar**	**2 1/2**	**cups vegetable oil**
2 1/2	**tablespoons soy sauce**		

- In blender or food processor, make mayonnaise by adding egg and yolks with vinegar, soy sauce and mustard. Slowly pour in the oils and blend until thick.

SAUCE FOR PASTA:

8	**green onions, chopped**	**1/4**	**cup peanut oil**
2	**cups Chinese snow peas**	**1/2**	**cup chopped cashew nuts**
2	**cups Sesame Mayonnaise**	**3**	**pounds thin pasta**
2	**dashes hot Szechwan pepper oil**		

- Sauté onions and snow peas in peanut oil for a few minutes. Add mayonnaise and Szechwan oil, stir to blend well. Fold in nuts. Pour over cooked pasta and serve immediately.
- Keep remaining sauce in refrigerator, or freeze.

PASTA SHELLS WITH PARSLEY PESTO

Serves 8

PARSLEY PESTO:

- **4 large cloves garlic, minced**
- **2 cups fresh parsley, chopped**
- **1 cup fresh basil, chopped**
- **2 cups olive oil**
- **Salt and pepper to taste**
- **1 cup walnuts, chopped**
- **1/2 cup Romano cheese**
- **1/2 cup Parmesan cheese**

- Chop garlic, parsley and basil in blender or food processor. Pour in olive oil, salt and pepper and blend until smooth. Fold in nuts and cheeses.

PASTA:

- **2 pounds pasta shells**
- **1/2 teaspoon salt**
- **1 teaspoon olive oil**

- Cook pasta just until tender in a large pot of water with salt and oil added.
- Pour 1 1/2 cup Parsley Pesto over cooked pasta shells and serve immediately. Refrigerate or freeze remaining pesto sauce.
- Makes 2 1/4 cups sauce.

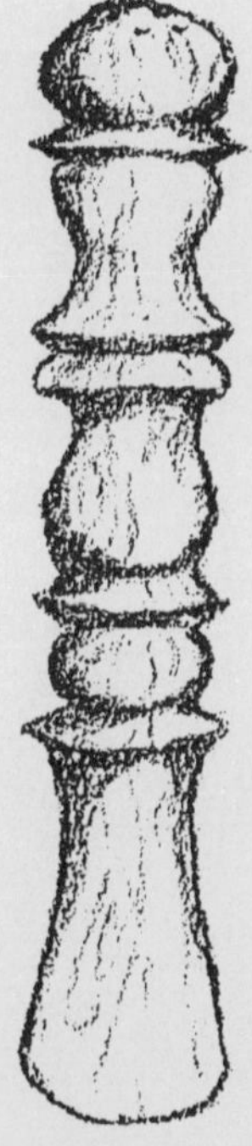

SPINACH PASTA

Serves 2-3

Just as pretty to look at as it is delicious to eat.

1/2 pound fresh spinach pasta
1/2 teaspoon salt
1/3 cup olive oil
3 cloves garlic
1/2 cup ham, chopped
1/2 cup parsley, chopped
2 tablespoons pimento, chopped
1/2 cup Parmesan cheese
1/4 teaspoon pepper

- Boil pasta for 4-5 minutes in a large pot of water; add a little salt if desired and 1 tablespoon of oil to prevent it from sticking. Drain well. Heat remaining oil in skillet; cook garlic until golden, about 3 minutes. Add ham, parsley and pimento and toss. Finally add cheese and pepper; toss to coat.
- Pour over cooked pasta.

ANGEL'S HAIR WITH CHERVIL SAUCE

Serves 6

6 cloves garlic, minced
5 cups fresh chervil leaves, minced
1 cup fresh basil, minced
2 lemons, juice of
3/4 cup olive oil
Salt and pepper to taste
3/4 cup Romano cheese, shredded
1/2 cup pistachio nuts
2 pounds Angel's Hair Pasta

- Using a food processor or blender, chop garlic, chervil and basil with lemon juice until smooth. Add olive oil, salt and pepper. Fold in the Romano cheese and pistachio nuts.
- Bring a large pot of water with a little salt to a boil and cook pasta just until tender. Drain pasta and add sauce.
- Serve immediately.
- Pass extra cheese at the table.

LORETO RICE RING

Serves 8

Thanks to Joanne Schiel, who showed us this way to use left-over rice. A tasty dish served with any Mexican or Alaskan caught fish.

2 1/2 cups cooked rice
1 pound shredded Jack cheese
6 green onions, chopped
1 can green chilies, chopped
1/2 to 3/4 cup sour cream

- Mix all the ingredients and fold into a greased aspic mold. Bake in a 350 degree oven for 45 minutes. Remove from mold and serve while hot.

LUMACHE PASTA WITH GORGONZOLA CHEESE

Serves 4

1/4 pound Gorgonzola cheese, shredded
2 tablespoons olive oil
1/4 cup heavy cream
1/2 teaspoon fresh ground pepper
1 teaspoon fresh basil, chopped
1 pound Lumache Pasta, (small snails)
1/2 teaspoon salt
1/4 cup walnuts, chopped

- Sauté cheese in olive oil; add heavy cream, pepper and basil. Cook pasta in large pot of boiling salted water. Drain, and toss sauce over. Sprinkle with walnuts.

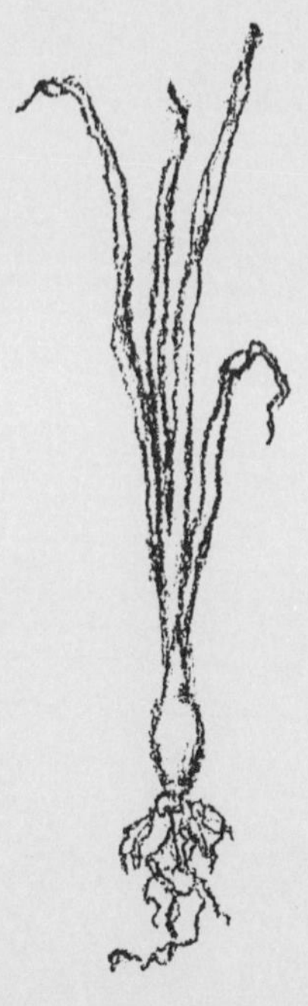

PASTA WITH FILBERT PESTO AND CHÈRVE

Serves 4-6

This has such unusual ingredients; the combination of flavors can't be described. A must to try.

FILBERT PESTO:

1/4 cup filberts, crushed
4 cloves garlic, minced
1 cup fresh basil leaves
1 cup good quality olive oil
1 tablespoon lemon juice
Salt to taste
1 tablespoon green peppercorns in brine, drained
3/4 cup Parmesan cheese

PASTA:

1 1/2 pounds spinach pasta

TOPPINGS:

1 cup imported Greek olives, pitted, in chunks
6 ounces chèvre, (goat cheese) crumbled
2 tablespoons filberts, coarsely chopped

- Use a food processor or a blender to chop nuts, garlic and basil and blend until smooth. Add olive oil and lemon juice. Season with salt and green peppercorns. Fold in the Parmesan cheese.
- Cook pasta until tender. Drain and top with olives, chèvre and nuts.

FETTUCCINI IN BELL PEPPER SAUCE

Serves 4

2 red bell peppers
1 cup fresh peas
2 tablespoons butter
3 green onions, sliced
1/2 cup cooked ham, in chunks
1 cup heavy cream
1/2 cup Parmesan, grated
Salt and pepper to taste
1 1/2 pounds fresh Fettuccini

- Roast bell peppers over flame, under a broiler or in the oven until skin is blackened. Remove skin under cold running water. Core peppers and slice into strips.
- Bring water with a few dashes of salt to a boil. Add peas, return to boil and immediately remove from heat; set aside for 5 minutes. In 2 tablespoons of melted butter, sauté green onions until limp. Add cooked peas, ham and roasted peppers. Blend in the cream. Add cheese and stir gently. Season with salt and pepper. Keep warm.
- Bring water to a boil in large saucepan and cook pasta until tender but still firm, about 4-5 minutes.
- Pour sauce over pasta and serve immediately.

SPICY SPAGHETTI DINNER

Serves 2

A colorful festive looking dish.

6	**tablespoons butter**
1/2	**green pepper, chopped**
4	**green onions, chopped**
3	**cloves garlic, minced**
1/2	**red pepper, chopped**
3	**small red hot peppers, minced**
1/2	**pound spaghetti**
1	**tablespoon oil**
1/2	**cup Parmesan cheese**
3	**tablespoons parsley, chopped**
1/2	**teaspoon salt**
1/4	**teaspoon pepper**

- In a large skillet heat butter over medium heat. Sauté peppers, green onion, garlic and red peppers 2 minutes. Boil spaghetti in large pot with salt and oil for 8 minutes. Drain well.
- Add spaghetti to peppers in skillet, toss well. Add the cheese, parsley, salt and pepper. Serve immediately.

CARBONARA

Serves 3-4

This classic Italian dish needs only a glass of good red wine and a loaf of French Bread. Given to us by the Hamilton's in New York City.

1/2	**pound bacon, crisp, crumbled**
1/2	**teaspoon salt**
4	**tablespoons olive oil**
1	**pound Linguini pasta**
2	**eggs**
1/2	**cup Parmesan cheese**
1/2	**cup parsley, chopped**
3	**tablespoons pine nuts**

- Fry bacon until crisp, set aside.
- In a large pot, boil water with salt and 1 tablespoon olive oil. Add pasta and cook for 3 minutes if using fresh, or follow package directions. Drain pasta and return it to pot. Add eggs and cheese, stirring vigorously to coat; the eggs makes the cheese cling to pasta.
- Add parsley and pine nuts, toss with the remaining olive oil, bacon and Parmesan cheese. Serve immediately.

FUSILLI PASTA AND STRAW MUSHROOMS

Serves 4

The Fusilli pasta, a small spiral pasta, comes in spinach flavor also. This is a hearty one-dish-meal.

MINT PESTO SAUCE:

3	**cloves garlic**	**1/2**	**cup lemon juice**
1 1/2	**cups mint leaves**	**1/2**	**cup Parmesan cheese**
1/4	**cup olive oil**	**1/4**	**cup pine nuts**
1/4	**cup basil oil**		**Salt and pepper to taste**

- Chop garlic and mint leaves with both oils and lemon juice in blender or food processor, using the on/off method. Add Parmesan cheese, pine nuts, salt and pepper. Store in refrigerator until serving time. This also freezes well.

4	**asparagus spears, cut in chunks**	**1**	**cup straw mushrooms***
1	**cup broccoli flowerets**	**2**	**cups cooked, cubed chicken breast**
1	**pound Fusilli pasta**		**Parmesan cheese**
1/4	**cup Spanish olives, chopped**		

- Cook asparagus and broccoli until tender. Drain and cool.
- Boil pasta according to directions. Toss with asparagus and broccoli, straw mushrooms, chicken chunks and Mint Pesto Sauce.
- Top with chopped olives. Pass additional Parmesan cheese.

* *Can be found in the gourmet section in most stores.*

KAM YEN JAN RICE AND PEAS

Serves 6-8

The flavor of Chinese sausage turns this rice dish into something spectacular.

- 2 cups rice
- 2 cups water
- 2 cups chicken broth
- 1/4 teaspoon Wy Hsiang Fun, Chinese Five Spice
- 1 tablespoon butter
- 1 teaspoon salt
- 1/2 pound Kam Yen Jan sausage
- 1 cup frozen peas, thawed

- Wash rice several times in cold water until water becomes clear. Soak rice for 30 minutes in 2 cups of water. Add broth, Chinese Five Spice, butter, salt, and sausage. Bring to a boil. Lower temperature and simmer for 30 minutes.
- When done, add peas. Keep lid on for 5 minutes to warm peas.

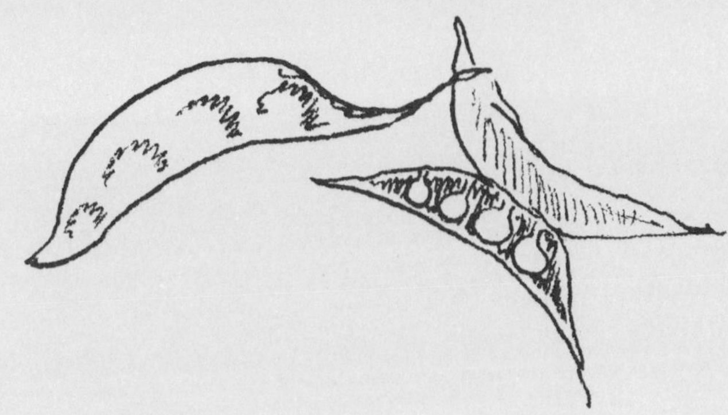

GREEN RICE CASSEROLE

Serves 6-8

- 1/2 teaspoon garlic, minced
- 2 tablespoons green onions, chopped
- 2 tablespoons butter
- 2 cups cooked rice
- 1/2 cup parsley, chopped
- 1/2 cup green olives, chopped
- 1 1/4 cups milk
- 2 eggs, beaten
- 1 cup sharp Cheddar cheese, grated

- Sauté garlic and onions in butter. Add rice, parsley, olives and milk. Blend in beaten eggs and cheese.
- Pour into buttered casserole and bake for 40 minutes at 350 degrees or until firm.

Off the Pastry Cart

OFF THE PASTRY CART

CAKES

PASTRYS

PIES

COOKIES

DESSERTS

CARROT CAKE WITH ORANGE FROSTING

Serves 6-8

Our good friend Brenda McGowan, permitted me to use this terrific cake recipe. Very nice, spicy and moist.

2 1/2 cups sifted flour
1 teaspoon baking soda
1 teaspoon baking powder
1 teaspoon salt
1 teaspoon fresh nutmeg, grated
1 teaspoon cinnamon
1 cup butter
1 1/2 cups sugar
4 eggs
1 1/2 cups carrots, shredded
2 teaspoons orange peel, grated
1 cup buttermilk
1/2 cup walnuts
1/2 cup raisins

- In a bowl combine fist six dry ingredients. Cream butter well, add sugar until smooth, blend in eggs, one at a time. Mix all the dry ingredients into this. Add carrots, orange peel and buttermilk. Finally stir in the walnuts and raisins. Grease a 13 x 9 x 2-inch. pan. Fold mixture into pan. Bake in a 350 degrees oven for 45 minutes to 1 hour. Cool on wire rack, frost with Orange Frosting.

ORANGE FROSTING:

Makes about 4 1/2 cups

1 8-ounce package cream cheese, softened
4 teaspoons cream
2 teaspoons vanilla
1 pound powder sugar
1 orange, peel of, grated

- Combine the cream cheese, cream and vanilla. Beat until smooth. Add sugar gradually and keep beating until light and fluffy. Fold in orange peel.

CLASSIC DANISH APPLE CAKE

Serves 8

This is not nearly as complicated as it might seem. This is often served at birthday parties in Denmark. It's not too sweet and it looks pretty with the currant jelly glaze.

1/2	**tablespoon butter**
3	**pounds cooking apples**
1/4	**cup water**
2/3	**cup sugar**
1	**orange, juice and rind of**
1	**teaspoon vanilla**
2	**cups fine bread crumbs**
1	**teaspoon cinnamon**
1/4	**cup brown sugar**
2	**tablespoons butter**
1	**8-ounce jar raspberry jam**
1/2	**cup butter**

- Butter an 8-inch round baking pan, 3 inches deep. Preheat oven to 350 degrees. Remove rind and squeeze the juice from orange.
- Cook the apples in water with sugar, orange juice, rind and vanilla for about 20 minutes. Mash and set aside. Mix together crumbs, cinnamon and brown sugar. Melt 2 tablespoons butter in sauce pan and add crumb mixture, brown for a few minutes.
- Sprinkle some of the crumbs in the buttered cake pan, alternating with apple mixture and raspberry jam, until all used up, ending with crumbs.
- Press down firmly with spoon. Pour 1/2 cup melted butter on top. Bake for 40 minutes or until firm.
- Cool and unmold on serving platter.

GLAZE:

2/3	**cup currant jelly**
2	**tablespoons sherry**
	Heavy cream, whipped, for decoration

- Heat jelly and sherry in small sauce pan. Cook, stirring until jelly is melted. Cool slightly. Spread over entire cake. Decorate with whipping cream.
- This must be served cool but not directly from refrigerator.

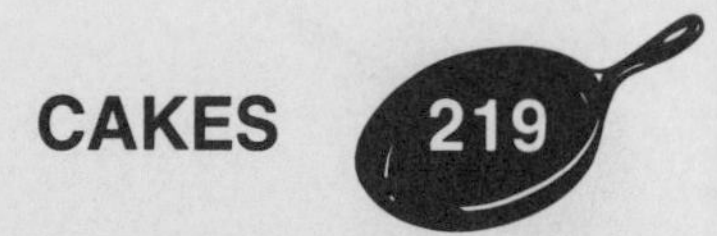

EVELYN'S CHEESECAKE

Serves 12

Rich with a wonderful full flavor of lemon juice and vanilla. Linda Andrews lent me a copy of this recipe, it's terrific.

CRUST:

- **1 package graham crackers**
- **3 tablespoons sugar**
- **1/2 stick margarine**

- Grind or crush crumbs well. Add margarine and sugar. Mix thoroughly. Press into bottom of a 10-inch, 2 1/2-inch deep springform pan. Set aside.

FILLING:

- **2 8-ounce packages cream cheese**
- **1 1/2 sticks margarine**
- **4 eggs**
- **1 1/2 cups sugar**
- **1 pound ricotta cheese**
- **2 tablespoons flour**
- **2 tablespoons cornstarch**
- **2 tablespoons vanilla**
- **2 tablespoons fresh lemon juice, or more**
- **1 pint sour cream**

- Combine eggs and sugar in mixing bowl; beat until lemon colored, light and fluffy. Set aside.
- Place cream cheese and margarine in saucepan. Melt over medium heat or low flame.
- Transfer the melted cream cheese mixture to large bowl. Slowly blend until margarine seems absorbed by cheese. Keep stirring until smooth. Add ricotta cheese and scrape sides of bowl to avoid any lumps. Combine this with the egg and sugar mixture, beat slowly at first, then increase speed and beat until smooth. Add flour and cornstarch, vanilla, lemon juice and sour cream to mixture, blending well after each addition.
- Pour into prepared crust.
- Bake at 325 degrees for 1 hour. After an hour, turn oven off and crack door open by placing a clothespin between door and oven. Let rest like that for 2 hours. Refrigerate without removing from pan until serving time, preferably 24 hours later.
- Serve with your favorite sauce.

CHEESE CAKE

Serves 12

Petersburg is a small town in Southeast Alaska, but it has the best cooks around. Arlene Otness once made and served this to her guests during the Norwegian Festival. On the 17th of May, people come to Petersburg from all over to join in the celebration. It is a weekend full of food, fun and many different events. The Kaffe Hus (Coffee House) serves the most delectable things. One of the best cheese cakes ever to pass your lips is this one.

CRUST:

2 cups graham crackers, finely crushed
2/3 cup butter, melted
1 cup pecans, chopped
2 tablespoons powder sugar

- Make the crust by combining everything.
- Press into a 15 x 10 x 1 1/2-inch pan. Bake for 10 minutes at 350 degrees.

FILLING:

2 8-ounce packages cream cheese
2 cups sugar
4 eggs

- Beat the cream cheese with sugar and eggs until nice and smooth. Fold into prepared crust. Bake 20 minutes at 350 degrees, cool.

TOPPING:

2 cups sugar
1 cup cold water
4 tablespoons cornstarch
2 tablespoons butter
2 tablespoons lemon juice
2 teaspoons lemon rind, grated
4 cups blueberries, or any favorite wild berries

- In sauce pan add the sugar, water, cornstarch, butter, lemon juice, lemon rind and 1 cup of the berries. Let this cook until thick. Carefully add the remaining 3 cups of blueberries, making sure not to crush them. Pour over the top of the cheese cake. Chill.
- Serve with freshly whipped cream or Cool Whip.

Note: Extra thickening is required if using frozen berries.

NORTH CAROLINA POUND CAKE

Makes 1 cake

From Laura Ann's files. This is moist and light. I believe it's the twice-sifted flour that makes it extra good.

2 1/2 sticks butter
3 cups sugar
6 eggs
3 cups flour, sifted twice
1 teaspoon baking powder
1/4 teaspoon salt
1 cup evaporated milk
1 teaspoon vanilla
1 teaspoon lemon extract

- Grease tube pan with butter and dust lightly with flour.
- Cream butter and sugar until light and fluffy. Add eggs one at a time, beating 1 minute after each addition. Combine flour, baking powder and salt. Combine milk with lemon extract and vanilla. Add dry ingredients and milk combination alternately to egg mixture, ending with flour mixture. Pour batter into pan and bake for 1 hour at 350 degrees. Allow cake to cool in pan for 10 minutes.
- Mrs. Brann said that she cools the cake in a covered Tupperware container, resulting in a very moist cake.

AUSTRALIAN FRUITCAKE

Makes 3 loaves

This is a most unusual fruitcake. It tastes even better toasted. It freezes well and is a nice change from the sticky kinds usually served.

1 1/2 cups whole Brazil nuts
1 1/2 cups walnuts, or pecans
1 cup dates, pitted, chopped
1 cup candied orange peel, chopped
1/2 cup candied red cherries
1/2 cup raisins
3 eggs
1 1/2 teaspoons salt
1 teaspoon vanilla
4 cups sifted flour
3/4 cup sugar

- Grease bottom and sides of 3 loaf pans. Mix all the fruit and nuts. Beat eggs lightly with salt and vanilla. Combine egg mixture with flour and sugar, blend thoroughly. Fill pans with fruit mixture, pressing down firmly. Pour the egg mixture over the fruit, it will barely cover fruit and nuts.
- Bake for 2 hours in a 300 degree oven. Keep an eye on the cakes to make sure they don't burn. Cover with foil if they get too dark.

CHEESE CAKE

Serves 8-10

Here is a copy of an old fashioned baked cheese cake. I borrowed this from Nancy Austin in Washington D.C.

4 8-ounce packages cream cheese
1 1/2 cups sugar
4 eggs
1/4 teaspoon salt
3/4 teaspoon vanilla
Graham cracker crumbs

- Beat cream cheese until soft. Add sugar and beat well. Add eggs one at a time. Beat until thick and lemon colored. Blend in salt and vanilla. Butter a souffle pan or spring form pan. Dust lightly with graham crumbs, and pour in cheese mixture. Place the pan inside another holding water that comes half way up the sides of spring form pan. Bake at 350 degrees for 2 hours. Cool. Invert on a platter to serve.

HEIRLOOM ALMOND TORTE WITH MERINGUE

Serves 6

Linda Andrews often enjoys making this torte from her mother's recipe files. It's one of those "light as a feather" desserts. The secret is the 3-times sifted flour.

1/2 cup butter
1/2 cup sugar
4 eggs, separated
1 1/3 cups cake flour, sifted three times
1 1/3 teaspoons baking powder
5 tablespoons milk
1/2 teaspoon almond flavoring
1/8 teaspoon cream of tartar
1 cup sugar
1/2 cup almond slivers
Heavy cream, whipped

- Cream butter and sugar until lemon-colored. Add one egg at a time and beat well. Sift flour with baking powder and add this to egg mixture alternating with milk and almond flavoring. Spread into two 9-inch greased pans.
- Whip egg whites until stiff. Add cream of tartar; beat sugar in slowly. Spread over cakes. Sprinkle almonds on top.
- Bake for 20 minutes in a 250 degree oven. Increase heat to 350 degrees and bake for another 20 minutes. Cool and serve with whipped cream.

TEA-TIME TASSIES

Makes 24

Delicate little "tassies" from the pantry of Violet Davis.

1 3-ounce package cream cheese
1/2 cup butter, softened
1 cup flour, sifted
1 egg
1 tablespoon butter, softened
3/4 cup brown sugar
1 teaspoon vanilla
Dash of salt
2/3 cup pecans, coarsely broken

CHEESE PASTRY:

- Let cheese and butter soften at room temperature. Cream together and blend in flour. Chill slightly. Shape into 24 1-inch size round balls. Place balls in ungreased 1 3/4-inch muffin tins. Press dough firmly to line cups. Set aside.

PECAN FILLING:

- Beat egg together with butter and brown sugar until smooth. Add vanilla and a dash of salt. Divide half of pecans among pastry-lined cups. Pour egg mixture over and top with remaining pecans.
- Bake for 25 minutes at 325 degrees.

EUROPEAN PEAR TART

Serves 8

One of many recipes sent from my family in Europe. This looks like it just came off a pastry cart.

PASTRY:

1/4 cup butter
2 tablespoons sugar
Dash of salt
1/2 teaspoon lemon peel, grated
1/2 teaspoon vanilla
1 egg yolk
3/4 cup flour
1/4 cup almonds, finely ground

FILLING:

4 tablespoons red currant jelly
1/2 cup flour
3 tablespoons sugar
1/4 cup butter
1/2 teaspoon lemon peel, grated
1/2 teaspoon vanilla
1 egg
3 ounces cream cheese
5 canned pear halves
1 cup fresh strawberries
Heavy cream, whipped

- Heat oven to 375 degrees.
- Combine all the ingredients for pastry and beat until light and fluffy.
- Roll into ball and press into bottom and up the sides of a 10-inch tart pan or a spring form pan.
- Bake for 10 minutes, then let cool.
- Brush 2 tablespoons of currant jelly on baked tart.
- In a medium bowl, combine flour, sugar, butter, lemon peel, vanilla, egg and cream cheese. Beat until light and soft. Pour filling over currant jelly. Arrange pear halves rounded side up, pointed end toward the center.
- Bake for 25 minutes or until center is set.
- Arrange strawberries between pear halves. In small sauce pan heat the remaining currant jelly over medium heat. Brush berries and pears with currant jelly mixture. Serve with a spoon-full of whipped cream.

DANISH MARZIPAN TART

Serves 8

A rich, flavorful dessert. The fruit gives it a wonderful balance between sweet and tart. Spoon a scoop of your favorite ice cream on top.

1 1/4 cups flour
1/4 teaspoon salt
5 tablespoons cold butter, cut into pieces
1 large egg, lightly beaten
1 7-ounce package Odense marzipan
7 small red plums, halved and pitted
4 apricots, halved and pitted
2 tablespoons butter, melted
1 tablespoon sugar
2 tablespoons almond slivers

- Using a 9 1/2-inch pan with a removable bottom makes this easier. Butter it lightly.
- In a medium-sized bowl, combine flour and salt. Cut in the cold butter until the mixture resembles fine bread crumbs. Stir in the egg; mix well and form into a ball.
- On a lightly floured board, roll out dough to form a roughly 13-inch circle. Gently press dough into bottom and sides of pan, cut off excess dough.
- Roll marzipan into a 9-inch circle and press it lightly on top of dough. Cut each fruit half into 3 wedges. Arrange wedges, skin-side down, in circles starting at the edge of the pan and working into the middle.
- Brush with melted butter; sprinkle with sugar and almonds. Place tart on cookie sheet and bake for 40 minutes at 400 degrees or until fruit is tender and tart is nicely browned.
- Unmold onto a flat dessert platter and cut like a pie.
- Top with ice cream or dollops of whipping cream.

SACHER TORTE

Serves 8

About 10 years ago, this torte was very popular in Europe. My mother sent me a magazine clipping with this outstanding dessert.

10 eggs, separated
1 cup sugar
2 tablespoons bread crumbs
2 cups pecans, ground
12 ounces semi-sweet chocolate
2 tablespoons hot, strong coffee

- Lightly grease three 9-inch cake pans. Beat yolks with half of sugar until lemon-colored and completely blended. Add crumbs and nuts. Set aside.
- Melt chocolate, stir in hot coffee, set aside to cool, then add to yolk mixture.
- In a separate bowl, whip egg whites until stiff; gradually add the remaining sugar. Fold whites into the yolk and chocolate mixture. Pour into pans and bake at 350 degrees for 35 minutes. Cool on wire racks.

FROSTING:

4 squares unsweetened chocolate
1/2 cup strong brewed coffee
1 cup sugar
2 yolks, beaten
1/2 cup butter, softened
1/2 cup apricot preserves

- Mix chocolate and coffee in saucepan. Heat until dissolved. Add sugar and cook until smooth, stirring frequently. Remove from heat, beat in yolks and butter, set aside to cool.
- Cover 2 layers of torte with apricot preserves, then with chocolate frosting. Place the third one on top. Cover entire cake with remaining frosting. When this dries, it's very shiny and glossy.

CRUNCH ICE CREAM PIE

Serves 8 chocolate lovers

Thanks to Donna Kurtti, we have enjoyed this many times.

1 cup semi-sweet chocolate morsels
1/4 cup butter
2 cups Kellogg's Rice Krispies cereal
1 tablespoon light corn syrup
1 quart coffee ice cream, slightly softened

- Melt chocolate and butter in double boiler, over hot but not boiling water, stirring until melted. Remove and reserve 3 tablespoons for later use.
- Add Rice Krispies to chocolate mixture, stir until well coated. Press evenly and firmly into pie pan to form crust. Add corn syrup to reserved chocolate mixture, blend well.
- Spread ice cream on top of crust. Drizzle with remaining chocolate.
- Freeze for 2 hours. Before serving, place pie pan on hot, wet towel for a few minutes and pie will lift right out.

BREN'S WALNUT PIE

Serves 8

1/3 teaspoon salt
1 cup dark brown sugar
1 cup white corn syrup
1 teaspoon vanilla
1/2 cup butter, melted
3 eggs
1 cup walnuts, chopped

- Combine salt, sugar, syrup and vanilla with butter. Add slightly beaten eggs. Pour into a 9-inch unbaked pie shell. Sprinkle walnuts over filling. Bake at 350 degrees for 55 minutes.

LEMON CHEESE PIE

Serves 12

The Page family is blessed with many great cooks. This one comes from Aunt Madge. It is truly a melt-in-your-mouth kind of pie.

9 eggs
3 cups sugar
1 1/2 sticks butter
5 lemons, juice of
1 teaspoon lemon rind
3 tablespoons white cornmeal
Egg whites for brushing shells

- Brush two deep dish pie shells with egg white. Cook for about 10 minutes before filling.
- Beat the eggs and the sugar together well. Add the remaining ingredients. Keep beating until light and smooth.
- Divide into two pie shells. Bake at 350 degrees for about 45 minutes or until set, but not dry.

SOUTHERN PECAN PIE

Serves 8

3 eggs
3/4 cup dark corn syrup
3/4 cup brown sugar
1/4 teaspoon salt
2 teaspoons vanilla
3 tablespoons butter, melted
1 1/4 cups pecan halves

- Beat eggs. Add the corn syrup, mix well. Add sugar and keep mixing. Stir in the salt and vanilla. Add the melted butter. Fold in the pecan halves. Pour into pie crust and bake at 375 degrees for 45 minutes. Serve with a dollop of whipping cream.

RHUBARB PIE

Serves 6

I have always thought rhubarb pies too tart. This one with a custard-type filling is different and very good. Cerena Cheek shared this recipe with me, along with others in this book.

- **3 eggs**
- **2 cups sugar**
- **1/4 cup flour**
- **3/4 teaspoon nutmeg**
- **4 tablespoons milk**
- **4 cups rhubarbs, cut into bite-size pieces**
- **2 tablespoons butter, for topping**
- **Pie Crust**

- Combine the first five ingredients, then add the rhubarb. Pour filling into a pie crust and dot with butter.
- Bake in a 400 degree oven for 55 minutes.

PIE CRUST

Makes 2 pie crusts

Making a really good pie crust is easy, but try making one that is the best-ever! My friend, Diane Howell let me submit this one.

- **3 cups flour**
- **2 teaspoons salt**
- **1/3 cup ice cold water**
- **1 egg**
- **1 tablespoon vinegar**
- **1 1/2 cups butter-flavored Crisco**

- Mix all the ingredients and form into a ball. Refrigerate for at least 1/2 hour, remove, and roll out.
- Bake crusts in two 8-inch pie pans for later use, or fill with your favorite filling. Bake according to the filling recipe.

RHUBARB AND STRAWBERRY PIE

Serves 8

- **3** **cups strawberries, cut up if fresh**
- **2** **cups rhubarb, cut into 1/2-inch pieces**
- **3/4** **cup sugar**
- **1/2** **cup brown sugar**
- **3** **tablespoons flour**
- **1/4** **teaspoon nutmeg**
- **1/4** **teaspoon cinnamon**
- **2** **eggs**
- **1** **tablespoon butter**
- **Pastry dough for double-crust 9-inch pie**
- **2** **tablespoons milk, to brush on top**
- **Heavy cream, whipped**

- Preheat oven to 400 degrees.
- In large bowl, combine strawberries and rhubarb. In another bowl, mix sugar, brown sugar, flour, nutmeg and cinnamon. Stir in eggs. Pour over fruit and blend well.
- Pour into pastry-lined pie pan. Dot with butter. Place second crust on top. Brush with milk. Bake at 400 degrees for 15 minutes. Lower temperature to 350 degrees and bake for another 45 minutes, or until pie is golden.
- Serve with unsweetened whipping cream.

DONNA'S PIE CRUST

Makes 2 crusts

This crunchy and crisp pie crust can be used for both desserts and quiche dishes.

- **2** **cups flour**
- **10** **tablespoons shortening**
- **1** **teaspoon salt**
- **1/3** **cup water**

- Measure flour into large bowl, add shortening and salt. Cut into mixture with pastry blender or two knives until pieces range from rice-size to navy bean-size. Sprinkle with cold water, whip quickly with fork. Separate and roll half of the mixture at a time, place other half in refrigerator while working. Try to work quickly, handling dough as little as possible; this will result in a flakier crust.
- Press into 2 9-inch pie pans. Use with your favorite filling.

JOE FROGGER'S COOKIES

Makes 3-4 dozen

The story of Joe Frogger was told to me by my friend Linda Andrews. She keeps a coffee can full of these great cookies during the summer when boating. The story goes:

Long ago in Marblehead, Massachusetts, an old Negro lived on the edge of a frog pond, on Gingerbread Hill. Fishermen would exchange a jug of rum for his cookies. The women packed the cookies in sea chests for the men to take to sea. "Uncle Joe" said that what kept the cookies soft was rum and sea water.

7 cups flour
1 tablespoon salt
1 tablespoon ground ginger
1 teaspoon ground cloves
1/2 teaspoon ground allspice
1 teaspoon grated nutmeg
3/4 cup water
1/4 cup rum
2 teaspoons baking soda
2 cups dark molasses
1 cup butter
2 cups sugar

- Sift flour with fist five spices, set aside. Combine water and rum. In a separate bowl, stir baking soda and molasses together. Cream butter and sugar in a mixer; add dry ingredients and beat well. Add rum and water, then fold in the molasses and soda mixture, blending well after each addition. Place in refrigerator overnight.
- Roll a portion of chilled dough into a 1/4-inch thickness on a floured board. Leave remaining dough in refrigerator until just before rolling. Use a 3-inch round cutter or tuna can to cut out cookies. Place on greased cookie sheet and bake at 375 degrees for 10 to 15 minutes. Let cookies rest on sheet for a minute or two after baking before removing them to prevent breaking.
- Store in airtight container with waxed paper between lid and cookies. These keep very well.

BUTTER-NUT COOKIES

Makes 2 1/2 dozen

1 cup flour
1/2 cup cornstarch
1/2 cup powdered sugar
1 1/2 sticks butter, room temperature
1/2 cup pecans, coarsely chopped

- Sift the first 3 ingredients into bowl. Add butter and mix well. Fold in pecans. Heat oven to 300 degrees. Drop cookies with a spoon onto baking sheet. Bake for 20 to 25 minutes or until golden brown.

LEMON BARS

Serves 8

My friend, Brenda McGowan, from Portland, and Loreto, shares these delicious treats with many people. All the ingredients are available in Loreto, so she makes them often. This has become one of our favorite things to have for dessert.

CRUST:

- 1 **cup butter**
- 1/2 **cup sifted powdered sugar**
- 1 3/4 **to 2 cups sifted flour**

FILLING:

- 4 **eggs**
- 2 **cups sugar**
- 1 **teaspoon baking powder**
- 1/4 **cup flour**
- 3 **tablespoons grated lemon peel**
- 1/4 **cup fresh lemon juice**

GLAZE:

- 2 **cups powdered sugar**
- 1/4 **cup fresh lemon juice**
- 1 **tablespoon grated lemon peel**

- To prepare the crust, beat the butter and powdered sugar until creamy. Stir in the flour until well blended. Spread evenly into well greased 13 x 9 x 2-inch baking pan. Bake in a moderate oven, 350 degrees for 15 minutes or until lightly browned.
- While crust is baking, prepare the filling. Beat eggs and sugar until light and fluffy. Stir in the baking powder, flour, lemon peel and lemon juice. Pour over hot crust. Return to oven for about 25-30 minutes, or until filling is set. Remove and cool for 10 minutes.
- Make the glaze by combining the sugar and lemon juice over low heat until sugar is completely dissolved. Add the lemon peel and spread over filling. Cool and cut into squares.

CRISPY LEMON COOKIES

Makes 8 dozen

- 1 **cup butter, softened**
- 1 1/2 **cups sugar**
- 4 **large egg yolks**
- 1 **lemon, juice of**
- 2 **teaspoons grated lemon rind**
- 1/4 **teaspoon lemon extract**
- 3 **cups flour**
- 1/2 **teaspoon salt**

- Cream butter and sugar until fluffy and lemon-colored. Add egg yolks, lemon juice, lemon rind and extract and continue beating until well-blended.
- Add flour and salt, just until blended. Roll dough in plastic wrap into 2 cylinders, each 2 inches in diameter. Chill overnight or at least for several hours.
- Slice cookies 1/8-inch thick; place on prepared sheet. Bake at 375 degrees for 8 to 10 minutes, or until lightly browned around edges. Cool on rack. Store in tightly sealed container.

TAMMY'S CHOCOLATE SQUARES

The recipe originated in Vermont, was given to me by Linda, and is liked by everyone on the DamnYankee.

- **2 squares unsweetened chocolate**
- **1/2 cup milk**
- **1 tablespoon butter**
- **1 cup sugar**
- **1 1/2 cups flour**
- **Pinch of salt**
- **1 teaspoon baking soda**
- **3 tablespoons boiling water**
- **1 teaspoon vanilla**

- Melt chocolate with milk and butter. Add sugar, flour and salt. Blend well. Combine baking soda with boiling water and add to mixture. Finally, add vanilla and stir well.
- Pour into greased jelly roll pan and bake for 10 minutes at 350 degrees.

FROSTING:

- **2 cups powdered sugar**
- **2 tablespoons butter**
- **1/2 teaspoon peppermint extract**
- **1 ounce unsweetened chocolate**

- Combine all the ingredients except chocolate, and frost cake.
- Melt chocolate with a little butter and drizzle on top.
- Cut into squares and enjoy!

VI'S BROWNIES

Makes 1 dozen

Not only the easiest, but also the best you will ever taste.

- **3 squares unsweetened chocolate**
- **2 eggs**
- **1 cup sugar**
- **1/4 pound butter**
- **1 cup flour**
- **1/2 teaspoon baking powder**
- **1 cup of your favorite nuts, chopped**

- Melt chocolate in double boiler, set aside.
- Beat eggs with sugar until light and fluffy. Add butter, flour and baking powder, mix well. Fold in the nuts and melted chocolate.
- Grease one 8-inch pan with a little butter. Pour mixture into pan.
- Bake at 350 degrees for 12 to 15 minutes.

CHOCOLATE TORTE WITH CHANTILLY CREAM

Serves 8

This dessert is very elegant looking when served.

TORTE:

1 1/2	**stick butter**	**1**	**cup sugar**
9	**ounces bittersweet chocolate, finely chopped**	**1/4**	**cup flour**
6	**eggs, separated**	**2**	**tablespoons powder sugar**
		1/4	**teaspoon salt**

- Butter a 9-inch round pan and dust with flour. Melt butter and chopped chocolate in double boiler over simmering water. In a separate bowl, whip yolks with 3/4 cup of sugar. Gradually stir in flour. Add the melted butter and chocolate mixture; blend well.
- Whip egg whites with salt and remaining sugar until peaks form. Fold whites into chocolate mixture. Pour batter into buttered cake pan. Bake at 325 degrees for 30 to 40 minutes or until cake is moist, but not at all runny.
- Cool and turn out onto platter. Cut into 1/2-inch slices.

CHANTILLY CREAM

1	**cup heavy cream, well chilled**	**1/2**	**teaspoon vanilla extract**
1 1/2	**teaspoons superfine sugar**		**Pinch of salt**

- Blend all the ingredients together and whip to soft peaks.
- Spoon onto dessert plates and top each with a slice of Chocolate Torte. Shake powdered sugar on top.

DESIGNER DESSERT

Serves 8

From a television show! This is rich, rich, rich.

- **3 pounds melted semi-sweet chocolate**
- **6 egg yolks**
- **2 tablespoons sugar**
- **1/2 pound butter, room temperature**
- **2 drops vanilla**
- **2 drops peppermint extract**
- **1/4 cup dark rum**
- **2 cups heavy cream**
- **Your favorite pound cake**

- Melt chocolate in a double boiler. Beat egg yolks and sugar until stiff and lemon-colored. Add butter, vanilla, peppermint extract and rum, beating after each addition. Combine this with chocolate and cool to room temperature.
- In a separate bowl, whip cream until stiff, then fold them into the cooled chocolate mixture. Pour into lightly butter-greased loaf pan. Refrigerate until set. Unmold and slice.
- Slice pound cake. Arrange alternately with chocolate loaf on dessert plates. Decorate with fresh raspberries, and a fresh mint leaf, if available.

PERFECT POACHED PEACHES

Serves 8

A refreshing ending to any meal.

6 cups water
1 cup sugar
2 teaspoons rum extract
8 medium peaches, peeled

- Combine water, sugar and rum extract in large saucepan. Bring to a boil. Add peaches, lower heat and let simmer for 10 minutes, basting several times.
- Remove peaches from syrup and refrigerate.

CUSTARD SAUCE:

1/4 cup sugar
1/4 teaspoon salt
1 tablespoon cornstarch
2 cups milk
2 egg yolks
1 teaspoon rum extract
Mint leaves

- In a heavy saucepan, combine sugar, salt and cornstarch. Blend well. Add milk and egg yolks; stir constantly over medium heat until mixture thickens. Add rum extract and remove from heat. Place waxed paper directly on top of custard to prevent a crust from forming. Cool to room temperature. Spoon custard over chilled peaches and garnish with mint leaves.

RIS A' L'AMANDE (Danish Rice Dessert)

Serves 8-10

This dessert is a Danish tradition. It is usually served during the Christmas holidays. The dish has a hidden surprise; among all the slivers of almonds one whole almond is placed somewhere in the dish, and the lucky finder receives a present, usually a marzipan pig with a red ribbon tied around it's neck. Start by cooking a rice porridge. When cooked, let it cool, then continue to follow the Ris a' l'amande recipe.

RICE PORRIDGE:

2	**cups rice**	**1**	**teaspoon salt**
6	**cups milk**	**1**	**cup Half-and-Half**

- Cook rice in milk over low heat for about 1 hour. Stir often. When done, add the salt and Half-and-Half. Set aside to cool.

2	**cups rice porridge**	**2**	**tablespoons sugar**
2	**cups whipped cream**	**2**	**teaspoons vanilla**
1/2	**cup almonds, blanched, chopped**	**1/2**	**cup dry sherry**

- Place the cold rice porridge in a bowl. Blend all the above ingredients thoroughly and chill again. Serve with fruit sauce.
- Don't forget the almond.

FRUIT SAUCE:

2	**cups red fruit juice**	**2**	**tablespoons cornstarch**
1	**tablespoon sugar**	**1**	**teaspoon water**
1/2	**teaspoon vanilla**		

- Bring fruit juice to a boil; add sugar and vanilla. Mix cornstarch with a little water and add to the hot juice. Stir mixture, and bring it to a boil for 2 minutes. Cool.
- This looks pretty served in clear dessert glasses with the sauce poured over top just before serving.

ZABAIONE

Serves 4

A light custard with Marsala. Often served cool over fresh strawberries or fresh raspberries.

5	**egg yolks**	**2**	**tablespoons sugar**
1	**whole egg**	**1/2**	**cup sweet Marsala**

- In a double boiler combine the egg yolks, egg and sugar.
- Over low heat beat the mixture with a rotary beater until it is pale yellow and fluffy.
- Add the Marsala a little at a time. Keep beating until the mixture becomes thick; it sometimes takes 15 minutes before it's stiff enough.
- Serve in large stemmed glasses while still warm.

ITALIAN CHOCOLATE LOAF

Serves 8-10

Absolutely sinful!!

1/2 pound semi-sweet chocolate, cut into small pieces
1/4 cup dark rum
1/2 pound unsalted butter, softened
2 tablespoons superfine sugar
2 eggs, separated
1 1/2 cups grated almonds
Pinch of salt
12 butter biscuits, cut into 1 by 1/2-inch pieces
Powdered sugar
1/2 cup heavy cream, whipped

- Grease sides and bottom of 1 1/2-guart loaf pan lightly with oil. Set upside down to drain.
- In double boiler or heavy sauce pan, melt chocolate over low heat, stirring constantly. When dissolved, remove from heat, add rum.
- In a separate bowl, cream butter until light and fluffy. Add the sugar and egg yolks, then stir in the almonds and cooled chocolate.
- Add a pinch of salt to egg whites and whip until stiff.
- Fold the chocolate mixture into this, then gently fold in the biscuits. Spoon mixture into loaf pan, smooth the top a with spatula.
- Cover and refrigerate.
- Remove the loaf 1 hour before serving time. Dip a sharp knife in hot water and run it around sides. Dip bottom of pan in hot water and turn loaf onto a serving platter. Cool again.
- Slice very thin and serve with powdered sugar and whipped cream.

TORTONI

Serves 6

Elegant and quick dessert.

- **1 quart vanilla ice cream, slightly softened**
- **1/2 cup dry macaroon crumbs**
- **1/4 cup miniature semi-sweet chocolate chips**
- **2 tablespoons almonds, chopped**
- **1/4 cup candied cherries**
- **1/2 cup heavy cream, whipped**
- **1 tablespoon brandy**

- Place paper liners inside muffin pan. Combine ice cream, macaroon crumbs, chocolate, almonds and cherries in bowl. Blend well. After whippin cream pour in brandy, then fold into ice cream
- Freeze until firm, or about 1 1/2 hour.

FRANGELICO DELIGHT

4 servings

- **1 pound fresh peaches, peeled and sliced**
- **2 1/2 tablespoons sugar**
- **2 tablespoons Frangelico liqueur**
- **1 1/2 tablespoons fresh lemon juice**
- **1/2 stick butter**
- **1/2 cup hazelnuts, ground**
- **1/2 cup fresh bread crumbs**

- Combine peaches, 1 1/2 tablespoons sugar and liqueur. Mix well. Stir in the lemon juice. Divide into 4 small au gratin dishes. Heat oven to 400 degrees.
- Meanwhile melt butter in sauce pan. Remove from heat and stir in the remaining sugar, the hazelnuts and the bread crumbs. Spoon mixture over peaches. Bake for about 15 minutes or until bubbly and brown. Serve at room temperature.

PEACH KUCHEN

Serves 12 peach lovers

Simply wonderful. Our pretty deckhand Valerie whipped this dessert up for us on the boat.

6	**fresh peaches, halved, peeled**	**1/2**	**cup butter**
2	**cups flour**	**1**	**teaspoon cinnamon**
1/4	**teaspoon baking powder**	**2**	**egg yolks**
1/2	**teaspoon salt**	**1**	**cup heavy cream or sour cream**
1	**cup sugar**		

- Mix flour with baking powder, salt and 2 tablespoons sugar.
- Cut in butter with a knife. Press dough into Pyrex pan or jelly roll dish. The dough is not very dense.
- Arrange peach halves in pan cut-side up. Sprinkle with cinnamon and remaining sugar.
- Bake at 400 degrees for 15 minutes.
- Mix together egg yolks and cream and pour over the baked peaches, return to oven and bake for another 30 minutes.
- Serve either warm or chilled.

APRICOT AND PECAN SLICES

Serves 6

2	**cups flour**	**4**	**eggs, separated**
1/4	**teaspoon salt**	**2**	**tablespoons milk**
1	**teaspoon baking powder**	**1**	**teaspoon lemon extract**
1	**cup sugar**	**1/2**	**cup apricot jam**
2/3	**cup sweet butter**	**1**	**cup pecans, chopped**

- Preheat oven to 350 degrees. Sift flour, salt, baking powder and 1/2 cup sugar. Cut butter in, as if for a pie crust. Combine slightly beaten egg yolks, milk and lemon extract. Add all dry ingredients and mix well. Place the dough in a 9 x 12 x 2-inch pan and press into bottom and sides to about a 2-inch thickness. Spread jam on top. Beat egg whites, gradually adding remaining sugar, and beat until stiff. Spread with more jam and sprinkle with chopped nuts.
- Bake for 25 to 30 minutes. Cool, cut into 2-inch slices.

CARAMEL CUSTARD (Flan)

Serves 6

Smooth as silk. One of our favorite desserts when in Mexico. Preheat oven to 300 degrees.

1/2 cup sugar
1/4 cup boiling water
1/2 cup granulated sugar
1/4 teaspoon salt
3 eggs
3 cups milk
Nutmeg

- Pour 1/2 cup sugar in small frying pan and melt over very low heat stirring constantly. Add the boiling water very slowly and simmer for 10 minutes.
- Pour 1 tablespoon of this syrup in each of 6 custard cups.
- Beat sugar, salt and eggs until fluffy.
- Add milk, stir until blended. Pour into cups, 1/2-inch from top. Shake a little nutmeg on each.
- Place inside shallow baking pan with 2 inches of hot water in bottom of pan. Bake at 300 degrees for 1 hour, or until a knife comes out clean.

DANISH APPLE DESSERT

Serves 6

A delicious, quick dessert.

2 cups graham cracker crumbs
1/2 cup butter
2 tablespoons sugar
1 cup whipped cream
2 cans French Apple pie filling
6 tablespoons raspberry jam

- Brown the crumbs with butter and sugar in skillet.
- Set aside to cool. Divide the crumbs into 6 dessert glasses.
- Whip the cream. Spoon the apple filling on top of the crumbs, top with whipping cream. Decorate with dabs of raspberry jam.

RUM FROMAGE

Serves 8

Another Danish delight.

6	egg yolks
1	cup sugar
1	tablespoon gelatin
1/2	cup boiling water
1/2	cup dark rum
4	egg whites
1	cup heavy cream

- Beat egg yolks with sugar until thick and lemon colored. Soak gelatin in 1 tablespoon cold water for 5 minutes. Add 1/2 cup boiling water to gelatin and stir until dissolved. Add this to the egg mixture and blend well. Add the rum and mix again.
- Whip egg whites and fold into yolk mixture. Whip the cream and fold in also; save a little for decorating.
- Chill for 2 hours.

CITRON FROMAGE (Lemon Fluff)

Serves 8-10

After a heavy meal, this light fluffy dessert is just right.

8	eggs, separated
1	cup sugar
2	tablespoons gelatin, unflavored
1/2	cup cold water
1	tablespoon lemon rind, grated
1/2	cup lemon juice, fresh
1	cup heavy cream, whipped

- Beat yolks with sugar until lemon colored. Soak the gelatin in water for 5 minutes, squeeze out excess water. Transfer to small pan and melt over direct heat, then cool slightly.
- When gelatin is soft add it to the egg mixture. Add the rind and lemon juice. Stir well.
- Whip the egg whites until peaks form.
- Whip the cream and carefully fold it into whipped whites.
- Refrigerate for several hours.
- Garnish with a few dollups of whipping cream and some finely shredded lemon peel.

INDIVIDUAL BAKED ALASKAS

Serves 6

- Bake 6 frozen patty shells according to package. Set aside until completely cool.
- Fill each shell with your favorite ice cream. Top with meringue, and bake on a wooden board at 450 degrees for 5 minutes or until delicately browned.

MERINGUE:

- Beat 2 egg whites until stiff.
- Gradually add 4 tablespoons sugar
- Flavor with 1/4 teaspoon vanilla.

HOT FUDGE SAUCE

Makes 1 cup

This is in my opinion the world's best hot fudge sauce. Label it ''brown gravy'' when you keep it in refrigerator the house sitters won't find it.

3 tablespoons butter
1/3 cup sugar
1/2 cup heavy cream
1/3 cup brown sugar, firmly packed
1/2 cup Dutch chocolate, sifted

- Combine butter and cream in heavy sauce pan over medium heat. Stir until butter is melted and mixture comes to a low boil. Add sugar and stir for a few minutes until the sugar dissolves. Reduce heat; add cocoa and whip with wire whisk until smooth.
- Serve over your favorite ice cream, or store in refrigerator. Can be reheated in microwave or in top of double boiler. Should be thick, but if too thick add a few drops of hot water.

Extra! Extra!

EXTRA! EXTRA!

MRS. DUTCH DERR'S POTATO CANDY

It wouldn't seem like Easter without the Derr family's delicious Easter candy. Romer is keeping up the tradition of making his mother's home-made treats every Easter.

1/2 cup mashed potatoes
3 parts powdered sugar
1 part coconut, shredded
Semi-sweet chocolate for dipping

- Beat mashed potatoes until liquified; the food processor works well for this. Slowly add powdered sugar and coconut to potatoes until moderately stiff. Shape into eggs. Let eggs rest overnight. Melt chocolate, dip eggs and let them dry. Share with your favorite people.

ROSEMARY OLIVE OIL

Makes 2 cups

Use this in your salad dressings that needs that little extra flavor.

2 thick branches fresh rosemary
2 dried hot chiles
2 cups olive oil
3 drops hot Chinese oil

- Break rosemary up between your fingers to release flavors. Bruise chiles; combine both with olive oil and hot Chinese oil in a jar with a tight-fitted lid. Let flavors blend for 10 days without refrigeration. Strain through 2 layers of cheese cloth. Return to jar. This oil will keep for several months.

NEWTON'S CHEESE FONDUE

Serves 8

A fun way to entertain good friends. Pour a glass of ruby red wine and enjoy.

- **1 clove garlic**
- **1 1/2 cups white wine**
- **1 tablespoon lemon juice**
- **1 pound Swiss cheese, shredded**
- **3 tablespoons flour**
- **Nutmeg and pepper to taste**
- **1 Baguette, or other French bread**

- Dredge cheese in flour by placing it in a plastic bag and shake. Wipe bottom of fondue pot with garlic, discard.
- Add wine and lemon juice to pot and bring to a boil. Immediately begin adding cheese and flour mixture. Stir with wooden spoon until all cheese is melted. Season with pepper and nutmeg to taste.
- To enjoy, break bread into chunks and dip in cheese.

MARZIPAN AND DATES

To be enjoyed around the holidays. Let the children help with this yummy task.

- **1/2 pound pitted dates, fresh and moist**
- **1/2 cup walnuts, broken**
- **1 package Odense Marzipan, about 7 ounces**
- **Chocolate for dipping**

- Mix almond paste and nuts. Divide almond paste into as many parts as you have dates.
- Remove pits; replace it with a small oval roll of Marzipan. Dip in melted chocolate. Cool. Store in tin canisters in a cold place.

SWISS FONDUE

Serves 8

- **1 pound Emmenthaler cheese, shredded**
- **1 clove garlic**
- **2 cups Riesling wine**
- **1 tablespoon lemon juice**
- **3 tablespoons flour**
- **3 tablespoons Kirsch**
- **Dash fresh ground nutmeg, or paprika**
- **2 loaves Italian bread, cut into cubes**

- Rub fondue pot with garlic, cut in half. Discard. Pour in white wine. Set over medium heat. When wine is hot without boiling, add lemon juice. Dredge cheese with flour and by the spoonfuls to the hot wine. Stir until cheese is melted. Add Kirsch and spices, stirring until blended. Keep hot over burner. Dunk and swirl the bread in cheese fondue.
- Serve with a hot spiced wine.

HOMESTEADER'S FIREWEED HONEY

Given to me by Vi Webb-Davis, of Juneau and Georgia. She did however, explain that she only makes it when in Alaska.

- **10 cups sugar**
- **1 teaspoon alum, powdered**
- **2 1/2 cups boiling water**
- **30 white clover blossoms**
- **18 red or purple clover blossoms**
- **18 fireweed floweretes, or red rose petals**

- Boil the first three ingredients for 10 minutes, remove from heat. Add the remaining ingredients, cover and steep for 10 minutes. Strain and pour into warm, clean jars. They do not have to be sealed.
- Later versions of this recipe were called "Alaska Honey" and Fireweed Honey. Exactly as if made by a real bee.

SERENA ANTIPASTO

It appears first to be a lot of work, but let me tell you it is worth every minute. There is enough to share with friends too. It lasts really well in the refrigerator if placed in jars with lids.

PART ONE:

3 packages frozen artichoke hearts
4 onions, sliced
6 tablespoons olive oil
8 cups water
4 cups cider vinegar
2 medium heads cauliflower, broken up
3 large green peppers, cut into strips
8 medium size carrots, thinly sliced
1 bunch celery, cut into pieces

- Cook artichoke hearts according to directions, set aside.
- Sauté onions in olive oil until limp. Drain. Set aside.
- Place water, vinegar and vegetables in a large soup pan and boil until tender, about 20 minutes. Drain, and set aside.

PART TWO:

4 7-ounce cans tomato sauce
Salt and pepper
3 16-ounce cans whole mushrooms, drained
1 5-ounce jar pimento stuffed olives
2 16-ounce cans black olives
2 16-ounce cans small white pearl onions
3 5.5-ounce cans mackerel in tomato sauce

- Mix sliced cooked onions with tomato sauce, season with salt and pepper to your taste. Place in pan with above drained, cooked vegetables, mushrooms, pearl onions, artichoke hearts and both kinds of olives. Gently stir all the ingredients, very gently, being careful not to break up vegetables. Simmer for 20 minute. Remove from heat.
- Finally, fold in the mackerel.
- Store in jars, this will keep in the refrigerator for up to 3 weeks; it can also be frozen.
- Serve with crackers or pumpernickel bread triangles.

DERR'S SAUERKRAUT

Makes 18 quarts

There appears to be enough for an army, but by the time Romer has shared with friends there is just enough until next years crop of cabbage can be picked and "krauted."

50 pounds cabbage
1 1/2 cups pure salt

- Clean cabbage. Shred into thin strips, about the thickness of a coin. In a large plastic bag, mix approximately 5 pounds of cabbage with 3 tablespoons salt. Place in crock, or heavy plastic container. Repeat with remaining cabbage. Leave about 3 to 4 inches of space on top of crock. Place 2 to 3 gallons of water in garbage bag. Set the water bag atop the cabbage as a weight. It must be heavy enough to keep constant pressure on cabbage.
- Let sit for 5 to 6 weeks or until desired taste is achieved. It should be tart.
- Fill jars 3/4 full. Place jars in hot water bath and prosess for 15 minutes for pint size jars and 20 minutes for quart size jars.
- This is excellent for any sauerkraut salad recipe you might have.

ZUCCHINI FREEZER PICKLES

Makes 6 pints

Another Brann family favorite, guaranteed to please.

2 medium carrots, cut into julienne strips
2 pounds zucchini, cut into julienne strips
2 small onions, sliced into rings
6 cloves garlic
4 cups white vinegar
3 cups sugar
2 cups water
1/2 teaspoon celery salt
1/2 teaspoon salt

- Cook carrots in small amount of water for 5 minutes, drain. Loosely pack zucchini and onions into 6 1-pint containers. Place 1 clove garlic in each jar. Combine the remaining ingredients; boil for 1 minute. Pour liquid over vegetables and seal jars. Tip jars with liquid to coat vegetables. Freeze up to 1 year.

GREENHOUSE BREAD AND BUTTER PICKLES

Makes 6 quarts

Cleaning up the greenhouse is a wonderful task when the reward is a pantry full of things to be enjoyed and shared later on when colder weather sets in.

2 gallons small cucumbers, sliced thin
6 quarts ice cubes
2 onions, sliced
1 cup salt

- Place above ingredients in layers of onions, cucumbers, ice and salt in a large container or use the sink. Place a plastic bag on top and weigh it down. Let soak for 4 hours.

Combine the following:

8 cups cider vinegar
8 cups sugar
3 teaspoons turmeric
3 teaspoons celery seeds
3 teaspoons mustard seeds
1 teaspoon ground cloves
1 teaspoon allspice
2 teaspoons whole cloves
Sprig of fresh dill

- Bring above ingredients to a boil. Remove cucumbers and onion slices, drain. Add cucumbers and onions to brine and cook for 10 minutes. Push down floating slices. Using a slotted spoon, transfer onions and cucumbers to hot sterilized jars, pour brine over cucumbers, filling jars to 1/4-inch from top. Wipe jar tops clean with hot towel and place lids on jars; seal tightly.
- Place jars in large pot of boiling water and boil with lid on pot for 20 minutes. Make sure the water is above jars.
- Remove and tighten lids again. Press each jar lid in the middle, if the lid stays down, jar is sealed.

ZUCCHINI RELISH

Makes 6 pints

This tasty relish recipe was given to me by Vi Davis, who is known as one of the better cooks in Juneau. With as many fresh zucchini as we have in the garden, it is a special treat to have a new way of preparing this fresh vegetable to be enjoyed long after the zucchini have stopped bearing.

10 cups zucchini, finely chopped
1 red bell pepper, finely chopped
1 green bell pepper, finely chopped
4 cups green onions, chopped
3 tablespoons salt

- Mix all ingredients together with salt and set aside overnight. The next morning, rinse and drain well. Set aside.

Combine the following:

2 1/2 cups vinegar
1 teaspoon turmeric
1 teaspoon nutmeg
1 teaspoon celery salt
1 teaspoon pepper
4 1/2 cups sugar

- Pour the above ingredients over vegetables.
- Bring to a boil, lower temperature and simmer slowly for 30 minutes.
- Pour into sterilized jars and seal.

VI'S CRAB APPLE PICKLES

Makes 6 pints

This is a nice compliment to any main course.

2 quarts crab apples with stems, wild Alaskan ones are great
2 sticks cinnamon
1 1/2 teaspoons whole cloves
3 cups water
6 cups sugar
3 cups white vinegar

- Start by running large needle through apples, from stem through apple; this will prevent them from bursting. Tie cinnamon and cloves inside cheese cloth. Combine all the ingredients except apples, boil 5 minutes. Add as many apples as liquid will hold and boil until apples are almost tender, about 10 minutes, depending of the size. Remove apples from liquid and repeat with the remaining apples. Remove apples and again bring syrup to a boil, then pour syrup over fruit. Let stand 12 to 18 hours. Remove spice bag. Pack apples inside sterilized jars. Bring syrup to a boil, but let it boil down a little. Pour over apples. Adjust lids. Process in boiling water bath for 15 minutes.

PEAR AND RASPBERRY JAM

Makes 12 half pints

When I received this recipe from North Carolina, the raspberries were perfect and ripe. Absolutely wonderful!

12 medium pears, about 4 pounds, cored, peeled
2 10-ounce packages frozen red raspberries, or fresh
12 cups sugar
4 tablespoons lemon juice
4 teaspoons orange peel, finely shredded
1 6-ounce package liquid pectin

- Coarsely chop pears in food processor or by hand. Combine enough raspberries with them to make 8 cups. In a large pot combine all ingredients except pectin with pears and raspberries. Bring to a rolling boil that you can't stir down and let boil for 1 minute. Remove from heat, stir in pectin quickly skim off foam with metal spoon. Ladle into hot sterilized 1/2-pint size jars, up to 1/4-inch from top.
- Place in water bath, bring to a boil and allow jars to remain in boiling water for 15 minutes.
- Adjust lids and set aside in cool, dark place to be enjoyed later.

LORETO JALAPEÑO JELLY

Makes 4 pints

Given to me by Dori Pallesen of Loreto. Wonderful served on a cracker with cream cheese, or use it as a condiment for lamb.

1 1/2 cups Jalapeño peppers, seeded
1 cup green peppers. chopped
6 1/2 cups sugar
1 1/2 cups cider vinegar
1/4 teaspoon green food coloring
1 6-ounce bottle pectin

- Remove seeds from both peppers. Grind to a pulp in food grinder or blender, not too fine.
- Mix peppers, sugar, and vinegar in sauce pan; bring it to a rolling boil and boil, for 15 minutes. Add pectin, return it to a boil, letting it boil for 3 minutes. Remove from heat and set aside for 1 minute. Remove foam. Add food coloring.
- Pour into hot sterilized jars and seal. Store in a cool, dark place.

PETER PAGE'S PEAR CHUTNEY

The most wonderful chutney around. Make it when the pears are still firm and not quite ripe. Make lots. This is a perfect addition to any Christmas basket. This is easy to double or triple.

2 medium pears = 2 cups
1 1/2 medium onions = 1 1/2 cups

1 1/2 cups thinly sliced onions
2 cups cubed pears with skin on
1/2 cup preserved ginger in syrup or the crystal kind
2 fat cloves garlic
3/4 cup cider vinegar
1 cup sugar
1 cup brown sugar
2 teaspoons mustard seeds
2 teaspoons salt
1 1/2 teaspoons cayenne pepper
1 cup seedless raisins

- Slice onions and cut pears into cubes. Slice ginger and garlic. Combine vinegar, sugars, mustard seeds, salt and cayenne pepper and bring to a boil. Cook until sugar has dissolved; add raisins, pears and onions. Bring to a boil. Lower heat and let simmer until thick, about 1 1/2 hours. Pour into hot sterilized jars and seal.
- This chutney is especially good poured over cream cheese and served on Melba toast.
- Also a terrific flavor for spicy curry dishes.
- Use chutney in fruit salad dressings.
- Mix 1/2 cup chutney with 1 cup mayonnaise for a dip with fruits.
- See other uses for chutney throughout book.

PETER PAGE'S WINE JELLY

Serves 10

This is always on the table for Christmas dinner at the Page's home.

2 envelopes unflavored gelatin
1/2 cup cold water
1 cup boiling water
2/3 cup sugar
Pinch of salt
1/4 cup fresh lemon juice, strained
1/4 cup orange juice, strained
2 cups sweet sherry

- Soak gelatin in 1/2 cup of cold water for 10 minutes. Bring 1 cup water to a boil. Add to gelatin and stir well; cool slightly. Add sugar, salt, juices and sherry. Mix well. Pour into your favorite shaped mold.
- Place in refrigerator until completely set.
- To unmold; dip mold in hot water for 4 seconds, and jelly slips right out.

MINT JELLY

Makes 2 pints

With a recipe from Mrs. Webb-Davis of Georgia and mint transplanted from Virginia, we manage to have mint jelly in Juneau year round to go with all the game we enjoy.

2 cups mint leaves
1 1/2 cups white vinegar
1/2 cup water
1 teaspoon lemon juice
3 drops green food coloring
3 1/2 cups sugar
3 ounces pectin

- Place mint and vinegar in blender or food processor. Chop and blend well. Add water. Place in pan and bring it to a boil. Remove from heat; set aside to rest with cover for 10 minutes.
- Strain mint leaves in fine sieve or cheese cloth, discard chopped mint. Place 1 and 3/4 cups of juice in large sauce pan. Add lemon juice, green food coloring and sugar. Bring to a rolling boil for 1 minute. Stir in pectin and fill into sterilized jars. Cover with wax according to direction.

SPICED BLUEBERRY JAM

There is endless ways to use fresh blueberries when in season. When the winter sets in we enjoy this wonderful jam.

5 cups blueberries
1/2 teaspoon cinnamon
1/2 teaspoon cloves
1/2 teaspoon allspice
1/2 teaspoon ginger
1/2 teaspoon vanilla
7 cups sugar
1 lemon, juice and zest of
1 bottle or pouch of pectin

- Combine all the ingredients and simmer slowly for 15 minutes. Remove from heat and stir in 1 bottle commercial pectin. Skim foam off top. Pour into hot sterilized jars.
- This is terrific on top of a bagel with cream cheese or Brie.

BAVARIAN GRAND MARNIER

Serves 6

- **2 tablespoons gelatin, unflavored**
- **1 3/4 cups water**
- **1/4 cup sugar**
- **1 6-ounce can frozen orange juice, concentrated, thawed**
- **Dash of salt**
- **1 cup heavy cream**
- **1/4 cup Grand Marnier**

- Sprinkle gelatin into a cup of the water. Add sugar. Heat over low heat until gelatin is dissolved. Add remaining water, orange juice, salt and Grand Marnier. Chill until mixture begins to thicken. Fold in the whipped cream. Pour into 6-cup mold and chill till firm.
- Unmold and garnish with a twist of orange peel.

FRONTIER SPICED CIDER

Serves 5

- **1 quart apple cider**
- **2 whole allspice**
- **2 whole cloves**
- **2 cinnamon sticks**
- **5 tablespoons brown sugar**
- **1/2 orange, sliced with skin**

- Combine everything in sauce pan over high heat and cook for 10 minutes, stirring half way through cooking time.
- If using a microwave oven, heat until temperature probe reaches 190 degrees. Strain into heated mugs.

SMOOTH GIN FIZZ

1 Serving

- 1 1/2 ounces vodka or gin
- 1 ounce lemon juice, fresh
- 1 tablespoon orange juice
- 1 teaspoon sugar
- 1 egg, well beaten
- 2 ounces heavy cream
- Dash of orange rose water
- 1/2 cup crushed ice

- Mix all the ingredients with ice in blender until frothy.

BRAZILIAN COFFEE DESSERT DRINK

Serves 4

- 1/2 cup heavy cream, whipped
- 1 teaspoon sugar
- 4 cups hot chocolate
- 1 1/2 cups strong coffee
- 1 cup dark rum

- Whip cream with sugar. Mix chocolate, coffee and rum. Pour into heated mugs and top with the whipped cream.

DANISH AKVAVIT

Makes 1

I will not be responsible for anyone having more than 1 of these dessert drinks. I serve this in see-through glass mugs, it looks very pretty, but they creep up on you.

- 1 cup strong coffee
- 1 teaspoon brown sugar
- 1 1/2 ounces Jubilaeums Akvavit
- Whipping cream for topping

- Stir sugar into cup with coffee. Add Akvavit; top with whipping cream.

HOT MULLED WINE

Serves 6

Perfect on a cold night in front of an open fire.

- 6 **tablespoons sugar**
- 1/4 **cup water**
- 10 **whole cloves**
- 6 **orange slices**
- 6 **lemon slices**
- 4 **cinnamon sticks**
- 6 **cups dry red wine**

- Combine all ingredients except wine in a cast iron pot. Heat slowly, stirring until sugar is dissolved. Add wine and continue heating until mixture is just below boiling point. Strain into heated mugs.

SPALDING FIZZ

Serves 6

This is named after Bob Spalding, a friend from Fairbanks. It is both tangy and smooth. One of our favorites when entertaining at brunch time.

- 1 **12-ounce canned, frozen lime or lemonade**
- 12 **ounces Half-and-Half**
- 12 **ounces gin**
- 4 **level teaspoons refined sugar**
- 1 1/2 **cups ice, crushed**
- 4 **teaspoons orange flower water**
- **Dash of nutmeg for garnishing**

- Combine all the ingredients except nutmeg in blender. Continue blending until the rattling stops and drink is smooth and velvety. Garnish with freshly grated nutmeg.

AMARETTO COFFEE

Serves 6

A perfect ending to any evening.

- 6 **ounces coffee liqueur**
- 2 **ounces Amaretto**
- 24 **ounces strong, hot coffee**
- 1/2 **cup heavy cream, whipped**
- 1 **teaspoon chocolate shavings**

- Combine liqueur and Amaretto with coffee. Top with heavy cream and sprinkle with chocolate shavings.

HERBS AND SPICES

There is no limit to what will grow in the garden or the greenhouse. My problem was always how to preserve herbs and spices so we could enjoy them when the weather turned sour and the winter set in.

Asking a lot of questions from the pro's helped. At their suggestions, I tried drying some herbs in the microwave, which worked well on several of them, but others I froze. Still others I just dried by hanging them upside down over the meat block.

I found that the very best way to freeze herbs is to set them initially in ice cube trays filled with water, freeze them, and then transfer them to zip-lock bags and remove them as needed.

The most important part of storing your herbs is picking them at their peak. They should be picked early in the morning before given a chance to wilt in the heat of the day.

I often tie an assortment of herbs in small cheese cloth bags and store them in Mason jars, or give them to friends in their Christmas basket. Here are some basic guidelines to storing herbs and spices I found worked well.

When microwaving herbs, I make sure to clean and dry them before placing them in the oven between several layers of paper towel. At medium heat, dry a few branches at a time for 2-3 minutes. Replace the top towel and continue until the herbs are completely dry. Keep an eye on them, as they can burn and start a fire. If, however, a fire does occur, turn to my fabulous roasted marshmallow recipe to take advantage of it.

To freeze your herbs, first dip them in boiling water for 3 seconds; this prevents them from turning dark and loosing their flavors. Pat dry on paper towel. Chop and place in ice cube trays with water.

Preserving in oil and vinegar is the very best method for storing some herbs. Wash the herbs, pat them dry between paper towels. Place them in either white wine vinegar or olive oil. To herbs with strong flavors like rosemary, I add a few green peppercorns and a pinch of salt. Store them this way for at least a couple of weeks before using, to give the oil or vinegar time enough to absorb the flavor of the herbs. Dried herbs should be stored in airtight containers.

BASIL

This flavors pesto for the most part. It freezes well. Also used for pasta, tomato salads, seafoods and stews.

CHERVIL

Freeze in ice cube trays. Add to soups, casserole dishes, egg dishes and sauces.

DILL

Dry in microwave oven. This is the most essential herb for a Scandinavian cook. Use in dressings, soups, potato salads and all seafoods.

GARLIC

Store this in olive oil for any recipe calling for garlic. You may also use the oil to add a wonderful garlic flavor to salad dressings, stews, meat dishes and many Oriental or Italian dishes.

MARJORAM

Dry in microwave oven, or freeze in ice cube trays. Use in all Italian dishes, stews, beef, pork or veal.

OREGANO

Dry in microwave oven or hang in bouquets somewhere dry and free of draft. Seasons most all Italian, Mexican or Greek dishes. Once dried, store in airtight container.

PARSLEY

Chop and freeze in ice cube trays. Used in almost all my recipes; fish, veal, game, beef, soups and sauces.

ROSEMARY

Preserve in white wine vinegar. Good in soups and salads as well as lamb, poultry and veal dishes. Also, drop a few sprigs on barbecue coals, to add flavors to meat.

SAGE

Hang to dry in bunches with lots of fresh air. Tasty seasoning for poultry and eggplant dishes, stuffings and sausages.

SHALLOTS

The elegant member of the onion family, more delicate than other onions, and a must in French cooking. Store in a net bag in cool place. Use for French cooking, salads, dressings and delicate sauces.

SAVORY

Freeze in ice cube trays. Add to many egg dishes, cream soups, meat and seafood stews.

TARRAGON

Preserve in white wine vinegar, or in oil. Use for dressings, soups, poultry, shell fish and sauces.

THYME

Dry in microwave oven between paper towels. Good in soups, sauces or casseroles.

Index

C

E

F

G

Q

PANNING FOR PLEASURE
Winni Page
18065 Trails End Drive
Juneau, Alaska 99801

Please send me ____ copies of **Panning For Pleasure** at $16.95 each, plus $1.50 per book for postage and handling.

TOTAL ___________

Enclosed is my check ☐ or money order ☐.
Make checks payable to **Panning for Pleasure.**

Please print or type

Name ____

Address ____

City ________________________ State ___________ Zip ___________

PANNING FOR PLEASURE
Winni Page
18065 Trails End Drive
Juneau, Alaska 99801

Please send me ____ copies of **Panning For Pleasure** at $16.95 each, plus $1.50 per book for postage and handling.

TOTAL ___________

Enclosed is my check ☐ or money order ☐.
Make checks payable to **Panning for Pleasure.**

Please print or type

Name ____

Address ____

City ________________________ State ___________ Zip ___________

PANNING FOR PLEASURE
Winni Page
18065 Trails End Drive
Juneau, Alaska 99801

Please send me ____ copies of **Panning For Pleasure** at $16.95 each, plus $1.50 per book for postage and handling.

TOTAL ____________

Enclosed is my check ☐ or money order ☐.
Make checks payable to **Panning for Pleasure.**

Please print or type

Name ____

Address ____

City ____________________ State ____________ Zip ____________

PANNING FOR PLEASURE
Winni Page
18065 Trails End Drive
Juneau, Alaska 99801

Please send me ____ copies of **Panning For Pleasure** at $16.95 each, plus $1.50 per book for postage and handling.

TOTAL ____________

Enclosed is my check ☐ or money order ☐.
Make checks payable to **Panning for Pleasure.**

Please print or type

Name ____

Address ____

City ____________________ State ____________ Zip ____________

Dear Readers,

We hope you have enjoyed this edition of **Panning for Pleasure.** We also would very much appreciate you sending us your favorite recipes from your kitchen which may be included in a future edition.

Should your recipe be published, you will receive full credit. Please use the space below and mail to:

Panning for Pleasure
18065 Trails End Drive
Juneau, Alaska 99801

Johnnys seafood Seasoni

Pickles 251
Candy 247
Jelly 255
Jam 256
Salad 59
Sauce 98
" 106
" 115

Chicken 120
" 121

Zucchini 159

Beans 163
Cabbage 170
Onion pie 174
Teriyaki sauce 198
Tartar " 200
Rice Dish 214

FOLD HERE

PLACE
STAMP
HERE

PANNING FOR PLEASURE
18065 Trails End Drive
Juneau, Alaska 99801